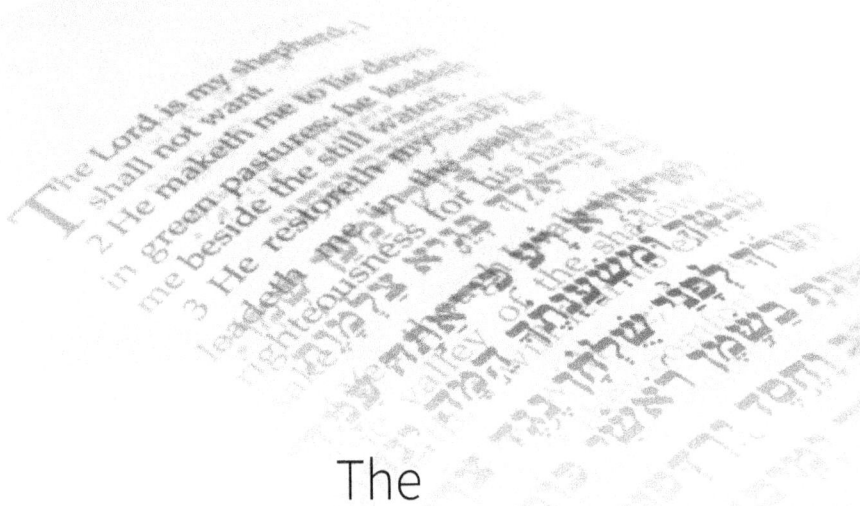

The

BIBLE

Was Not Written in English

How Church Traditions
Have Kept Us in the Dark

Easy to Understand Bible Guide
For The Undecided to The Senior Pastor

David Murdoch

WingSpan Press

Cover Design by: David Pollock
www.pollockmedia.com
davepollock@me.com

Published in the United States and the United Kingdom
by WingSpan Press, Livermore, CA

The WingSpan name, logo and colophon are the trademarks
of WingSpan Publishing.

ISBN 978-1-59594-569-3 (pbk.)
ISBN 978-1-59594-902-8 (ebk.)

First edition 2015
Second edition 2016

Printed in the United States of America

www.wingspanpress.com

Library of Congress Control Number: 2015956034

1 2 3 4 5 6 7 8 9 10

"Dedicated to all those who have always known there was more"

TABLE OF CONTENTS

INTRODUCTION 1

PREFACE 3

SECTION I

Overcoming Obstacles.. 11
1. Three Heaven and Earth Ages 12
2. Part of God's Plan 15
3. The Original Languages.. 17
4. Understanding the Beginning............................... 20
5. Who the Serpent is 22
6. The Family of Cain 23
7. Not Skilled in the Manuscripts 26
8. Overcoming Traditions... 28

SECTION II

Myths and Facts 35
Questions and Answers.. 113

SECTION III

God's Food Laws 233

BIBLIOGRAPHY 250

INTRODUCTION

I met David Murdoch early in my teenage years after my parents bought the land adjacent to the Murdoch ranch. We built a home there where I lived with my parents from 1984 to 1988. After school I got into the insurance business and around 1992, I wrote David's insurance and developed a close friendship that has grown stronger over the years. I have spent hours discussing the Bible and his in depth research of the original manuscripts. These conversations have greatly impacted my life in many ways. I have also read David's books and have learned that there have been more than a few misinterpretations of different versions of the Bible. When I began studying information from the original manuscripts, God's Word has taken on a whole new meaning in my life. I understand myself and a lot of the major events in the Bible much better.

I have made more than my share of "wrong turns" and "bad choices" in life, one of which almost cost me my life. About five years ago I had a tragic accident in which I should have been killed. God spared my life and I spent months in the hospital recovering from my near death experience that my Heavenly Father has used to get my attention. During this time in the hospital, David spent a lot of time at my bed side talking and praying with me and my family.

I know in my heart that my relationship with David was by

Divine design and in God's Plan for my life. I now might truly have the chance to learn fully about God's Living Word and what it means to have a personal relationship with my Heavenly Father on a daily basis. Please, as you start to read this book, don't make any quick assumptions and keep an open mind. If there is any part that you don't understand or disagree with, take the time to use a Strong's Exhaustive Concordance of the Bible and you will be completely amazed of the accuracy of this book.

II Corinthians 4:1 says *"Therefore seeing we have this ministry, as we received mercy, we faint not; 2. But have renounced the hidden things of dishonesty, not walking in craftiness, nor handling the Word of God deceitfully; but by manifestation of the truth commending ourselves to every man's conscience in the sight of God. 3. But if our gospel be hid, it is hid from them that are lost; 4. In whom the god of this world hath blinded the minds of them which believeth not, lest the light of the glorious gospel of Christ, who is the image of God, should not shine unto them. 5. For we preach not ourselves, but Christ Jesus the Lord; and ourselves your servants for Jesus sake. 6. For God who commanded the light to shine out of darkness, hath shined in our hearts, to give the light of the knowledge of the glory of God in the face of Jesus Christ."*

My prayer as you read this book is that God will remove the scales from your eyes and that His Living Word will take on a whole new role and meaning in your life!

God Bless
Greg Harmon

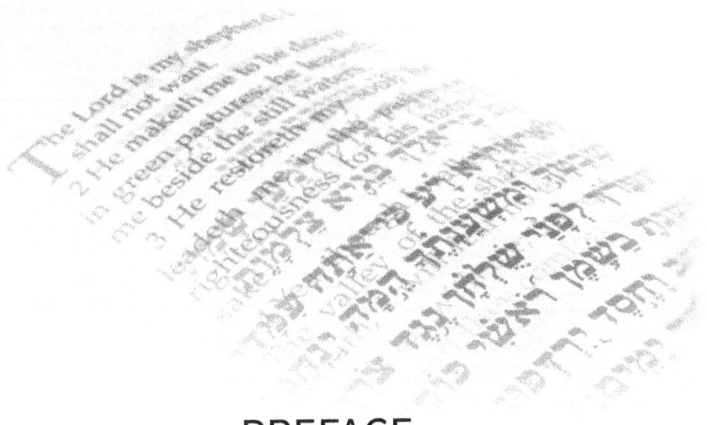

PREFACE

This writing is dedicated to those who believe the Bible is the Word of God, yet sometimes have trouble understanding what it is really saying. This is caused many times by mistranslations from the original manuscripts to English. Simple clarification by correctly translating the subject and object will many times be the difference as in daylight and dark. When the proper intended meaning is set forth, the entire Bible begins to make more sense. Areas of conflict that seemed unanswerable in English are now crystal clear with a new corrective light of truth for these end times. The Bible flows in concert when God's original message is stated. The truth of God's letter to us is truly a history of one man's family, a love story, a prophetic message and an instruction book for our lives. Some of the Bible was hidden until the time appointed. This end time Fig Tree Generation is the time. Many things are coming to light just on time, in God's time. Daniel and others were told not to write some of the things God revealed to them. They were to be revealed in the last days. Scales are coming from eyes and God's mysteries are being made simple for those that are intended to see and understand. Just as most of Jesus' disciples were not considered scholars in their day, God is revealing His end time truths to servants who are not necessarily of high ranking in academia, but have a teachable spirit and unquestionable loyalty to our Father. This simple book will answer questions you

3

may have always wondered about. For those of you who have always known there was more, this may be the key of David to open the lock in your mind. Once this hurdle is crossed, the entire Bible will become a living thing to you. For you see, *"In the beginning was the Word and the Word was with God, and the Word was God and the Word became flesh and dwells among us."*

In **Section I** we will begin by listing some obstacles that confront most Christians when they get serious about trying to find more about God. For a long time there seemed to be a barrier that caused me to think there were no solutions to finding out about God's overall plan. If you are like most people, you have been frustrated at times in your search for deeper truth about God. Having been a pastor of a small church for a few years and having counseled with people for over 45 years, I know religion is one of the big hang ups. Three main problem areas for most people are money, sex and religion. The better we understand the Bible, the better we are able to deal with any of life's problems. In **Section II** we will move into the Myths and Facts, then Questions and Answers portion and endeavor, with scriptures, to show how man's traditions have impacted our belief structure to the point of us being taught and believing a number of falsehoods. You may ask why this work should be believed? What makes this writing any more than this writer's opinion? Those questions are reasonable and will be answered. First, you are given the subject and then the scripture. Second, you are given the materials that you can use to do your own research and prove it for yourself.

My opinion is not worth much if it can't be backed up with scripture taken from the manuscripts. Let me make it clear from the start, you do not have to be a Greek/Hebrew scholar to be able to learn from the manuscripts. A Strong's Exhaustive Concordance of the Bible, a King James version of the Bible and a good Webster's Dictionary will start you out well. For those of you who do not place much value in the Bible or believe it to be myth, let me give an example or two for your consideration. In the early days of NASA's attempt to orbit a space craft, something unusual happened for the scientific community. It seems the way to project where everything in space will be at a certain time is to go back in time and find out the locations of planets and stars in the past. Since everything repeats itself in precise time, you go back, then project forward. Now get this picture in your mind. You have PhD's in white coats. These are the brightest of the bright. They were having trouble getting their readings to come out correctly. This was also the early days of the computer and they just could not get it to come out right. One of the PhD's said, "I remember when I was boy in Sunday School, we read in the Bible where the earth stood still." So they got a Bible and started looking. They found where the Earth stood still and entered that in the computer. This information helped, but it was still not perfect. So they looked and found another time where the time was changed. (actually the sun dial went backward) They entered all the information that the Bible has on this subject and it came out perfect. How do we know this happened? Well, in an official NASA publication the article theme read: "NASA Scientist use Bible to Solve Space Problem." I have personally seen this paper and had a copy of it at one time. So the accurateness of the Bible was used to benefit modern man. The National Geographic Society found years ago that they could save time and money by using the information in the Bible to help them on ancient archaeological digs. Some areas mentioned in the Bible, covered with the sands of time, were thought to be myth until uncovered and documented. These are just two examples that show that there is more to the Bible than many believe. If these things are true, then we must consider that more of it is true. If there is a God and He left us His book of instruction, we really need to do an in depth search and find out what we are missing when we don't follow the instructions in His book. We also need to factor in the greed and vanity of man slanting the information in the Bible for his or her benefit. This greed and ego factor, I believe, is one of the reasons we have all the different religions and beliefs today. After all if there is only one God, why do we have so much confusion about Him if there are not negative forces at work? This is allowed by God and it is up to each of us to search out the truth for ourselves. We must learn to eat the grapes and spit out the seeds.

The Pastors of Shepherd's Chapel, opened up some of the doors that I was unable to get through on my own. Once these areas had light shined on them, the Bible has really come alive. It is this writer's hope that this work will also open up God's truth in a deeper way for you. I thank God for the few that use the gifts that God gives them. Everyone has a gift. Sometimes we spend a lifetime trying to find what it is. Very few actually use the gifts God gives them for God. If you have memorized the Bible and can quote it, yet are relying on just the English translation, you still do not know the overall plan of God. You know far more that most, but getting into the manuscripts will open many other doors for you. If you have never studied from the manuscripts and have relied mostly on the English translations of the Bible, you will doubtless disagree at first with many of the things discussed. All that is asked of you is to keep an open mind and check it out in the manuscripts. Many good people have thought they found areas that were incorrect. However, when they took the time to check it out, most changed their mind. Once you get into the manuscripts and learn how they have been protected through the years, your opposition will melt with the light of truth. It is up to each of us to study for ourselves to prove what is true and acceptable to God by rightly dividing His Word. Jesus said it best when asked about some of His teachings. His reply was, **"It is written, have ye not read?"**

I will close this preface with an example of what is happening this day and time. My publisher sent one of my books to a seminary professor to proof read and get his opinion. I still had a land line at the ranch and he called one afternoon and after identifying himself, he said; "Murdoch, where did you come up with some of this stuff?" I asked him if he was comfortable using a Strong's Concordance and he replied, "absolutely, I have one right here on my desk." I then asked him what he had a problem with and he asked about what happened in the garden of Eden. I asked him to look up the word **"touch"** where God told them not to even touch the *"tree of knowledge of good and evil."* He looked it up and found the definition to be **"to lie with a woman."** I asked him to look up **"beguiled"** where Eve responded to God's question, *"woman, what is this thou hast done?"* Eve answered, *"the serpent beguiled me"* with the meaning **"to seduce"** I then asked the professor, what has any of this got to do with eating an apple? He then asked several other questions with the same results. After a forty-five minute talk, he paused and said, **"I have a masters degree, I pastor a church and am a seminary professor and I have learned more Bible in the last hour than I learned my entire life; how can this be? How can this happen?"** My reply was the same to everyone that asked that question. You have been taught the traditions of men by good, well meaning people that meant only the best for you. The problem is much of what is taught is handed down generation to generation and is now taught as gospel. The majority of churches today regardless of the denomination, do not teach the Bible chapter by chapter and verse by verse. They read a scripture or two and then speak their own words which may be heart rendering, but they are not the truth from God's Word. The sad result is people don't really understand the Bible. This man went from skeptic to believing in less than an hour and ended up writing the Forward for my second book.

In my opinion, the way to get the most out of this book is to read it all the way through, making notes and underlining as you go. Then go back, read it again and look up all those scriptures you wondered about or are convinced could not be true.

This writer will make you a promise, if you are able to find anything in this writing that is not in agreement with the manuscripts, I will apologize and immediately change it. We are not talking about the English translations of the Bible. We are talking about the original languages as found in the manuscripts. You can easily obtain the tools to check out this work and in doing so, you will learn more Bible in a short time than you have learned in your entire life.

David Murdoch

"WITH ALL THY GETTING, GET UNDERSTANDING, GET WISDOM"

"I was set up from everlasting, from the beginning,
Or ever the earth was. When there were no depths,
I was brought forth; When there were no fountains
abounding with water. Before the mountains were settled,
Before the hills was I brought forth:
While as yet He had not made the earth, nor the fields,
Nor the highest part of the dust of the world.
When He prepared the heavens, I was there: When he set
a compass upon the face of the depth: When he established
the clouds above: When He strengthened the
fountains of the deep: When He gave to the sea His decree,
That the waters should not pass His commandment:
When He appointed the foundations of the earth:
Then I was by Him as one brought up with Him:
And I was daily His delight, Rejoicing always before Him.
Rejoicing in the habitable part of His earth;
And my delights were with the sons of men."

Proverbs 8:23-31

SECTION I

OVERCOMING OBSTACLES
TO BETTER UNDERSTAND
GOD'S OVERALL PLAN

"In the beginning was the Word,
and the Word was with God,
and the Word was God.
And the Word was made flesh
and dwelt among us."

John 1:1, 14

A SERIOUS STUDENT MUST OVERCOME THESE OBSTACLES IN ORDER TO UNDERSTAND GOD'S ETERNAL PURPOSE.

1. NOT UNDERSTANDING THE THREE HEAVEN AND EARTH AGES WRITTEN ABOUT IN THE BIBLE.

2. PLACING OUR FOCUS ON JUST A PART OF GOD'S PLAN WITHOUT LOOKING AT THE WHOLE PLAN.

3. NOT UNDERSTANDING THE IMPORTANCE OF GETTING INTO THE ORIGINAL LANGUAGES.

4. NOT UNDERSTANDING THE BOOK OF GENESIS ESPECIALLY FROM THE BEGINNING THROUGH NOAH AND HIS FAMILY.

5. NOT UNDERSTANDING WHO THE SERPENT WAS, IS AND SHALL BE.

6. NOT KNOWING ABOUT THE DESCENDANTS OF CAIN.

7. NOT KNOWING THAT A LARGE MAJORITY OF CHURCH LEADERS OF ALL FAITHS ARE NOT SKILLED IN THE MANUSCRIPTS AND WHAT THE BIBLE REALLY SAYS.

8. OVERCOMING THE TRADITIONS AND TEACHINGS OF WELL MEANING FAMILY FRIENDS, TEACHERS AND CHURCH LEADERS IS ONE OF THE MOST DIFFICULT THINGS IN REALLY UNDERSTANDING GOD.

Now let's take each one and give enough details for the serious student to be able to remove the roadblocks set in place by poor scholarship and traditions. Please understand these are not the only drawbacks, but some of the more difficult ones that you will have to educate yourself about if you want to grow as a Christian.

1. NOT UNDERSTANDING THE THREE HEAVEN AND EARTH AGES WRITTEN ABOUT IN THE BIBLE.

Many people are not even aware that the Bible speaks to us about three ages, much less where to find them. The Bible tells us many are willingly ignorant of the ages.

a. II Peter 3:5-7 *"For this they willingly are ignorant of, that by the word of God the heavens were of old and the earth standing out of the water and in the water. 6. Whereby the world that then was, being overflowed with water, perished. 7. But the heavens and the earth which are now, by the same word are kept in store, reserved unto fire against the day of judgment and perdition of ungodly men."*

b. Jeremiah 4:23 *"I beheld the earth and lo, it was without form and void and the heavens and they had no light. 24. I beheld the mountains and lo, they trembled and all the hills moved lightly. 25. I beheld and lo, there was no man and all the birds of heaven were fled. 26. I beheld and lo, the fruitful place was a wilderness and all the cities there of were broken down at the presence of the LORD and by His fierce anger. 27. For thus hath the LORD said, "The whole land shall be desolate, yet will I not make a full end."* This is clearly not Noah's flood, but the earth that was. Pilots have to use isogonic or magnetic deviation to adjust their heading for true north. The reason is that when God shook the earth, true north was thrown out of line about six degrees. There were no man or birds remaining after this shaking. Careful study will show this first earth age will explain the disappearance of prehistoric animals, birds and some sea creatures. It was also the time when cities like Atlantis, things like the Sphinx and other unexplained mysteries happened.

God talks about this time in **Job 38** when he asked Job, *"Where were you when the morning stars sang together and the sons of God shouted for Joy?"* Many places in the Bible are referred to as *"of old."* We are most familiar with the earth that is, for we are living in that time now. **Isaiah 45:18** *"For thus saith the LORD that created the heavens, God Himself that formed the earth and made it. He hath established it, He created it not in vain, He formed it to be inhabited. I AM THE LORD, and there is none else."* GOD did not create the earth in vain. The Hebrew word **"tohu"** is used for the word void in **Genesis 1:2. Verse 1** tells us that *"In the beginning God."* The Creator is separate from His creation. A better understanding would be **"In the very beginning, God created the first heaven and earth."** Verse 2 of **Genesis 1**: *"And the earth was without form and void"* should be translated. **"And the earth became void."** For it was created perfect and then became void as described in **Jeremiah 4:23.** *"Yet I will not make a full end."* After this begins the beginning of the earth that is now.

c. **Revelation 12** tells us the reason the first heaven and earth age was destroyed. **Verse 3.** *"And there appeared another wonder in heaven and behold a great red dragon, having seven heads and ten horns and seven crowns upon his heads. 4. And his tail drew the third part of the stars of heaven and did cast them to the "Earth."* The Dragon, who is the Devil, is the reason God destroyed the First Heaven and Earth Age. Ezekiel gives us more details about some of the names given to the devil and his part in the Garden of Eden. **Ezekiel 28:1** *"The word of the LORD came again unto me, saying, 2. 'Son of man, say unto the prince of Tyrus, Thus saith the LORD GOD; because thine heart is lifted up and thou hast said, I am a God, I sit in the seat of God, in the midst of the seas;' yet thou art a man and not GOD, though thou set thine heart as the heart of God."* Here we find the devil referred to as the prince of Tyrus. He had already been demoted (in the first earth age) from King of Tyrus which you will find if you continue reading. Let's continue to see his role in the garden. **Ezekiel 28:13** *"Thou hast been in Eden* (as the serpent) *the garden of God; every precious stone was thy covering, the sardius, topaz and the diamond, the beryl, the onyx and the jasper, the sapphire, the emerald and the carbuncle and gold: the workmanship* *of thy tabrets and of thy pipes was prepared in thee in the day that thou wast created. Thou art the anointed cherub that covereth; and I have set thee so: thou wast upon the holy mountain of God; thou has walked up and down in the midst of the stones of fire."* (At the very altar of God) *15. "Thou wast perfect in thy ways from the day that thou wast created, till iniquity was found in thee."* God created him the full pattern and he earned his way up to being one of two cherubs who guarded the Mercy Seat of God. God loved him, but that was not enough for "old pretty boy" he wanted to sit on the Mercy Seat and be God. You can read on and find more about this good creation that chose to turn bad. Satin is the only one in the Bible called by name that has been sentenced to die. More about the devil under item 5 in this chapter.

d. Man's traditions have taught us that the earth age we are living in now is the age that was created in **Genesis 1:1**. Many let their ignorance show when they say the earth is only six thousand years old. As mentioned, **Jeremiah 4** makes it clear that this is not the case. God was very displeased with Satan and his bunch, but could not bring Himself to destroy one third of His children. He chose to destroy the earth age that existed at that time. He destroyed the cities and He shook the earth off its axis to where true north is about six degrees off course. (from Ft. Worth) He destroyed the birds and animals living at that time. This is what happened to the dinosaur. There are some animals and things that made it through this terrible shaking. The crocodile for one and other sea creatures. This also accounts for the city of Atlantis and others still a mystery to most today.

The following is a scientific explanation of how the earth is now. The rotation of the earth is now on an inclined axis west to east every 24 hours at the rate of 1,000 mph. Earth is also racing over its course around the sun from east to west at a speed of 1,000 miles per minute. There is another motion in conjunction with these two called "wabbling." This is illustrated by the swaying action of a top after the speed of rotation is no longer sufficient to keep it perfectly upright. This wabbling of the central axis of the earth is due to its lopsidedness or uneven distribution of bulk along the equatorial belt, causing a periodic increase and decrease of the attraction

14

exerted by the sun and moon. Were the earth a perfect sphere this wabbling would not occur. It is however, flattened at the poles and over-bulged along the equator. This wabbling was started at the katabloe where God destroyed the first earth age. We all look forward when the Third Heaven and New Earth Age is restored to its original perfection. (taken from unknown author)

2. **PLACING OUR FOCUS ON JUST A PART OF GOD'S PLAN WITHOUT LOOKING AT THE WHOLE PLAN.**

a. Most Christian denominations place their emphasis on salvation. **John 3:16** makes it clear what is necessary for salvation. This is the first step and is both necessary and wonderful. Paul made it clear in **Hebrews 6:6** that to preach salvation to those who are already saved is like putting Jesus to an open shame, because it is like saying He did not do it right the first time. Paul, who wrote most of the New Testament, also was upset with those who were still teaching the basics after two years. He said it was like adults still on a milk bottle. Let's read Hebrews 6:1-6 as a good example that we need to move past a salvation message. **Verse 1.** *"Therefore leaving the principles of the doctrine of Christ, let us go on unto perfection, not laying again the foundation of repentance from dead works and of faith toward God, 2. Of the doctrine of baptisms and of laying on of hands and of resurrection of the dead and of eternal judgment. 3. And this will we do, if God permit. 4. For it is impossible for those who were once enlightened and have tasted of the heavenly gift and were made partakers of the Holy Spirit, 5. And have tasted the good word of God and the powers of the world to come, 6. If they shall fall away, to renew them again unto repentance; seeing they crucify to themselves the Son of God afresh and put Him to an open shame."* Wow! In these six verses we find that we are to move on to the deeper things of God. And when we do so and taste of these deeper riches in the Holy Spirit it is difficult to just play church again. These verses also talk about the Third World Age which is to come. Most Christians agree that salvation is the foundation of their belief system. I think we can all agree on that. Let me give an example of what this must look like to God when we keep going back to this type of message over

15

and over. Picture in your mind trucks pouring cement into a foundation form. Now the lot has been prepared, the rough-in plumber is already done. The designer of the house is there to be sure everything is correct. The cement people pour the foundation and then finish it to the specifications of the designer and owner. When they finish their work everyone stands back and admires this perfect foundation. After a few days to allow the cement to cure properly, the house is now ready to begin the framing of the house. Instead of starting on the walls, the cement truck is ordered back out. The cement people take a look and see this perfect foundation and leave because their job has been done. They ask, "Why did you want us to come back and do it again?" People drive by and see this perfect foundation anticipating the beautiful house that is to be built. After a few months the owner uses a small portion of the foundation to erect a lean-to. It really looks funny with this big beautiful slab and this small fragile excuse for a house sitting in the middle of it. Every time a storm comes the lean-to is blown away. Now the foundation is still there and still good, but the potential of what could have been is not fulfilled. No wonder Paul was so upset with these people who were still on a milk bottle. If we expand on this just a little we can compare many church congregations to driving by a sub-division with hundreds of slabs ready to build, but no completed houses. The wonderful thing about the mercy of our Heavenly Father is that no matter how old our foundation is we can still start building upon it. Even if it has been months, years or even decades since our slab was poured, we can start building now. If there are no completed houses in the whole sub-division we may find that the people who own them may not know how to build. If you are in a church that does not go much past salvation, it may be time to either find another pastor or another church. Either way it is really up to you to build on your foundation. If you have a pastor that is well studied in God's word and teaches about the whole plan of God, then you are blessed. Even if you don't have such a pastor, you can *"study to show yourself approved unto God."* You can not only build the house, you can also furnish it with just the right decor so that you will know that God is pleased with you. I really don't think there are too many liberties taken in this modern parable. Kind of sad isn't it. This writer has found only two Bible teachers in his life time that don't beg for money and do teach from the manuscripts. Try your local television listing under Shepherd's Chapel. They have been teaching over 50 years. Give them a look in the early A.M.

b. In order to understand God's overall plan we must first look at it from a distance. At one time my wife and I raised Arabian horses. (By the way we can trace these horses back to Abraham in the Bible). If I really want to appreciate a horse, I first back off and view it from a distance where I can really see the whole horse. Once I see the balance, symmetry and movement of the whole horse, then I can move closer and appreciate the individual parts that make up the whole. If I only view the horse up close and focus on the area right in front of me, I can learn a great deal about that part, but will not know much about the entire horse. I will not understand how all of the parts come together to make this animal one of God's most beautiful creations. Likewise, if I spend my whole life on salvation, I will miss out on the completeness of GOD. I may not find out why salvation was necessary in the first place or go back to before mankind was created in this flesh realm. I won't know that the Bible talks about dinosaurs and UFO's. I won't know about eternity past where the Sons of God and the Morning Stars sang together. I won't understand how the High Priest that questioned Jesus was not really a Priest of God at all, but rather a Priest of the Synagogue of Satan. **Revelation 2:9, 3:9**

3. **NOT UNDRSTANDING THE IMPORTANCE OF GETTING INTO THE ORIGINAL LANGUAGES.**

a. The Bible was not written in English, it was translated from Hebrew and Greek. There is much lost by honest mistakes. There is more lost through deliberate changes. We can still dig out the truth if we go to the manuscripts.

b. The vast majority of people in this country make the mistake of accepting the English translations as all they need to understand God and His ways. All the while deep down inside knowing there is more. Let's take a verse in Genesis to illustrate why getting into the original language is so important. **Genesis 3:13** *"And the LORD God said unto the woman, What is this thou hast done? And the woman said, The serpent beguiled me and I did eat."* If we go to the Strong's Main Concordance and look up the word **"BEGUILED"** we find the number 5377. If we then go to the Hebrew Dictionary in the back of the Strong's Concordance and look up 5377 we find the primitive root word **"NASHA"** with the meaning **"TO LEAD ASTRAY, TO SEDUCE."** If we go to the New Testament, **II Corinthians 11:3** we find Paul talking about the same subject. **Verse 3.** *"But I fear, lest by any means, as the serpent beguiled Eve through his subtitle, so your minds should be corrupted from the simplicity that is in Christ."* The number in the Greek for **"BEGUILED"** in the Strong's is 1818 **"EXAPATAO,"** with the meaning to **"SEDUCE WHOLLY."** So we can easily see what most churches teach about what happened in the garden is way off base and has nothing to do with eating an apple. This, by the way, is one of the parts that is needed to understand God's overall plan. It also opens the door to understanding why Cain is never found listed in the off-spring of Adam. It does not take too much to understand why Jesus told the religious leaders of that time in **John 8:44** *"Ye are of your father the devil and the lusts of your father ye will do. He was a murderer from the beginning and abode not in the truth, because there is no truth in him. When he speaketh a lie, he speaketh of his own: for he is a liar and the father of it."* Who was the first recorded murderer in the Bible? Cain!

c. Let's take another example of what happens when we don't go to the original languages. We will deal with the same subject so we have another witness. **Genesis 3:3** *"But of the fruit of the tree which is in the midst of the garden, God hath said, ye shall not eat of it, neither shall ye touch it, lest ye die."* Again going to the Strong's and looking up the word **"TOUCH"** we find the number 5060 which in Hebrew is **"NAGA"** with the meaning **"TO LIE WITH A WOMAN."** We can see with just these words how we as a people have been led down the wrong path. A famous painting showing Eve eating an apple given to her by a snake is not even close to what really took place.

The veil that has been over the eyes of well meaning Christians is now blown away by truth that was there all the time.

d. Now using a different subject we will look at **Luke 14:26** where the English Bible tells us we must hate our loved ones in order to be Jesus disciple. Jesus is talking: *"If any man come to Me and hate not his father and mother and wife and children and brethren*

and sisters, yea, and his own life also, he cannot be My disciple."
This sounds terrible for Jesus to tell us we have to hate our loved
ones and our self in order to be His disciple. First of all this does
not make sense and is not in keeping with the nature of God. The
word hate in the Greek is **"MISEO"** and translates **"TO LOVE
LESS."** Hey, I can live with that, I'm supposed to love God more
than these others, not hate them. We see again how important it is
to go to the manuscripts to find out what is really meant. With this
information the Bible starts to make more sense in areas that have
been clouded in mystery. Now we can better understand from the
first two examples why God told His people to do away with the
people that inhabited the promise land. These people were descendants of that old serpent, the devil. Cain was not the son of Adam. I
know this sounds radical if this is the first time you have ever heard
such a thing, but the Bible has the information if we are willing to
dig it out; to *"Study to show ourselves approved that we might not
be ashamed when we stand before God."*

Let me close this part by paraphrasing some information giv-
en in the Green's Interlinear Hebrew Bible, by Jay P. Green Sr.,
General Editor and Translator. For centuries the Biblical text was
only available to a few. There first had to be a standard tool created
with which to work. This came to us in 1611 with the King James
version of the Bible with the final form of it being established in
1730. Now it was possible to make a concordance which could be
used by everyone; whether learned or unlearned with only the ability to read necessary for its use. After another century or so, lexicon-
dictionaries and grammars found fertile soil and added their input to
the growing knowledge of the Bible. These works were mostly for
the learned or formally trained. Then came two big concordances,
one by James Strong first published in 1890 (in my opinion the best.
DM) and Robert Young's published in 1884. With this work much
needed help was available to those who only knew the English language. With the aid of computers and all the Biblical information
available today you would think everyone would have a better understanding of what our Father's Word is saying. Let me now quote,
with permission, from Volume I of the Interlinear Bible: "It should
be kept in mind in the use of this work that there is a wide difference
in time and culture and language, not only between Hebrew and

Greek, but also between those languages, times and cultures and those of our day. In rendering the Biblical languages into English we particularly found it difficult to deal with the following:

a. Figures of Speech: The Hebrew speaks of the 'lip' of the river, rather than the 'Bank' sometimes the 'mouth' of Jehovah, rather than the 'word' or 'command' of Jehovah;' lifting the heads' rather than counting, etc.

b. Parts of Speech: It is not always possible to render the parts of speech in literal form and at the same time convey the meaning to the English reader.

c. Interpretation: It is not always possible to render the parts of speech in literal form and at the same time convey the meaning to the English reader.

d. Untranslated words: There are some Hebrew words which are not translated in any work. A sign defining the direct object of a verb and at places a little different sign, the relative particle, which is sometimes redundant.

e. Punctuation and Capitalization: It should be noted that in the original Biblical languages, both Hebrew and Greek, all letters were capital letters. It should also be noted that there was no punctuation in the original manuscripts, either in Hebrew or Greek. The Masoretic punctuation (c 700 AD.) have placed certain punctuation marks for the benefit of the Hebrew reader. For this reason the punctuation may seem strange." (to the English reader. (DM) Green's comments certainly point out some of the obstacles confronting the serious student. These things lead us to the next reason why we have trouble understanding God's plan. (The next three obstacles, 4,5, and 6, are really a part of number 3, but are important enough to be listed separately.)

4. NOT UNDERSTANDING THE BOOK OF GENESIS, ESPECIALLY FROM THE BEGINNING THROUGH NOAH AND HIS FAMILY.

a. The first part of Genesis covers many events and a considerable amount of time. Here we find the First Earth Age in **Genesis 1:1** Careful study will show that this was the time when *"the morning stars sang together and the sons of God shouted for joy"* as discussed in **Job 38** and the destruction of the First Earth Age discussed in

Jeremiah 4. The earth became void during this destruction and God started over with this Earth Age.

b. We see the recreation of birds, animals, fish and man through the first six thousand years. We see God resting on the seventh day and forming "Adam" on the following day.

c. We see this man **"ETH HA-ADAM"** and his wife, Eve, disobeying God and getting involved with the serpent (who is the devil) with the resulting off-spring being a son of the devil, Cain, being born to Eve. We see how easy it is for Satan to fool man with his lies by misquoting what God has said. In this writers opinion all lies are about ninety percent truth, otherwise it would be obvious that they were lies. We see God revealing some of His plan by telling us about the **"SEED"** of the **"SERPENT"** and the **"SEED"** of the **"WOMAN."** Careful study will show God was talking about Jesus dying for us and the devil being destroyed in the end.

d. We find the bad angels coming directly to earth as talked about in **Jude.** Let's look at **verse 4.** *"For there are certain men crept in unawares, who were before of old ordained to this condemnation, ungodly men, turning the grace of our God into lasciviousness and denying the only LORD God and our Lord Jesus Christ. 6. And the angels which kept not their first estate, but left their own habitation, He hath reserved in everlasting chains under darkness unto the judgment of the great day."* They found the daughters of Adam fair and caused them to bare giants in the land. This caused God to regret He had made man in the flesh.

e. God found Noah and his family were the only ones that had not had sexual relations with these bad angels and were pure in their generations or pedigree. God instructed Noah to build an ark and take two of every flesh. Careful study will show this was also two of every race of people, not just animals. For the serious student, let's go to **Genesis 1:31** and it reads: *"And God saw every thing that He had made and behold, it was very good. And the evening and the morning were the sixth day."* **Genesis 2:1** *"Thus the heavens and the earth were finished and all the host of them."* Stop and think how many are in a host. If you are gaining eyes that see, you were just told that all the races were created by the end of six thousand years from the start of the second heaven and earth age. The First Earth Age lasted millions of years and the scientist and the Bible do not disagree. Now go to **II Peter 3:8** *"But beloved, be not ignorant of this one thing, that one day is with the LORD as a thousand years and a thousand years as one day."* Now go to **II Peter 3:5.** and see for yourself how God is telling you about all three Heaven and Earth ages and how most people do not have knowledge of this. *"For this they willingly are ignorant of, that by the word of God the heavens were of old and the earth standing out of the water and in the water: 6. Whereby the world* (first earth age) *that then was, being overflowed with water, perished: 7. But the heavens and the earth which are now,* (this earth age) *by the same word are kept in store, reserved unto fire against the day* (third earth age) *of judgment and perdition of ungodly men."* These are just some of the highlights in the first part of Genesis that if not understood make it almost impossible for you to understand God's Eternal Purpose for your life. He will still love you as He loves all His children, but you won't be of much use to Him. Since He made all things for His pleasure: **Revelation 4:11** *"Thou art worthy, O LORD, to receive glory and honor and power: for Thou hast created all things for Thy pleasure they are and were created."* When is the last time you gave Him pleasure by telling Him you love Him and showing Him you love Him by getting into the letter He left for you, the Bible. If you wrote a letter to your child and advised them of all they would ever need to know and they never even went to the trouble to try to read and understand it, how would you feel?

5. NOT UNDERSTANDING WHO THE SERPENT WAS AND IS AND HOW HE OPERATES.

Without a clear understanding of who your enemy is makes it impossible to know much about your enemy, whose job is to keep you from learning about God's plan. **Revelation 12:9** *"And the great dragon was cast out, that old serpent, called the Devil and Satan, which deceiveth the whole world."* We must understand *"that old serpent"* is the same serpent discussed In Genesis that beguiled Eve. His deception started long before in the "First Earth Age" when and where he fooled one third of God's creation into following him and rebelling against God. This rebellion is the reason for the destruction of the "First Earth Age." to give those rebels another chance to choose again. He allows Satan to live somewhat restrained. God's plan was constantly under attack by "that old serpent." Satan tried to mess up the Adamic line by seducing Eve. Satan tried to alter God's plan; by taking over the promise land; by sending his descendants through Cain and the fallen angels to take over the land first. **Genesis 7:15** *"two of every flesh went on the ark."* He is still confusing God's people today by subtle changes done to our Bible by his henchmen and scribes who were and are Kenites or sons of Cain. Whether a person is consciously aware or not, that they are doing the work of the devil does not change the fact that the work gets done by his or her hands. Satan causes many to buy into a radical agenda that in the person's mind has nothing to do with religion, yet it serves the devil's purpose well. I will give you an example of how even some of our Bible's have been altered. Let's go to **Ezekiel 13:20** in the Original King James Bible. *"Wherefore thus saith the LORD GOD; 'Behold, I am against your pillows, wherewith ye there hunt the souls to make them fly and I will tear them from your arms and will let the souls go, even the souls that ye hunt to make them fly."* Some of the newer revised additions change the meaning to *"birds flying."* "You say, so what difference does that little change make." You see this is one of the places in His book of instructions where God makes it clear there will be no "fly away" or "rapture." Yet with this seemingly innocent little change, one of God's warning is taken away. (We get into the rapture theory later.) In the Old Testament before "Grace," no wonder God told His people to kill all the people in the land when they went in. God knew if these devil worshipers were allowed to live they would corrupt His people; which they did, but not all. Reading **Ezekiel 28:1-19** with understanding will help shed light on the devil.

6. **NOT KNOWING ABOUT THE FAMILY OF CAIN AND THE FALLEN ANGELS.**

Sad to say, most Christians have never heard of the off spring of Cain, much less completed an in depth study of them. Kenites are sons of Cain, who was a son of "that old serpent." They are a race of people whose descendants are still in the earth today. When you stop and consider this fact, many things become clear. It explains why some people are so evil and why many things that happen have no logical explanation. They can be saved if they repent and accept Jesus as their Lord instead of the devil; this poses a challenge if you ever encounter a Kenite. God is fair to everyone and they will have their chance during their walk on earth to accept God's truths instead of Satan's lies.

a. Jude tells about the fallen angels that came directly to earth and had sexual relations with women and produced children. Careful study shows *"and again"* after Noah's flood, so they are still here. **Genesis 6:2** *"That the sons of God saw the daughters of men that they were fair; and they took them wives of all which they chose."* **Verse 4.***"There were giants in the earth in those days; and also after that (after the flood)when the sons of God came in unto the daughters of men and they bare children to them, the same became mighty men which were of old, men of renown."* **Numbers 13:33** *"And there we saw the giants, the sons of Anak, which came of the giants: and we were in our own sight as grasshoppers and so we were in their sight."* the word giant is from the Hebrew **"nephilim"** or fallen angel. Please note: The **Genesis 6:2** account would be better understood if the manuscripts were consulted. Properly translated we find a clearer meaning. *"That the fallen angels of God saw the daughters of ha Adam that they were fair: and they took them women of all which they chose."* This is emphatic "the man Adam" not mankind. These were the daughters of Adam that these fallen angels seduced "beguiled" in order to attempt to mess up God's plan for the Christ to come through the Adamic seed line. These nephilim did not marry these daughters of Adam as this poor translation indicates by stating: *"and they took them wives of all which they chose."* The devil's first known attempt to thwart God's plan was to seduce Eve. If this second attempt or any of his attempts were to succeed, he would prove he was wiser than God and thus reverse his death sentence and miss the lake of fire. Now to be sure it is clear to the reader. The nephilim (fallen angels) came directly to earth as discussed in the book of Jude. The off spring of the nephilim were the giants born to the daughters of Adam. David a descendant of Adam, fought and killed one of these descendants, a giant of about ten feet tall (six cubits and a span), named Goliath.

24

You can read about this enormous man in **I Samuel 17**, his size is given in **Verse 4**. There have been a number of giants even in more recent times. The skeleton of a man nine feet tall was found in a cemetery in England not too many years ago. Ignoring the facts does not change the facts. The Bible tells us they existed and bones and history verify they did. The enlightened Bible account of these hybrid beings in much more plausible, even to the skeptic, than some of the fairy tales taught by the so called intellectual elite who don't believe in God.

b. Jesus talked about a more normal size off-spring of Cain in the parable of the sower. This is very descriptive and leaves no doubt if the reader is looking for truth. Let's see what Jesus has to say about this race of people. **Matthew 13:24** *"Another parable put He forth unto them, saying, the kingdom of heaven is likened unto a man which sowed good seed in his field: 25. But while men slept, his enemy came and sowed tares among the wheat and went his way. 26. But when the blade was sprung up and brought forth fruit, then appeared the tares also. 27. So the servants of the householder came and said unto him, Sir, didst not thou sow good seed in thy field? From whence then hath it tares? 28. He said unto them, an enemy hath done this. The servants said unto him, wilt thou then that we go and gather them up? 29. But he said, Nay: lest while ye gather up the tares, ye root up also the wheat with them. 30. Let both grow together until the harvest: and in the time of harvest I will say to the reapers, Gather ye together first the tares and bind them in bundles to burn them: but gather the wheat into my barn."* Jesus disciples came later and said *"please tell us what you were talking about."* People say today, "I just don't understand the Bible, please tell me what it really says." The answer Jesus gives can be understood by a first-grader if they just listen. **Matthew 13:37** *"He answered and said unto them, 'He that soweth the good seed is the son of man; 38. The field is the world; the good seed are the children of the kingdom; but the tares are the children of the wicked one; 39. The enemy that sowed them is the devil; the harvest is the end of the world; and the reapers are the angels. 40. As therefore the tares are gathered and burned in the fire; so shall it be in the end of this world."* Now, so there is no doubt about what Jesus is talking about, let's look up the word *"seed"* as used in the parable. The explanation is the Greek word in the Strong's number 4690 "**Sperma**" or "**Male Sperm.**" This is directly telling you about this race of people. If you don't understand this from the mouth of Jesus, it's probably not meant for you to understand at this time. Let's drop on down in this same chapter of **Matthew to Verse 49**. *"So shall it be at the end of the world: the angels shall come forth and sever the wicked from among the just, 50. AND SHALL cast them into the furnace of fire: there shall be wailing and gnashing of teeth." 51. Jesus saith unto them, "Have ye understood all these things?" They say unto him, "Yea, Lord."* You might look in the mirror and ask yourself, "do I understand?" If you have to say no, it is time to really look at your life and belief system.

7. NOT KNOWING THAT A LARGE MAJORITY OF CHURCH LEADERS OF ALL FAITHS ARE NOT SKILLED IN THE MANUSCRIPTS AND WHAT THE BIBLE REALLY SAYS.

If your pastor gets up and says, "my text for today is" and then reads a scripture or two and then starts telling sad or humorous stories and refers to the Bible, but does not teach chapter by chapter and verse by verse, you are being cheated out of your full potential as a child of God. He or she is only doing what they were taught in seminary. Most are taught to never teach beyond a forth grade level and never talk about anything that is controversial. Sad to say many people go to church all their lives and have never been taught the Bible all the way through with understanding. This can only be accomplished when the pastor or teacher is very familiar with the original languages in which the Bible was written. It was not written in English. I have been counseling for over forty years and have counseled with pastors, their wives, their children, church leaders and teachers and sad to say, not many if any at all, knew what the Bible really says or God's over-all plan. This by no means is saying there are not any, only that there are very few and that has been my experience. After I read and understand the book of Ezra do I realize that times are not much different than about thirty-five hundred years before Christ. **Ezra 2:62 *These sought their register among those that were reckoned by genealogy,*** *but they were not found: therefore were they, as polluted, put from the priesthood."* If you will study the books of Ezra and Nehemiah, you will find that out of the six hundred priest that were traveling with them, they did not find one single legitimate priest. How many truly called of God servants of God, do you know? I'm not talking about good sincere people trying to do what is right. We are talking about "God Called, Anointed" men and women of God that are teaching with understanding the "Word of God." What was found in Ezra's time trying to pass themselves off as Priests of God, were scribes and Nethinims. (temple servants) They had worked their way into the Priesthood, because the real Priest were lazy and had them cut wood and do other chores the Priest did not want to do. Over time and after generations they had gradually taken more and more of the Priests' duties until they took over all the duties.Too many pastors are not called of God. Most pastors go to school to learn how to manage a church. They learn how to marry and bury. They learn how to take in money. They learn the traditions of men. Most learn enough Bible to get by. Most don't spend time in the manuscripts to find out what the Bible really says. If their school is one of the few that may still teach Hebrew, (very few if any left) it is modern Hebrew, not ancient Hebrew or Greek. If a pastor does not have a knowledge of at least how to study with understanding he or she will not be able to teach the people that attend their church about the total plan of God. They will spend most of their time on salvation and never get into the deeper truths of God.

The next time you go to church, pay attention to how much time is actually spent on the teaching of God's word. Don't get me wrong, most of these people are great speakers and can make chills run up your back at times. It takes about four to five years for a good Bible teaching pastor to go through the Bible if they are teaching chapter by chapter and verse by verse at three services a week. The sad thing for me, I have been counseling for over forty years and I have yet to meet a regular church attender that has ever had their denomination teach the Bible from cover to cover. Check them out the next time they use a verse in the Bible. Do yourself a favor, when your pastor says "My text for today is" and then quotes a verse or two, write the date beside the verse and then see how long it is before they return to that verse. It is usually not long. Common sense tells us that if they only teach a verse or two each week, you won't live long enough to cover the entire Bible. You will have enough to understand your denominational slant on why "they have the truth." How sad. Let me close this part by being very clear: If you have a pastor who teaches the Bible with understanding on a regular basis and covers the entire Bible in about four years, you are very blessed and the things we are discussing here are no surprise to you. If you are not being taught you can make up your mind to teach yourself. A few simple tools, mentioned in the Preface of this book, are all you need.

8. OVERCOMING THE TRADITIONS AND TEACHINGS OF WELL MEANING FAMILY, FRIENDS, TEACHERS AND CHURCH LEADERS IS ONE OF THE MOST DIFFICULT THINGS IN REALLY UNDERSTANDING GOD AND HIS WAYS.

If there is any doubt, man will always trust tradition before trusting what the Bible really says. Some traditions are based on God's Word, many are not. Let's look at a few.

EASTER

One tradition that most churches observe is Easter, which is not in the manuscripts. Even a good college dictionary will tell you Easter comes from the word "EASTRE" which was a pagan fertility festival. Eggs certainly have to do with fertility, but it makes one wonder how they worked their way into the Holy Day of Passover. The word Easter is wrongly used one time in the book of Acts. In the manuscripts the correct word "Paschal" is used, not Easter. Was this change accidental or on purpose? Ask yourself, "what does Passover have to do with hard boiled eggs?"

CHRISTMAS

Another tradition is celebrating December 25 as Jesus' birthday. It is indeed a day for celebrating, but it is the conception or day Jesus began to dwell with man. This is easily proven even with a King James Bible. Ask yourself why would shepherd's be tending their flocks in winter when there was nothing for the sheep to eat? Why would the Roman government be taxing the people in winter when travel was difficult and months after the crops had been harvested? This will be covered in more detail in the Myths and Facts portion of this book.

RAPTURE

One of the most dangerous traditions which is not scriptural in the rapture doctrine. **Proverbs 10:30** tells us very plainly that *"The righteous shall never be removed from the earth."* **Ezekiel 13:20** tells us that *"God is against those who teach His people to fly in order to save their soul."* Why did the rapture story begin in AD 1830 after a woman in Scotland, by the name of Margaret MacDonald, had an evil dream? (her words) This doctrine is dangerous because it teaches God's people that they are to worship the first Jesus that comes on the scene and does not inform them that this is really Satan as a Jesus look-a-like. The shame of those fooled by "instead of Jesus" will cause many to pray for mountains to fall on them because they will be so ashamed that they worshiped the devil. Jesus' parables make it very clear that the people taken first are the people fooled by Satan.

If you are familiar with God's overall plan, then you have the scales off your spiritual eyes and ears. You are and will be aware of who you are, what your are doing here and you will be about your Father's business. You will see God's hand in all of life. He is the Creator of Heaven and Earth, He is the giver and sustainer of all life. If most of the things we are discussing are not familiar to you then I suspect you are not familiar with the manuscripts or God's overall plan. You have been told that all you have to do is believe. You have bought into the idea that you don't have to understand God's word; that you don't have to understand the book of Revelation. The preacher tells you to just listen to him and he will get you there. How sad so many have fallen for this doctrine so that through the years good sincere people obey the traditions of their church or family rather than following the Word of God. The majority of church goers today go to a building with pretty windows and listen to music that sounds so religious. They wonder and know deep inside there has to be more to God's Word than they have been taught. Most just shrug their shoulders and continue listening to traditions. Let me ask you, do know about the three heaven and earth ages? Do you know about what happened in the rebellion in the world that was; or what this earth age is all about? Do you know what happened in the garden of Eden? Does your church teach or even know the difference between Adam and Eth Ha Adam or why Cain is never listed in Adam's pedigree? You are not alone, most don't have a clue about what the polished metal vehicles described in Ezekiel are. Did you know the high priest at Jesus' trial was a disciple of the synagogue of Satan as spoken of in **Revelation 2:9**? *"I know the blasphemy of them which say they are Jews and are not, but are of the synagogue of Satan."* Have you ever looked up the word *"seed"* that was planted by the enemy in Jesus' parable in **Matthew 13** and found it is the Greek word for male sperm in the manuscripts and that Jesus is referring to a race of people?

Many pastors of most denominations are not taught and don't know that the food laws given by God in **Leviticus 11** are still in effect. Stop and ask yourself why are so many good people having so many health problems? Why is the average age of a medical doctor, to die in this country, 58 years old? Why are there so many overweight people including preachers? Let's go to **I Timothy 4:1** *"Now the Spirit speaketh expressly, that in the latter times some shall depart from the faith, giving heed to seducing spirits and doctrines of devils; 2. Speaking lies in hypocrisy; having their conscience seared with a hot iron; 3. Forbidding to marry and commanding to abstain from meats, which God hath created to be received with thanksgiving of them which believe and know the truth. 4. For every creature of God is good and nothing to be refused, if it be received with thanksgiving:"* We may deal with "forbidding to marry" later and focus our attention to the food laws. Many make the mistake of rushing over the above verses. You can make a case that as long as you receive it with thanksgiving, (you bless it) that you can eat anything. *"Which God hath created to be received."* is one of the keys to understanding what is really said here. God did not create scavengers to be eaten. They are good and there purpose is to cleanse the earth. Let me ask you, would you eat a buzzard? No way! Why not, I'm sure there is a chef somewhere that could prepare it to be eaten? We don't eat buzzard because it is obvious that it was not intended to be eaten. The same is true of all scavengers whether fish, fowl or animal. Their purpose is to clean the refuse from the water and earth. Now don't shoot the messenger, but the biggest abuse is the swine. Bacon and ham can be made to taste so good. The problem even if you want to leave God's laws out of it, is that the swine has almost no sweat glans with which to rid its body of poisons. Most animals, including humans move out much of the toxins from their bodies through their sweat. Other than a few in their nose, the hog has no sweat glans and stores the poisons in their bodies in their fat.

This writer found an article in the New England Journal of Medicine about thirty or so years ago that stated that pork could cause some forms of arthritis. I had some arthritis in one of my hands at the time and made the decision to abstain from eating pork for a while. (this was before I got into the Greek and Hebrew and studied from the manuscripts) The results were within about three months, I no longer had discomfort in my hand. So I made the decision before I found what the Bible really had to say about what we eat. I had been taught that the food laws had been done away with when Jesus died on the cross. God is the same yesterday, today and forever. He does change his method of dealing with us as we grow and mature. Let's read **Isaiah 65:3** *"A people that provoketh Me to anger continually to My face; that sacrificeth in gardens and burneth incense upon alters of brick; 4. Which remain among the graves and lodge in the monuments, which eat swine's flesh and broth of abominable things in their vessels; 5. Which say, "Stand by thyself, come not near to me; for I am holier than thou." "These are a smoke in My nose, a fire that burneth all the day."* If you don't understand how God feels about eating swine's flesh and broth of abominable things, after reading these scriptures, you have scales on your eyes and it is not intended for you to see at this time. Human bodies are the same today as they were when God gave the food laws. The reasons God did not want His children to eat scavengers then are the same reasons He does not want us to eat them now. He loves His children and does not want to see them in ill-health. Eating pork or other scavengers will not cause you to go to hell. Long term, it will however cause you to not be as healthy as you could be. There is a difference between rituals, ordinances and laws. Some of the rituals and ordinances were done away with when Jesus fulfilled them making them no longer necessary. For instance blood sacrifices are no longer required by God, because Jesus paid the price by shedding His blood once and for all. The Ten Commandments and others, including the food laws are still in effect.

If you study with understanding as directed in **Nehemiah 8:2,3 & 8** you will learn the hidden mysteries that are there for those who dig it out. Those who set aside the time to find out; those who are not willing to trust their souls to some other earthly person. If you don't have a good teacher, then you can study for yourself. If you are serious enough about finding out about God and His ways, many questions will be answered. You will learn that there will be animals in heaven as found in **Isaiah 11.** You will know that you will recognize your family as shown in **Ezekiel 44:25.** You will learn that God uses tough love many times to teach His children. You will know that there will be no rapture for it is Satan that comes at the sixth seal, sixth trump and sixth vial deceiving all those who have not studied and know his plan. Like the five foolish virgins who did not have enough oil (truth) in their vessels (minds). You will learn that Satan has offspring living in the earth today. You will learn his method of operation will be and you will not be fooled by this Jesus look alike. The word Anti-Christ in the Greek should be translated "instead of Christ." He is coming first, before the true Christ, who comes at the seventh trump. Contrary to popular teaching Satan is coming peaceable and prosperously. He would not fool very many if he came looking like the devil and killing people. He will lead the greatest revival the world has ever known. The vast majority of the world including the Christian world, will believe he is Christ and think they will fly away with him.

We will leave Section I on this note: I have a friend who is always telling me, "That's not in my Bible." When I show him where it is he always says, "I never saw that before." Once we realize that our Father's Word is complete and covers all of life's situations and problems, we are able to relax and know He is truly in charge. If you have a disagreement with your Father's Word, you will have to change your mind. Go to the manuscripts, search and dig until you find the answer. Then you will know that He is always right. If it appears on the surface that the Bible is contradicting itself, keep looking and sooner or later you will find it is in perfect harmony in the manuscripts. The Bible not only has the answers to problems, but more importantly it has the road map for success to help you become healthy, wealthy and wise.

Note: The poem on the back of **SECTION II** was found in an old Bible many years ago. It was in a white envelope and written on paper that had turned yellow with age. It is so beautifully written that it reminds me of one of the Psalms. I hope you enjoy it as much as I do.

SECTION II

TRUTHS AND MYTHS
ABOUT THE BIBLE

Religious Confusionists

All the organized confusion that confronts us day by day,
With its myriad of preachers, preaching we have found the way.
Now the writer's been a seeker since the days of early youth,
Ever learning, never able to say, "this church has the truth."
With three hundred ways to travel in the Gospel's firey race;
Are we on our way to heaven with the planets out in space?
The Amana, The Adventist, some wielding Aaron's Rod.
Apostolic Overcoming and The Holy Church of God.
Now the Baptist, Independent? Regular and Free Will.
Evangelical and Separate and Seed in The Spirit too.
Plymouth Brethren, River's brethren, Dunker's Brethren,
Open-Closed, seventeen if I count them,
All are right and all opposed. With some Witness
of Jehovah ever knocking at my door.
"We've received The Great Commission, holy gospel to Restore."
Commandment Keepers, Judaism, Daniel's Band, Pillar of Fire.
Everything at my disposal to suffice my heart's desire.
The disputed Book of Mormon, oh the picture the Priest paints.
By Divine Revelation we are "The Latter Day Saints."
As I read The Book of Mormon, I enjoyed it, truth or myth,
But I don't know who to follow, Brigham Young or Joseph Smith
Man, polygamist by nature, (oh my unruly tongue)
If my wife has no objections, I might follow Brigham Young.
But it leaves me kind of baffled when I read about their plights.
Mormons, patriarchs, Apostles, Brickerstones and Culterites,
Mennonites, Krimmer and Brethren too. Amish, Hitlerite,
Reformed, even Unaffiliated, Wisler; Old Order-transformed.
Methodist and Open Bible, Presbyterians and Jew. Christian
Science, with the latest, Muslims and Buddhism too. With so
many winds of doctrine,
But for which one should I fall? In this whirlwind controversy,
Maybe God's not there at all! B-o-o-k-s, no mortal man can
read them. So the Bibles still my choice. And through all this
controversy,
I can hear the "still small voice."

(Author unknown)

MYTHS THAT THE MAJORITY OF CHURCHS BELIEVE TO BE TRUE

TRUTHS AND MYTHS ABOUT THE BIBLE

As we have found that many things we believe to be Biblical may not be based on the Bible, but rather traditions of our church or family. Be honest and ask yourself; Is what I believe based on my personal study and research or have I accepted on faith what has been taught to be true? God tells us to *"study to show ourselves approved that we might not be ashamed at judgment."* **2 Timothy 2:15.** Some of the things we have discussed might upset you or even make you mad. However, careful study of the original languages and manuscripts will show that many of our beliefs are not based on God's Word. There is a cartoon in my office that shows a board meeting of a church. The head deacon is standing and stating to the others, "Our bylaws specifically state that the will of God can not be overturned without a two thirds majority vote." While this is a very funny cartoon it conveys a lot of truth. Many times church leaders vote rather than study. This could also be said of some of our Supreme Court's recent rulings. **Isaiah 3:4** *"And I will give children to be their princes and babes shall rule over them."* Isaiah was inspired by God to let those with eyes that see what would take place in the last days. We certainly have immature people in high places making decisions that effect all of us. You know we have a problem when a decision is made ruling in favor of about two percent of the population that offends over half of this nation. As a nation founded on Christian ideals, we should be ashamed to put people in office that do not believe in God. We have "In God we Trust" on our money, but many have shifted their trust to the government. For those who don't believe there is a God, hide and watch, God will not be mocked. God needs no vote, He is always

36

correct. He is slow to anger, but those who ridicule and make fun of Him will regret their poor decisions sooner than later.

Now let's go over some of the Myths that the majority of church people believe to be true. The scriptures used are taken from a King James Bible

1. MYTH: The earth is only six thousand years old.

FACT: The earth is millions of years old. The manuscripts and science say so. (This subject is discussed several times in this work.)

2. MYTH: The Bible does not discuss a world that existed before the world as we now know it.

FACT: The manuscripts and The King James version do indeed talk about the world that was, the world that is and the world that is to come. We find in **II Peter** that many people including church goers are willingly ignorant of the three heaven and earth ages. **II Peter 3:5** *"For this they willingly are ignorant of, that by the word of God the heavens were of old and the earth standing out of the water and in the water: 6. Whereby the world that then was, being overflowed with water, perished:"* (first heaven and earth age) **7.** *"But the heavens and the earth which are now, by the same word are kept in store,* (this present age) *reserved unto fire against the day of judgment and perdition of ungodly men.* (third age) *8. but, beloved, be not ignorant of this one thing, that one day is with the LORD as a thousand years and a thousand years as one day."* (the six days of Genesis were six of God's days.) Now let's deal with a poor translation in **Genesis 1:2** *"And the earth was without form and void; and darkness was upon the face of the deep."* Now we go to **Isaiah 45:18** to find that the earth was not created void. **Verse 18.** *For thus saith the LORD That created the heavens; God Himself That formed the earth and made it; He hath established it, He created it not in vain. He formed it to be inhabited: I Am the LORD.* Staying in **Isaiah 45,** go up to **verse 12.** *"I have made the earth and created man upon it; I, even My hands, have stretched out the heavens and all their host have I commanded."*

Now let's go to the book of **Revelation** and find what happened to cause God to destroy the first heaven and earth age. **Chapter 12: Verse 3.** *"And there appeared another wonder in heaven; and* *behold, a great red dragon, having seven heads and ten horns and sevens crowns upon his heads. 4. And his tail drew the third part of the stars of heaven and did cast them to the earth:"* Satan has many names including dragon. The book of Job tells us who the stars of heaven are and then we see that the devil caused one third of God's children to follow him. God could not bring Himself to destroy one third of his children so He destroyed the first heaven and earth age instead. **Job 38:7** *"When the morning stars sang together and all the sons of God shouted for joy."* Let's take the time to translate this chapter with understanding. It is one of the best accounting's of the Creator of the Universe telling a man about his workings. For a moment place yourself in Job's place and imagine God is talking to you. We will be using the notes from The Companion Bible. God is speaking directly to this man. **Job 38:3** *"Gird up now thy loins now like a man; for I will demand of thee and answer thou Me. 4. Where wast thou when I laid the foundations of the earth? Declare, if thou hast understanding. 5. Who hath laid the measures thereof, if thou knowest? Or who upon it stretched the line upon it? 6. Whereupon are the foundations thereof fastened? Or who laid the corner stone thereof; 7. When all the morning stars sang together, and all the sons of God shouted for joy? 8. Or, who fenced in with doors the [roaring] sea, When bursting forth from [Nature's] womb it came? 9. What time I made the clouds its covering-robe, and darkness deep the swaddling-band thereof; 10. When I decreed for it My boundary, And set its bars and doors and it said, 11. "thus far-no further, Ocean, shalt thou come: Here shalt thou stay the swelling of thy waves?" 12. Hast thou called Morning forth since thou wast born; Or taught the early Dawn to know its place? 13. [Bid Morn] lay hold on outskirts of the earth? [Taught Dawn] to rout the lawless from their place? 14. [Bid Morn] change earth as clay beneath the seal; 15. Thus Morning robs the wicked of their prey, And stays, arrested, the uplifted arm. 16. The fountains of the sea has thou explored? Or hast thou searched the secrets of the deep? 17. The gates of Death: have they been shown to thee? Or hast thou seen the portals of its shade? 18. The utmost breadths of earth hast thou surveyed? Reply, if thou hast knowledge of it all. 19. Where lies the way that leads to Light's abode? And, as for Darkness, where is found its place; 20. That thou shouldst bring each to its proper* *bound, And know the paths that lead unto its house? 21. [Thou know'st [of course]: Thou must have then been born, And great must be the number of thy days! 22. The treasuries of Snow hast thou approached? Or, Hast thou seen the storehouse of the hail, 23. Which against a time of trouble I have kept, Against the day of battle and of war? 24. The Light: by what way do its rays break up? How drives the east wind o'er the earth its course? 25. Who cleft a channel for the floods of rain? Or passage for the sudden thunder-flash? 26. So that it rains on lands where no one dwells, On wilderness where no man hath his home, 27. To saturate the wild and thirsty waste, And cause the meadow's tender herb to shoot? 28. The Rain, hath it a father [beside Me]? The drops of Dew: who hath begotten them? 29. Whose is the whence cometh forth the Ice? And heaven's hoar-frost: who gave it its birth? 30. As, turned to stone, the waters hide themselves: The surface of the deep, congealed, coheres. 31. Canst thou bind fast the cluster Pleiades? Or, canst thous loosen [great] Orion's bands? 32. canst thou lead forth the Zodiac's monthly Signs? Or canst thou guide Arcturus and his sons? 33. The statutes of the heavens: know'st thou these? Didst thou set their dominion o'er the earth? 34. The clouds: canst thou to them lift up thy voice, That plenteousness of rain may cover thee? 35. Canst thou send lightnings forth, that they may go, And say to thee "behold Us! Here are we?" 36. Who hath put wisdom in the inward parts? Or understanding given to the heart? 37. Who by his wisdom piles the clouds in tiers? Or, who inclines the rain-clouds of the skies, 38. When dust, like metal fused, becometh hard, And clods cleave fast together solidly? 39. The Lion: wilt thou hunt for him his prey? Or satisfy the hunger of his young, 40. What time within their dens they lay them down, Or in their jungle lairs they lie in wait? 41. Who is it that provides the raven meat; When unto GOD his young ones lift their cry, And wander forth abroad from lack of food?* That is the end of Chapter 38. Let me ask you could you answer these questions that God is asking? Have you ever considered the awesomeness of your closest living relative? Being able to see our Father in the light of these scriptures is indeed rare. We will continue this insight by reading a while longer. Remember we are using this translation in order to make it easier for most to better understand. Don't let this old spelling of some words detract you from staying on course. **Job Chapter 39:1.** *"Know'st thou the time the Rock-Goat gendereth? Observest thou the calving of the Hinds? 2. The months they fill, didst thou their number set, And know the time when they to birth should bring? 3. they bow themselves: they bring their offspring forth; And to the winds cast all their pangs away. 4. Strong grow their young; they fatten on the plains; And to their parents never more return. 5. Who is it that sent forth the Wild Ass free? Or who hath loosened the swift runners bands? 6. Whose dwelling I have made the wilderness; His haunts the salt and arid desert waste. 7. The city's busy tumult he doth scorn; The driver's shouts and cries he doth not hear. 8. The mountains are his ample pasture ground; There roameth he in quest of all things green. 9. The Wild Bull: will he be thy willing slave, Or pass the night, contented, by thy crib? 10. Canst thou in harness lead him forth to plow? To harrow, will he follow after thee? 11. Wilt thou, for all his strength, confide in him? Or leave to him the tillage of thy ground? 12. Canst thou be sure he will bring home thy seed, Or gather corn to fill thy threshing-floor? 13. The Ostrich wing, admired tho' it be: Is it the pinion of the kindly Stork? 14. Nay! She it is that leaves to earth her eggs, And in the dust she letteth them be warmed; 15. Unmindful that the passing foot might crush, Or that the roaming beast might trample them. 16. She dealeth sternly with her young, as if Not hers: and fears not that her toil be vain. 17. For God created her devoid of sense; Nor gave her in intelligence a share. 18. Yet, when she lifteth up herself for flight, The horse and rider both alike she scorns. 19. The War-horse: didst thou give to him his strength? Or clothe his arching neck with rustling mane? 20. Make him leap lightly, as the locust does? The glory of his snorting fills with dread: 21. He paws the plain, rejoicing in his strength; He rusheth on to meet the armed host: 22. He mocks at fear and cannot be dismayed; Nor from the sword will he turn back or flee, 23. Though against him rain the arrows of the foe, The glitter of the lance and flash of spear. 24. With noise and fury stampeth he the earth: Nor standeth steady when the trumpet sounds. 25. He saith among the trumpets, 'Ha, ha; and he smelleth the battle afar off, the thunder of the captains and the shouting. 26. Is it by thine instruction that the Hawk Soars high and spreads his pinions to the south? 27. Is it at thy command the Eagle mounts, And builds his eyrie in the lofty* *heights? 28. The rock he makes his home; and there he dwells On crag's sharp tooth and [lonely] fastnesses: 29. And thence he keenly spieth out the prey: His piercing eye beholds it from afar. 30. His young ones learn full soon to suck up blood; And where the slain are lying, there is he. 40:1 Moreover the LORD answered Job and said, 2. "Shall he that contendeth with THE ALMIGHTY instruct Him? He that reproveth GOD, let him answer it."* We will stop here with this rare look at our Creator. For your own study, please continue to read and find more information about our Creator, Redeemer and Master of the Universe.

3. MYTH: Adam and Eve were the first humans created by God on earth.

FACT: Mankind was created on the sixth day. **Genesis 1:26.** *"And God said, Let Us make man* (Hebrew manuscripts = mankind) *in Our image, after Our likeness. 27. So God created man* (mankind) *in His Own image, in the image of God created He him; male and female created He them."* The Hebrew is very specific here. The word for man has no article as it does in the next Chapter of Genesis where God formed man. **Genesis 2:7** *"And the LORD GOD formed man of the dust of the ground and breathed into his nostrils the breath of life; and man became a living soul."* (this man in Hebrew is eth-Ha'adham with the article and particle) The first man was all mankind and also womankind. If we go to **Genesis 2:1** *"Thus the heavens and the earth were finished and all the host of them."* This verse speaks of the end of the sixth day and included all the races of people. One of the definitions of host is: a multitude; great number. Adam and Eve would not be considered a multitude. Male and female were created on the sixth day. Eth-Ha'adham was not created until after God rested on the seventh day. At the beginning of the eighth day God needed a husbandman (farmer) and created Adam and Eve. Ask yourself, if Adam and Eve and Cain (after he killed Able) were the only ones on earth, who did Cain marry when he was kicked out of the garden? If there had been men and women on earth since the sixth day (six thousand years) there would have been a large number living on the earth after over a thousand years.

4. MYTH: Eve was talked into eating an apple by a snake.

FACT: Eve was seduced by Satan and bore a son named Cain as a result. If we check the word **"beguiled" as used in Genesis 3:13**

41

we find the Hebrew word "Nasha" with the meaning: "to seduce." If we go to Genesis 3:3 and check out the word. "touch" we find the Hebrew word "Naga" with the meaning "to lie with a woman." The tradition that has been handed down (that was changed by the enemy) has no reality base. Ask yourself, what has this got to do with a snake talking Eve into eating an apple? For more proof that there was no apple eaten, let's go to Genesis 3:7. *"And the eyes of them both were opened and they knew that they were naked; and they sewed fig leaves together and made themselves aprons."* You notice they did not cover their mouth from eating an apple, but rather their private parts. Remember the Bible was not written in English and through the years it has past through unholy heads and hands with time enough to tamper with it. Remember serpent is just one of the names of the devil. Now let's go to Ezekiel 28 to confirm that Satan was in the Garden of Eden. Verse 13 reads: *"Thou hast been in Eden the garden of God: 14. Thou art the anointed cherub that covereth and I have set thee so. 15. Thou wast perfect in thy ways from the day that thou wast created, till iniquity was found in thee."* We are given a description of the cherub before he fell. We are given another witness that he was in Eden. He earned his way up to be the anointed cherub that guarded the Mercy Seat of God. The tree of knowledge of good and evil is another of his names and he had no problem seducing Eve. He had been given the death sentence by God when he caused one third of God's children to turn away from God and follow him. In his mind, the only way he could get out of this death sentence was to interfere with God's plan of using the seed line of Adam (Eth-ha'adahm) to bring forth the Messiah. If he could change that by impregnating Eve, he might not be destroyed as discussed in Ezekiel 28:18 *"Thou hast defiled thy sanctuaries by the multitude of thine iniquities, by the iniquity of thy traffic; therefore will I bring forth a fire from the midst of thee, it shall devour thee,* (in the lake of fire) *and I will bring thee to ashes upon the earth in the sight of all them that behold thee."* While he still has a roll to play in these end times, he is a dead man walking; try to remember that in the days ahead. He is afraid of you if you know who you are in Christ and exercise the power of the name of Jesus Christ with authority. There are no half measures here, you either know and believe or you don't.

5. MYTH: Cain and Abel are full brothers.

FACT: Cain and Abel are half brothers that happen to be twins with different fathers. As we found earlier Eve was seduced by the serpent who was the father of Cain. Adam also knew his wife and bare Abel. Let's go to **Genesis 4** where we find what really happened when we go to the original language. *"And she again bare his brother Abel."* The Hebrew word for **"again"** is yacaph with the meaning to **"continue to do a thing."** If you just had a baby and continued in birth, you are having twins. If you don't believe it is possible to have twins with two different fathers, ask your doctor about it. I assure you it has happened many times over the years. If you are still having trouble getting your arms around this, let me ask you why you never find Cain's listed in the off-spring of Adam as listed in the fifth chapter of Genesis. Please read the forth chapter of Genesis and learn the off-spring of Cain. If Cain were Adam's son, he would be listed in Adam's pedigree which would include Cain's pedigree as well.

OPINION: The Pastor of Shepherd's Chapel shed light on this subject for this writer. This along with studying God's word for more than fifty years has brought a much needed explanation to a universally believed myth. We also know that God is always just and fair with everyone. We know that man and woman had been on the earth at least a thousand years before Adam and Eve. We know that sexual activity occurred and there were children produced. That being the case Adam and Eve may not have engaged in sex before the encounter with the serpent. It appears they were both very naive and innocent. God had warned them not to have anything to do with this evil one, but they were conned into believing a quote from God by the serpent, that was twisted just enough to convince them it was OK to get involved with "ole pretty boy." I believe whatever happened was an act of perversion. When Eve showed Adam what had happened, Adam partook as well. That's all that I will say and for those who have eyes and ears that see and hear that is enough.

6. MYTH : Cain married one of his sisters when he was banned from the garden.

OPINION: Cain married one of the sixth day creation (when all the races were created). **Genesis 4:16** *"And Cain went out from the presence of the LORD and dwelt in the land of Nod,* (believed to be Asia=Wandering=the Manda of the Cuneiform Inscriptions=the land

43

of the Nomads.) *on the east of Eden." 17. "And Cain knew his wife; and she conceived and bare Enoch: and he builded a city and called the name of the city after the name of his son, Enoch."* Another thing to consider is the fact Cain was worried about all the people that would slay him when he was driven out of Eden. Who were these people if only Adam and his family were on earth? Staying in **Genesis 4:14** with Cain speaking *"Behold, Thou hast driven me out this day from the face of the earth; and from Thy face shall I be hid; and I shall be a fugitive and a vagabond in the earth and it shall come to pass, that every one that findeth me shall slay me."* There is ample evidence given here to at least cause the serious reader to consider that Cain did not marry his sister. If you want to stay with that tradition, have a good trip, but be careful you don't fall in the ditch.

7. MYTH: The Bible doesn't say anything about Conservatives and Liberals as we know them today.

FACT: Ecclesiastes 10:2 *"The heart of the wise inclines to the right, but the heart of the fool to the left."* That is a pretty clear definition that was written a thousand years before Christ.

8. MYTH: Noah never sinned and that is the reason he was chosen to build the ark.

FACT: Genesis 6:9. *"THESE are THE GENERATIONS OF NOAH: Noah was a just man and perfect in his generations and Noah walked with God."* Noah was pure in his generations or pedigree. He and his wife and his sons and their wives did not have sexual relations with the bad angels that came directly to earth as mentioned in the book of Jude. Noah is also referred to by Jesus in Matthew in the parable of the wheat and tares in **Matthew 13:24-42.** My wife and I raised Egyptian Arabian horses and know how important it is to keep the blood pure if you have specific goals in mind. I have talked to pilots that flew over Mount Ararat and read about others that reported seeing what looked like a large wooden ship near the top of this mountain during World War II.

9. MYTH: God knows what everyone will decide about choosing God or Satan.

FACT: In order for there to be true love, there must be free will to choose. God did not create us like programed robots. Those that have free-will sail their own ship. Some by making conscious decisions and others just following the path of least resistance. Either way each person is responsible for his or her choices in life. The main purpose for this heaven and earth age is to find out what choice people will make with regard to choosing God or Satan. This is especially true of the one third that chose to follow Satan in the first heaven and earth age. The book of **Matthew 19:30** tells us *"many that are first shall be last"* and there is much evidence that tells us the vast majority of that first one third who followed Satan in the first earth age are alive in this final "Fig Tree Generation." Following the devil always leads to perversion and we have more perversion in the earth today than we find in recorded history. There have always been pockets of perversion throughout history. Because of the vast numbers of population and the many social media outlets and instant access to anything going on, wrongful thought and conduct run rampant around the world.

10. MYTH: God has never made a mistake.

FACT: God told Moses that He was sorry He had made man and threatened to destroy them and start over with Moses. Moses talked God out of it. **Exodus 32:9** *"And the LORD said unto Moses, "I have seen this people and behold, it is a stiff-necked people: 10. Now therefore let Me alone, that My wrath may wax hot against them and that I may consume them: and I will make of thee a great nation" 11. And Moses besought the LORD his God and said, Lord, why doth Thy wrath wax hot against Thy people, which thou has brought forth out of the land of Egypt with great power and with a mighty hand? 12. Wherefore should the Egyptians speak and say for mischief did He bring them out, to slay them in the mountains and to consume them from the face of the earth? Turn from Thy fierce wrath and repent of this evil against Thy people. 13. Remember Abraham, Isaac and Israel, Thy servants, to whom Thou swarest by Thine own Self and saidst unto them, "I will multiply your seed as the stars of heaven and all this land that I have spoken of will I give unto your seed and they shall inherit it forever. 14. And the LORD repented of the evil which He thought to do unto His people."*

11. MYTH: The Bible does not talk about dinosaurs.

FACT: The book of Job describes massive animals with a tail as large as a cedar tree. This description fits only the dinosaurs. **Job 40:16** *"Lo now, his strength is in his loins and his force is in the navel* (muscles) *of his belly. 17. He moveth his tail like a cedar: the sinews of his bones are as strong pieces of brass; his bones are like* *bars of iron.*" What other creature has a tail shaped like and as large as a cedar tree? By realizing there was a first heaven and earth age we are not conflicted by attempting to fit these animals into a six thousand year old earth. The first age lasted millions of years and science and the Bible are in agreement when you go to the manuscripts.

12. MYTH: The Bible does not discuss what we call UFO's.

FACT: The book of Ezekiel describes them very well when you consider the fact that the man describing them was only familiar with wagons and ox carts. He related his description to what he knew and actually did a very good job. God is the God of all creation including things we don't understand. Let's go to **Ezekiel 1:4** *"And I looked and behold, a whirlwind came out of the north, a great cloud and a fire infolding itself and a brightness was about it and out of the midst thereof as the color of amber, out of the midst of the fire."* If we go to the Strong's Concordance and look up the word **"amber"** we find the number 2830: **"bronze or polished spectrum metal"** If you will continue to read the rest of chapter one you will have Ezekiel's impressions of what he had witnessed. Careful study will indicate that Enoch was taken to heaven by one of these vehicles. Let's read where Elijah was taken with more detail. **II Kings 2:11** *"And it came to pass, as they still went on and talked, that, behold, there appeared a chariot of fire and horses of fire and parted them both asunder; and Elijah went up by a whirlwind into heaven."* Elisha was with Elijah when this happened and was allowed to see these vehicles. Since we are dealing with another dimension that normally can not be viewed by man let's find an example of many of these vehicles observed by Elisha and his servant. Elisha ask God to open his spiritual eyes that he might see into this very real dimension. **II Kings 6:17** *"And Elisha prayed and said, 'LORD, I pray thee, open his eyes, that he may see.' And the LORD opened the eyes of the young man; and he saw: and behold, the mountain was full of horses and chariots of fire round about Elisha."* Now go to the New Testament and see another incident that Paul is describing. **Hebrews 12:1** *"Wherefore seeing we also are compassed about with so great a cloud of witnesses."* The word cloud is also a part of this subject. Now for the deeper student, we go to **Revelations 19:11** *"And I saw heaven opened and behold, a white horse; and He that sat upon him was called Faithful and True and in righteousness He doth judge* *and make war. 14. And the armies which were in heaven followed Him upon white horses, clothed in fine linen, white and clean."* For those of you who have their eyes open and will do more investigation on their own, you will find that chariots, horses of fire and clouds as used in these verses and others, all have to do with what man calls UFO's. If you cannot see it, just put it on the back burner for now. There may come a time when events of the day will cause you to revisit these scriptures.

13. MYTH: Satan will be saved in the end.

FACT: Some churches teach this and many people believe this to be true. Let's look at where this might come from by not dividing the Word correctly. **II Corinthians 11:13** *"For such are false apostles, deceitful workers, transforming themselves into the apostles of Christ. 14. And no marvel; for Satan himself is transformed into an angel of light. 15. Therefore it is no great thing if his ministers also be transformed as the ministers of righteousness; whose end shall be according to their works."* If we go to the manuscripts by way of the Strong's Concordance, we find the word transformed has a meaning of "disguised." Satan and his crowd disguised themselves as angels of light; they were not transformed. Now, so there is no doubt what God has to say on this subject, we find in **Ezekiel 28:18** *"Thou hast defiled thy sanctuaries by the multitude of thine iniquities, by the iniquity of thy traffic; therefore will I bring forth a fire from the midst of thee, it shall devour thee and I will bring thee to ashes upon the earth in the sight of all them that behold thee."* God is telling us in no uncertain terms that Satan is a walking dead man and all those that have chosen to follow him will see his destruction with their own eyes. This will happen at the end of **"The LORD'S Day"** at the **"Great White Throne Judgment."**

14. MYTH: If you don't accept the truth while in this flesh body, you will not get a chance to do so.

OPINION: With what is being taught today many people have never heard the truth and will be taught the truth during the millennium. This includes people who have gone to church all their lives, yet have only been taught the traditions of men. There is more written about the millennium in the book of Ezekiel than anywhere in the Bible, including the book of Revelation. Let's see what we find in **Ezekiel 44:25.** *"And they shall come at no dead* (spiritually dead) *person to defile themselves: but for father, or mother, or for son, or for daughter, or for brother, or for sister that hath had no husband, they may defile themselves."* (a married sister would be a part of another family just like your mother is now a part of your family) Let us see if we can make this a little more clear. If you are one of God's elect, you will be able to go to your immediate family and show them how to get their act together. Remember we are in spiritual bodies at this time. The elect may not go to anyone who is spiritually dead except the members of his or her own family. After your visit, you will have to stay away from God for seven days to be cleansed. *26. "And after he is cleansed, they shall reckon unto him seven days."* I am convinced the main thing that will be taught to those who did not make it, will be discipline. The type discipline that does not put off learning about God and His ways. While in this flesh body these people always found an excuse to put off learning about the things of God. They put off the most important aspect of life, mainly because of the traditions of men and poor scholarship by their church leaders, but the ultimate responsibility belongs to each individual. The following scripture applies to everyone that has had the privilege of hearing about God. **II Timothy 2:15** *"Study to shew thyself approved unto God, a workman that needeth not to be ashamed, rightly dividing the word of truth."* The shame will be realized when the individual finds them self worshiping Satan, all the while believing they are worshiping Christ. This visitation also applies to all who have or will have died before Christ returns and find themselves on the wrong side of the gulf as discussed in the book of **Luke Chapter 16:19 thru 31**. You might like to read the entire parable, but we will focus on verse *26. "And beside all this, between us and you there is a great gulf fixed: so that they which would pass from hence to you cannot; neither can they pass to us, that would come from thence."* Please note in this case there will be no visitation until the millennium.

15. MYTH: Most preachers and churches are teaching God's truth.

FACT: The book of Revelations states that over 70% of churches are not approved by God. Only two out of seven are approved. You can read of the seven church types in **Revelation Chapters 2 and 3**. We will focus on the two who God approved of. **Revelation 2:8** *"And unto the angel of the church in Smyrna write; 'These things* *saith the First and the Last, which was dead and is alive; 9. I know thy works and tribulation and poverty (but thou art rich) and I know the blasphemy of them which say they are Jews and are not, but are the synagogue of Satan." Revelation 3:7 "And to the angel of the church in Philadelphia write; 'These things saith He That is Holy, He That openeth and no man shutteth and shutteth and no man openeth; 8. I know thy works: behold, I have set before thee an open door and no man can shut it; for thou hast a little strength and has kept My word and hast not denied My name. 9. Behold, I will make them of the synagogue of Satan, which say they are Jews and are not, but do lie; behold, I will make them to come and worship before thy feet and to know that I have loved thee."* Sad to say the vast majority of churches today don't have the foggiest idea what was just said. Let me ask you, does your church teach you about the one common denominator from both these churches; the *"synagogue of Satan?"* You notice that the leaders of these churches say they are Jewish priests, who are suppose to be appointed by God. Our Father tells us they do lie and in fact are the *"synagogue of Satan"* working for the devil. How could this be possible, that these men who represent that they are God's men are as phoney as a three dollar bill. Not only that, but these so called priest have been in power for a long time. Let's find out what Jesus Himself had to say about these men. **John 8:42** *"Jesus said unto them, 'If God were your Father, ye would love Me: for I proceeded forth and came from God; neither came I of Myself, but He sent Me. 43. Why do ye not understand My speech? Even because ye cannot hear My word. 44. Ye are of Your father the devil and the lusts of your father ye will do. He was a murderer from the beginning and abode not in the truth, because there is no truth in him. When he speaketh a lie, he speaketh of his own: for he a liar and the father of it."* If this is the first time you have heard this, you have a lot of catching up to do. You can do it, but you better get started or you will be left behind. The other thing most people don't see is that if your mind has been sealed by the truth of God and you know that the false messiah comes first, no man can close that truth to you. Many teach we will have a mark placed on our forehead or a computer chip placed under our skin. They teach the mark is 666. Let me assure you that if they tattooed 666 all over your body it would not change the fact that you love God and will never worship this "instead of Jesus." Many have asked, "How will I know if it is anti-Christ?" This is very simple, you see anti-Christ comes at the 6th trump and everyone is still in flesh bodies. If you see someone that is telling everyone that he is Christ and you can pinch yourself and it hurts, you are looking at a Jesus look-a-like. Christ comes at the last or 7th trump and we will be changed into our spiritual bodies. **I Corinthians 15:51** *"Behold, I shew you a mystery; We shall not all sleep, but we shall all be changed, 52. In a moment, in the twinkling of an eye, at the last trump: for the trumpet shall sound and the dead shall be raised incorruptible and we shall all be changed."* These are just a few examples of how most churches are not going beyond a salvation message and are actually teaching their congregations to worship the one who comes at the 6th trump. So the answer to your question about most churches and preachers are teaching God's truth is false, most are not.

16. MYTH: You should believe a man or woman if they say they are called of God.

FACT: Matthew 7:15. *"Beware of false prophets, which come to you in sheep's clothing, but inwardly they are ravening wolves. 16. Ye shall know them by their fruits, Do men gather grapes of thorns, or figs of thistles?"* By their fruits you shall know them. Try the spirits to see if they be of God. Using the percentage in the book of Revelation only two in seven pass muster. Since God does not use beggars, this eliminates most of them from the get-go. Let me say again, if you have a called of God minister that teaches God's word, support them in any way you can. There are so few really good scholarly Bible teachers that teach from the manuscripts, they are rare indeed. When an unsuspecting public is taught the traditions of men and believe they are being taught God's word, this has been and is a tragedy that God will require an accounting from the false teachers. **I Peter 4:17** *"For the time is come that judgment must begin at the house of God: and if it first begin at us, what shall the end be of them that obey not the gospel of God?"* Peter, that old fisherman, is telling us that God will judge the church leaders before He judges everyone else. Remember God is always fair, you will receive everything you have coming to you, good or bad.

17. MYTH: The Bible teaches that there will be a great famine in the end time.

FACT: Amos tell us the famine at the end of this present earth age will be hunger for the Word of God. **Amos 8:11** *"Behold, the days come, saith the LORD GOD, that I will send a famine in the land, not a famine of bread, nor a thirst for water, but of hearing the words of the LORD."* That famine has been in the land for quite a while now. People are starving for the true word of God. Our schools, our government, our military and even many of our churches have removed or are attempting to remove God and Jesus from everything we hold dear. Even the courts are making laws instead of allowing the legislature to do their job. Most of the religious stations on TV and radio have people passing themselves off to be doing God's business and they spend the majority of their air time begging for money. God does not send out beggars and no matter how well they disguise their trying to get your money, God did not send them. That is about as plain as it can be said. Stop and think a minute, if they are "about their Fathers business" don't you think God would see to it that they were blessed? He has always throughout the Bible blessed His true servants and He still does today.

18. MYTH: The Bible teaches there will be a rapture before anti-Christ comes.

FACT: The word rapture is not in the Bible. The any moment doctrine, speaking in unknown tongues and flying to save your soul was started in the year 1830 in Scotland by a woman by the name of Margaret MacDonald. **Ezekiel 13:20** *"Wherefore thus saith the LORD GOD; Behold, I am against your pillows, where with ye there hunt the souls to make them fly and I will tear them from your arms and will let the souls go, even the souls that ye hunt to make them fly."* The manuscripts make it even clearer, God said you have covered up my out-reached knuckles in order to teach this false doctrine of telling people that I will fly them out. **Proverbs 10:30** *"The righteous shall never be removed: but the wicked shall not inhabit the Earth."* Many denominations teach their congregations that they don't have to understand the book of Revelation because they will be out of here. Since this rapture doctrine has been taught for almost two hundred years, it has been accepted by many as being true. In fact this writer was in that camp until I got into the manuscripts and found there is no basis in fact to back it up. In fact, when an in depth study is done, the exact opposite is true. We are to put on the whole armor of God in order to withstand the fiery dart of the enemy. Instead of being unprepared by believing we will be gone, let's look at what Paul has to say on the subject in his letter to the **Ephesians 6:11** *"Put on the whole armour of God, that ye may be able to stand against the wiles of the devil. 12. For we wrestle not against flesh and blood, but against principalities, against powers, against the rulers of the darkness of this world, against spiritual wickedness in high places. 13. Wherefore take unto you the whole armour of God, that ye may be to with stand in the evil day and having done all, to stand."* Why would you need all that armor if you were not going to battle the enemy? When do you think the "evil day" is going to be? I can tell you for certain, it is when anti-Christ comes at the 6th trump telling his followers that he is going to fly them out of here. The true believers will need all the armor listed to battle against the subtle wiles of this smooth talking, good looking Jesus look-a-like. For you see he is coming back looking and acting like you think Jesus would look and act like. If he came killing people, it would be obvious he was a fake, but if he is doing miracles and comes peacefully and prosperously he will fool everyone except those who already know what he will be doing. All religions will accept him as their messiah. Even mothers will ask him to forgive their son or daughter who does not believe he is the real Christ, thus fulfilling the scripture in **Luke 21:16** *"And ye shall be betrayed both by parents, and brethren and kinsfolks and friends;"* The only way for this to happen is for these people to actually believe "ole pretty boy" is the Christ. A parent or friend would never knowingly betray you unless they are convinced he is Christ. Now let's go to the scripture that most rapture believers use to convince themselves and others that this has to be true. **I Thessalonians 4:17.** *"Then we which are alive and remain, shall be caught up together with them in the clouds, to meet the Lord in the air: and so shall we ever be with the Lord."* In order to know what is being discussed we first must get the sub-ject and object for this verse. We must go to **verse 13** in order to do this. It reads: *"But I would not have you to be ignorant, brethren, concerning them which are asleep,* (dead) *that ye sorrow not, even as others which have no hope."* (those that don't know the Lord. There is nothing sadder than going to a funeral where the person does not know the Lord) 14. *"For if we believe that Jesus died and rose* *again, even so them also which sleep in Jesus will God bring with Him. 15. For this we say unto you by the word of the Lord, that we which are alive and remain unto the coming of the Lord, shall not prevent* (precede) *them which are asleep."*(They are already gone, their true spirit man left when they died. **II Corinthians 5:8.***"We are confident, I say and willing rather to be absent from the body and to be present with the Lord."* Go back to **I Thessalonians 4:16.** *"For the Lord Himself shall descend from heaven with a shout, with the voice of the archangel and with the trump of God: and the dead in Christ shall rise first: 17. Then we which are alive and remain, shall be caught up together with them in the clouds, to meet the Lord in the air: and so shall we ever be with the Lord."* According to Paul we find that the trump of God that Christ will return is the last or 7th trump. **I Corinthians 15:51** *"Behold, I shew you a mystery; We shall not all sleep, but we shall all be changed, 52. In a moment, in the twinkling of an eye, at the last trump: for the trumpet shall sound and the dead shall be raised incorruptible and we shall be changed."* The mystery that Paul is talking about is the fact that the rapture believers don't understand the scriptures that are explaining what is going to happen. They take one verse, **17** and make a false claim that this means rapture. They are saying that Christ comes at the 6th trump, but this is the anti-Christ that comes at the 6th trump. They say we will meet the Lord in the air without going trouble to see what the Greek says about this word "air." This is not atmosphere, this is your breath of life body. You will not float around in space in your physical body. Those who make it will be with the Lord forever in their spiritual body right here on earth, but this will happen at the last trump as we saw in **I Corinthians 15.** Now let's review and consider this with a clear head. First, God does not change, He is the same yesterday, today and forever. He has never taken His people out of anything. He was with them in the Ark, but they were still here. He was with His people as they went through the Red Sea. He was with the Hebrew children in the fiery furnace, He was with Daniel in the lions den. He demonstrated His presence with Elijah when the profit defiled the false priest. The point is God gets the glory if he keeps us in the midst of trouble and He is not going to change His MO at the end of this earth age. Why would He require us to put on armor in these last days if we were going to be gone. Why would people pray for mountains to fall on them when they realize they had been deceived. They thought they had been worshiping Christ only to find out, when the two witnesses come back to life, that they had been worshiping anti-Christ. The shame will be more than they can bare and they will wish to hide and be able to die. The rapture doctrine has made a lot of people wealthy by selling their books and tapes, but it is a very dangerous doctrine that can lead to hell.

19. MYTH: It shows a lack of faith to pray the Father's will.

FACT: I John 5:14 *"And this is the confidence that we have in Him, that if we ask anything according to His will, He heareth us."* You notice it did not say you can ask for anything your heart desires, rather, *"if we ask anything according to His will."* The rewards for "being about our Fathers' business" are many, including peace of mind.

20. MYTH: Super-natural events are always of God.

FACT: Super-natural means it is not of man. **Revelation 13:13** *"And he doeth great wonders so that he maketh fire come down from heaven on the earth in the sight of men."* It can be from God or the devil. Calling fire down from heaven is super-natural, but as we see in the verse above, this is done by anti-Christ, who is the devil. Let's read the next verse and see the reason he is doing this. *14. "And deceiveth them that dwell on the earth by the means of those miracles."* He will deceive all those who do not have the truth of God sealed in their minds. Unfortunately this will be the vast majority of all peoples.

21. MYTH: God's love is always sweet and nice.

FACT: Real love is sometimes tough love. Correction is necessary and sometimes painful in order to set things straight. How many times have you heard someone ask, "What would Jesus do in this situation?" This usually happens when someone is trying to allow themselves or someone else to not be responsible for their actions. Their mindset is that Christians are suppose to turn the other cheek in all situations. Well, let's see what Jesus did do, let's answer once and for all that there are times when you don't turn the other cheek and you show that Christians are not second class citizens and they have a backbone and take care of wrong doing. **John 2:15** *"And when He (Jesus) had made a scourge of small cords, He drove them all out of the temple and the sheep and the oxen; and poured out the* *changer's money and overthrew the tables.* " Remember He did this in church and not only beat them with a cat of nine tails, He also humiliated the leaders of the church to the point that they wanted to kill him, but He did it anyway. Now for another witness, let's see what the man who wrote most of the New Testament did to handle a trouble maker. **I Corinthians 5:5** *"To deliver such an one unto Satan for the destruction of the flesh, that the spirit may be saved in the day of the Lord Jesus."* Here Paul turned a seemingly hopeless case over to Satan that this man might be saved. Paul could have done what most people would do and that is to attempt to get back at him for causing Paul much grief. Now, this is one of the best examples of "tough love." You see, always trying to be the "nice guy" and never rocking the boat will sometimes allow a person go to hell. If you call yourself a Christian, a "Christ Man" or "Christ Woman," then when a person's soul is at stake, follow the leading of the Holy Spirit instead of trying to be politically correct. The Holy Spirit will never lead you wrong, but He might lead you in a different direction than you are comfortable with or have been taught to respond. This does not happen every day, but if you follow God, it will happen and if you allow that soul to go to hell, God will require that person's blood to be on your hands. Where much is given, much is required.

22. MYTH: Rich people can not go to heaven.

FACT: If a person is rich with ill gotten gains this may make it impossible. If we please God, He promises to bless us. God has always blessed those who followed Him. Do you really think Abraham, Isaac, Jacob and David and the like are not in heaven? These were some of the wealthiest on earth. We do know those who came by their wealth dishonestly, unless they repent and change their ways, will not be in heaven. If you really want to know who will not go to heaven, let's look at the Bible and find out. **Revelation 21:8** *"But the fearful and unbelieving and the abominable and murderers and whoremongers and sorcerers and idolaters and all liars, shall have their part in the lake which burneth with fire and brimstone; which is the second death."* Most of us understand murderers, idolaters and liars, but let's look at Sorcerers: in the Greek it is the Strong's number 5332 **"pharmakeus"** from which we derive our English word **"pharmacist"** or druggist. There will be no drug dealers in heaven. Whoremonger has to do with perversion. There will be no perversion in heaven. Just because you murdered someone and the jury and judge found you not guilty, you have not had your real trial yet. Just because you have made millions ruining the lives of thousands of people by selling them illegal drugs and have not been caught, your real trial awaits you. Just because the Supreme Court ruled that there is nothing wrong with same sex marriage, does not make it right in the eyes of God. Unless you repent and change your ways, you will not be in heaven, but rather all of these shall have their part in the lake of fire. Don't shoot the messenger, these are not my words, these are rules found in God's letter to all His children. He may not like how you live or what you are doing, but He does love you. If you want to go to heaven, get your act together and stop playing church. Christianity is not a religion, it is a reality. The only reality that brings peace of mind. If you believe that what you have done is so bad, there is no hope for you. I will remind you that all through the Bible, God's people have messed up, some of them big time and yet for those who ask for forgiveness and turned to God were forgiven. Divorce is not the unforgivable sin. Adultery is not the unforgivable sin. Lying, cheating, stealing are not unforgivable if you repent and ask God for forgiveness and change your ways. You see, if God only used perfect people, He would work alone. All of the sinful things mentioned here have never caused a person to be happy and have peace of mind.

Establishing a relationship with the Creator of the universe, your real Father, is the most fulfilling, exciting and lasting thing you can do in your lifetime. God will always do His part, it is up to you where you will spend eternity. Your mother, dad, sister, brother, grandparents, friends, teachers or preachers will not stand with you when you stand before God at judgment. Judgment is a good thing for those who love the Lord, they will receive their rewards. Judgment is a frightful thing for those who continue to follow the devil.

23. MYTH: Ignorance of God's word is protection from His wrath.

OPINION: It is not a sin to not know. It is a sin to stay that way. Willing ignorance can send you to hell. Let's see what that old fisherman has to say about this subject. **II Peter 3:1** *"This second epistle, beloved, I now write unto you; in both which I stir up your pure minds by way of remembrance; 2. That ye may be mindful of the words which were spoken before by the holy prophets and*

of the commandment of us the apostles of the Lord and Saviour:
(Peter is saying, I want to remind you that both the prophets of the Old Testament and those of us who are writing the New Testament are telling the same story) *3. Know this first, that there shall come in the last days scoffers, walking after their own lusts,* (In this writers opinion, there has never been a time in history where the mocking, contempt, scorn, derision, doubt, cynicism, irreverence, coarse remarks, mocking laughter and openly insulting behavior have been so wide spread in all the earth. I am convinced the one third that followed Satan in the first age are alive today. They call truth lies and lies truth.) *4. "And saying, 'Where in the promise of His coming? For since the fathers fell asleep, all things continue as they were from the beginning of the creation."* (By their words and actions they do not believe that the Bible is true are even important and everything will continue as is and they really don't believe there is a God.) *5. "For this they willingly are ignorant of, that by the word of God the heavens were of old and the earth standing out of the water and in the water: 6. Whereby the world that then was, being overflowed with water, perished:"* (Pay attention this was the first of the three ages and with a little study we find this was not Noah's flood) *7. "But the heavens and the earth which are now,* (this is the second age that we are living in now) *by the same word are kept in store, reserved unto fire against the day of judgment and perdition of ungodly men."* (third age) *8. But, beloved, be not ignorant of this one thing, that one day is with the LORD as a thousand years and a thousand years as one day."* In **verse 5** he is calling to our attention that most are willingly ignorant of God's word. In **verse 8** he is saying, if you want to begin to learn at least don't be ignorant that one of God's days is a thousand years. When you understand this, then you are able to make more sense of the time period of the creation of this earth age in **Genesis 1**. God deals with each person individually, so no matter what your family or peers think or do about their relationship with God, it is up to you to establish a real bond between you and your Creator.

24. MYTH: Some say that God was unfair to have loved Jacob and hated Esau while they were still in their mother's womb.

FACT: Let's read **Malachi 1:2** *"I have loved you, saith the LORD. Yet ye say, 'Wherein hast Thou loved us?' Was not Esau*

Jacob's brother? saith the LORD: yet I loved Jacob, 3. And I hated Esau." Let's go to the New Testament to get a better picture. **Romans 9:11** *"For the children being not yet born, neither having done any good or evil, that the purpose of God according to election might stand, not of works, but of Him that calleth; 12. It was said unto her,* (Rebecca) *"The elder shall serve the younger." 13. As it is written, "Jacob have I loved, but Esau have I hated." 14. What shall we say then? Is there unrighteousness with God? God forbid."* Most Bible readers are left in the dark at this point, because they have not been taught about the first heaven and earth age. Without a clear understanding of all three ages, you will continue to have problems navigating through God's letter to you. You see God knew what Esau did in the first heaven and earth age. Esau did not care anything about his heritage then and as we study his life in this earth age, we find he sold his heritage for a bowl of mush. He gave up the rights of the first born which was a double portion of his father's inheritance because he was hungry. How foolish, Esau followed Satan in the first earth age, he sold his heritage in this earth age and God hated him for it and can not use him. Are you giving up a relationship with your real Father over what this world has to offer? Dying on the cross is what Jesus did for you, the question is, what are you doing for him? Isn't it time to make Him a priority in your life and get into His Word and find out what you are suppose to do with your life. Are you content to flounder around, up one minute and down the next, never really knowing who you are or what you are suppose to do to please God?

We also notice in **Romans 9**, quoted above *"the purpose of God according to election might stand."* This word "election" is another area that most church goers today are ignorant of, some willingly and some who are taught by poor scholars. Many teach this is talking about all Christians; this is not the case. Let's consider **Ephesians 1:3** *"Blessed be the God and Father of our Lord Jesus Christ, Who hath blessed us with all spiritual blessings in heavenly places in Christ: 4. According as He hath chosen us in Him before the foundation of the world, that we should be holy and without blame before in love: 5. Having predestinated us unto the adoption of children by Jesus Christ to Himself according to the good pleasure of His will."* There were a few of God's children in the first age that fought with God when Satan talked one third of God's children into following him.

58

As found in **Revelation 12:4.** God is always fair and he always give you everything you earn. These who earned it are now referred to as "elect," have already passed muster so to speak, because they have already proven their allegiance is to God. Our Father knows who they will worship when anti-Christ shows up and it won't be anti-Christ. Contrary to most teachings, not everyone has free will. For example, Saul's will was to persecute the believers in Jesus Christ and he was sanctioned by the churches and high priest of the day. God's will was for him to write most of the New Testament and his mission was important enough that Jesus appeared to him and changed his attitude and life's work. He went from Saul to Paul, he went from a mission of destroying this new religion to being one of its most important spokesman. Paul did not choose to do this, God chose it for him. If you are one of God's elect, you may or may not be aware of it at the present time. If you love the Lord and know that the anti-Christ comes first and will be telling all his followers that he has come to fly them out of here, you may be one of the elect that will stand before anti-Christ and allow the Holy Spirit of God to speak through you. Here is the difficult part for many to understand. You say you love God, but are ignorant that "instead of Christ" comes first. He looks and acts like what you believe Christ will be doing and you worship him. You may have spent your entire life in church and believe that you know the Bible and call yourself a Christian. Do you really believe God will be pleased with you? Look in the mirror, the person looking back at you is responsible for being sure you have spent the time to learn what the Bible really says by going back to the original languages. Just as those who ask about the unfairness of God regarding Jacob and Esau, many will say it is unfair for God to turn His back on those who believed they were worshiping Christ. Let's look at what Jesus will reply to these in that hour. **Matthew 7:21** *"Not every one that saith unto Me, Lord, Lord, shall enter into the kingdom of heaven; but he that doeth the will of My Father which is in heaven. 22. Many will say to Me in that day, Lord, Lord, have we not prophesied in Thy name: and in Thy name have cast out devils: and in Thy name done many wonderful works: 23. And then will I profess unto them, 'I never knew you: depart from Me, ye that work iniquity." 24. Therefore whosoever heareth these sayings of Mine and doeth them, I will liken him unto a wise man, which built his* *house upon a rock: 25. And the rain descended and the floods came and the winds blew and beat upon that house; and it fell not: for it was founded upon a rock. 26. And everyone that heareth these sayings of Mine and doeth them not, shall be likened unto a foolish man, which built his his house upon the sand: 27. And the rain descended and the floods came and the winds blew and beat upon that house; and it fell: and great was the fall of it." 28. And it came to pass, when Jesus had ended these sayings, the people were astonished at His doctrine: 29. For He taught them as one having authority and not as the scribes."*

Do you understand what Jesus just said? He must have been talking about church going people because what other group of people would prophesy in His name: or cast out devils and have done many wonderful works in His name. Probably not going to see that at Joe's Bar or your bank or business or a government office. No, those things mentioned are talked about and done by church going people. So how is it that people who are trying to do the right thing are going to lose the race because they unintentionally mess up? We will talk about it later, but this is what happened to the five foolish virgins who did not have enough oil (truth) in their vessels. This is what can happen when a person plays church and depends on another person to tell them what they believe. Don't allow yourself to continue to be willingly ignorant of God's overall plan.

25. MYTH: Ham sinned by seeing his dad naked in **Genesis 9:22** *"And Ham, the father of Canaan, saw the nakedness of his father and told his two brethren without."*

FACT: Seeing your hairy legged dad naked may not be pretty, but it is not a sin. Let's ask the Bible what is meant by this verse. It is also an example of the poor scholarship that has prevailed throughout the ages. **Leviticus 20:11** *"And the man that lieth with his father's wife hath uncovered his father's nakedness: both of them surely be put to death: their blood shall be upon them."* **Leviticus 18:6.** *"None of you shall approach to any that is near of kin to him, to uncover their nakedness: I am the LORD. 7. The nakedness of thy father, or the nakedness of thy mother, shalt thou not uncover: she is thy mother; thou shalt not uncover her nakedness. 8. The nakedness of thy father's wife shalt thou not uncover: it is thy father's nakedness."* **Genesis 9:22** *"And Ham, the father of Canaan, saw* *the nakedness of his father and told his two brethren without. 23. And Shem and Japheth took a garment and laid it upon both their shoulders and went backward and covered the nakedness of their father; and their faces were backward and they saw not their father's nakedness.* " Here is another case that if you depend on just English, this all seems strange. God is telling you in His letter to you, that you are not to have sexual relations with your kinfolk. We see that Shem and Japheth covered their step-mother's nakedness after Ham had intercourse with her. It was not their dad they were covering up, for he was not even there. It was there mother or step-mother. The result of this union produced Canaan, whom Noah kicked out of their household. This is understandable since Noah did not want to be reminded of his wife getting drunk and sleeping with his own son every time he saw Canaan. Most men would have kicked the wife out too.

26. MYTH: Easter is approved by God.

FACT: I Corinthians 5:7 *"Christ is our Passover."* The word Easter does not appear in the manuscripts. It is the name of a pagan sexual orgy festival. Easter is a heathen term derived from the Saxon goddess Eastre, the same as Astarbe, the Syrian Venus, called Ashtoreth in the Old Testament. The Greek word "paschal" is listed in the manuscripts as the Paschal Lamb slain and eaten at Passover. Easter is a grand tradition adopted by most all Christian churches. It does make one wonder how hard boiled eggs, which have a lot to do with fertility, worked their way into the highest Holy-Day of the year for Christians? God initiated "Passover" as the death angel "Passed Over" the children of Israel that were in bondage in Egypt. Jesus became our Passover Lamb as His blood keeps us day by day. Jesus is our Kinsman Redeemer, our closest living relative. You can still use Easter for good, but you should also know its true origin.

27. MYTH: The religious church leaders that had Jesus arrested and interrogated were Priests of God.

FACT: When talking to these church leaders Jesus tells us who they really were. **John 8:42.** *"If God were your Father, ye would love Me: for I proceeded forth and came from God. 44. Ye are of your father the devil and the lust of your father ye will do. He was a murderer from the beginning and abode not in the truth because there is no truth in him. When he speaketh a lie, he speaketh of his own: for he is a liar and the father of it."* Jesus told them "You do not know Me because you don't know My Father. If you knew My father you would know Me. You are not of my Father you are of your father, the devil. Jesus knew these people were not Priests of God, but Kenites or descendants of Cain. Notice Jesus identified them by telling us that they were of their father the devil. If you look up Kenite in your Strong's you will find Cain who was the first recorded murderer in the Bible.

28. MYTH: The parable of The Fig Tree, told by Jesus, beginning in Matthew 13 tells us that Christians want to be the first ones taken.

FACT: The ones taken first are deceived by anti-Christ. He will be telling everyone he has come before the tribulation to fly people out. The truth is the ones left shall resist this "instead of Christ" and wait for the true Christ five months later as found in: **Revelation 9:5** *"And to them it was given that they should not kill them, but that they should be tormented five months: and their torment was as the torment of a scorpion, when he striketh a man. 10. And they had tails like unto scorpions and there were stings in their tails: and their power was to hurt men five months. 11. And they had a king over them, which is the angel of the bottomless pit, whose name in the Hebrew tongue is Aabaddon, but in the Greek tongue hath his name Apollyon.* Let's take a moment and see if we can make sense of this. Symbolic words are used throughout the Bible and especially the Book of Revelation. Let's take the word "scorpions" as used above and see if we can better understand what God is showing us. First, a scorpion has no stomach and it stings its victim to addle it, then it uses it pincers to hold its victim and the victim becomes the stomach for the scorpion. Its digestive juices turn the victim's backbone to mush as he then ingest his prey. Not knowing who anti-Christ is will turn men's backbones to mush and they will be paralyzed with fear that will render them helpless. Only God's people who have the truth of God in their minds will be able to continue to do God's work and allow the Holy Spirit to speak through them. The book of Mark tells us that for the elects sake God will shorten the days, because if He does not, no flesh will be saved.

29. MYTH: The tribulation period will last three and one half years shortened from the original seven years.

FACT: There will be two tribulations. Satan's tribulation has been shortened from seven years, to three and one half years and as we found in **Revelation 9**, it is now shortened to five months. This is the time period for Satan's entire tribulation period. We find also in the Book of Revelation that the time for an individual's trial is only ten days. **Revelation 2:10** *"Fear none of those things which thou shalt suffer: behold, the devil shall cast some of you into prison, that ye may be tried; and ye shall have tribulation ten days: be thou faithful unto death and I will give thee a crown of life."* Now for those who have their eyes open, let's go to the Book of Luke to tie some of this together. **Luke 21:12** *"But before all these, they shall lay their hands on you and persecute you, delivering you up to the synagogues* (of Satan) *and into prisons, being brought before kings and rulers* (Satan's leaders) *for My* (Jesus) *name's sake. 13. And it shall turn to you for a testimony. 14. Settle it therefore in your hearts, not to meditate before what ye shall answer: 15. For I will give you a mouth and wisdom, which all your adversaries shall not be able to gainsay nor resist. 16. And ye shall be betrayed both by parents and brethren and kinfolks and friends; and some of you shall they cause to be put to death, 17. And ye shall be hated of all men for My name's sake. 18. But there shall not an hair of your head perish. 19. In your patience possess ye your souls."* Now go to **Mark 13:9** *"But take heed to yourselves: for they shall deliver you up to councils; and in the synagogues* (of Satan) *ye shall be beaten: and ye shall be brought before rulers and kings for My sake, for a testimony against them."* Now at first blush, this sounds pretty bad; persecuted, beaten, put to death and betrayed by your family and friends. On the other hand it seems to contradict itself by saying, *"But there shall not an hair of your head perish."* How can this be that you are beaten and put to death and yet not one hair of your head will perish. This definitely needs a little help to understand. First, why would your family and friends, who love you, betray you? The only reason this can happen is that a mother believes that anti-Christ is the real Christ, and that mother or friend thinks they are doing you a favor and turning you over to this bunch in order to save you. For the elect, this is their destiny. This is the reason God has allowed them to live at this time. The elect stood against the devil in the first earth age and God knows He can trust them to stand against him again. Since not one hair will be harmed, let's look closer at the word beaten. Have you ever been intimidated or brow-beaten. The elect will be brought before Satan and/or his lieutenants (the rulers and kings with the small k and small r) and they will attempt to brow-beat you in order to make you worship anti-Christ. Instead, you will allow the Holy Spirit to speak through you and even the talking heads in the media will not be able to punch a hole in what will be spoken. The language will be the Pentecostal tongue spoken of in both the Old and New Testaments. This language will be understood by everyone on the face of the earth. Unlike the United Nations where they have interpreters, this message will be directly understood when spoken; only God can do this. You say, "how about being put to death?" *"And ye shall be betrayed both by parents and brethren and kinsfolks and friends; and some of you shall they cause to be put to death,"* is what we read in **Luke 21:16.** Death is one of Satan's names and some of God's elect will be brought before him and will be faithful to give testimony to him for all the world to see and hear. Make no mistake these events will demand world wide attention and every major and minor news media will be covering the happenings taking place in the middle east, in a place called Jerusalem. Every, I repeat, **every religion in the world** will accept this anti-Christ as their messiah. Buddhist, Muslims, Hendos and even the majority of people that call themselves Christians will worship who they believe is Jesus the Messiah. They will believe it because the majority of the churches are teaching the fly-away doctrine know as "rapture." People are afraid of the unknown and you are now being given a glimpse of what will take place shortly upon the earth. So if you understand what is being said, you are probably one of God's elect and there is no reason to fear because you know what is going down. Don't be too hard on your family or friends for what you could call a betrayal, but really they are only doing the one thing that has the possibility of you fulfilling your ultimate destiny. *"Be thou faithful unto death and I will give thee a crown of life."* If you cannot understand what we are talking about, you will remember it when these things start to happen. We can spend more time on this, but either you are beginning to see the clever plan that the devil has devised to seduce unstudied people or you don't. All of this so far has been about Satan's tribulation. We said at the beginning there will be two tribulations. The first is the tribulation of anti-Christ. The second tribulation will be the tribulation God. The first will last five months.

The second, or God's tribulation, will consist of two battles fought simultaneously and be over quickly.

30. MYTH and PART TRUTH: The battle of Armageddon will be fought by Israel and her enemies at Megiddo and the battle will last three and a-half years.

FACT AND OPINION: The battle of Armageddon will be fought at Megiddo, in the area of Megiddo Pass (wadi Ara) inside the Jezreel Valley, also pronounced Har-Megedon. **Revelation 16:16** *And He gathered them together into a place called in the Hebrew tongue Armageddon.* **16:21** *"And there fell upon men a great hail out of heaven, every stone about the weight of a talent: and the men blasphemed God because of the plague of the hail; for the plague thereof was exceeding great."* Depending on what is being weighed a talent was anywhere from 117 pounds to 180 pounds. There is no weapon of war that can withstand being hit with hail stones weighing up to 180 pounds.

OPINION: Most Christians are not aware that there will be two tribulations and two battles. The first will be the tribulation of anti-Christ and the second will be God's tribulation. Most Bible scholars are looking strictly in the middle east. I realize at the moment, there is not much support for the second battle. So when you see these things start coming to pass you will know that God's tribulation battle will be fought up in the area of Alaska where Gog (Russia) will cross the 56 miles of the Bering Strait from the Chukotka Peninsula in Russia to the Seward Peninsula in Alaska to enter this country from the north.

As of this writing, there is considerable effort to build a tunnel under the Bering sea, in order to operate a high-speed train. This would greatly reduce the time and cost of transporting goods from China and others. The time would be reduced to days rather than weeks or months by ship. Whether the tunnel is completed before the battle makes no difference, as God will send hail stones that weigh up to one hundred and eighty pounds that will bring any army to its knees in a matter of minutes. We find the multitude of Gog known as Hamon-gog in the great Book of **Ezekiel 39:11** *"And it shall come to pass in that day, that I will give unto Gog a place there of graves in Israel,* (USA see below) *the valley of the passengers on the east of the sea:* (Bering Sea) *and it shall stop the noses of the passengers: and there shall they bury Gog and all his multitude:*

and they shall call it The valley of Hamon-gog. **Revelation 19:19** *"And I saw the beast and the kings of the earth and their armies, gathered together to make war against Him That sat on the horse and against His army. 20. And the beast was taken and with him the false prophet that wrought miracles before him, with which he deceived them that had received the mark of the beast and them that worshiped his image. These both were cast alive into a lake of fire burning with brimstone. 21. And the remnant were slain with the sword of Him That sat upon the horse, which sword proceeded out of His mouth: and all the fowls were filled with their flesh."* For the deeper student, most all of the promises that God made to Israel have been fulfilled in this country between the Pacific and Atlantic oceans. This is another subject for another time, but many who call themselves Caucasians have never checked their heritage to find that the term Caucasian comes from those tribes of Israel who traveled north over the Caucasus mountains and settled in Europe especially England, Scotland and Ireland, then migrated to this country. This is the land of milk and honey populated by a large number of people who don't even know who they are. The Battle of Ha-mon-gog will be fought in Alaska. The Russian army and its allies will enter Alaska by way of the Bering Sea.

31. MYTH: When a person dies, they immediately go to heaven or hell.

FACT: II Corinthians 5:8 *"To be absent from the body is to be present with the LORD."* **Ecclesiastes 12:7** *"Then shall the dust return to the earth as it was; and the spirit shall return unto GOD who gave it."* If we go to the Book of **Luke** and read of the rich man and the beggar named Lazarus in **Chapter 16: 26** *"And beside all this, between us and you there is a great gulf fixed: so that they which would pass from hence to you cannot: neither can they pass to us, that would come from thence."* When a person dies, regardless of their station in life, they go to paradise and either go to the good side where Lazarus went or they go to the bad side where the rich man went. They will both wait for the end of the millennium where the rich man will stand before God and reap his reward which will be the lake of fire unless he changes as a result of the teaching that is done by God's elect during the millennium. Lazarus will have no part in this second death and Judgment for him will be rewards he has earned by his works while on earth. If you are familiar with these events as recorded in Luke and you just stay in English, you will never realize the word hell that is mentioned with the rich man in the manuscripts is grave. The discomfort he is complaining about is the fact he went from a life of pleasure and comfort, where he called all the shots, to a very austere existence and he realizes that he will be there for a long time. The Gulf referred to is a medical term for an open wound used by Luke, who was a Physician. Jesus is the water of life and what the rich man was asking for was for the message of the Water of Life be told to his brothers and that he might be told as well so he could get out of there. There is no burning fiery hell at this time. God, who is a consuming fire will be present with the lake of fire at the great white throne judgment. This subject will be discussed in more detail in "Where are the dead" later in this book.

32. MYTH: The food laws listed in the Old Testament were done away with by Jesus.

FACT: Jesus said in **Matthew 5:17** *"Think not that I am come to destroy the law, or the prophets: I am not come to destroy, but to fulfill. 18. For verily I say unto you, Till heaven and earth pass, one jot or one tittle shall in no wise pass from the law, till all be fulfilled.* The health laws in **Leviticus 11:1-47** and **Isaiah 65:4** are still in effect. God said I created some scavengers to clean the earth and they are not for you to eat. Jesus did not do away with the commandants. He did do away with the ordinance of blood by dying once and for all. Dr. Ray Alexander stated, "If we abide by **Leviticus 3:16-17** we do not need to worry about coronary artery disease or cancer." God said don't eat the fat in **Leviticus 3:16** *"All the fat is the LORD'S."* 17. *"It shall be a perpetual statute for your generations throughout all your dwellings, that ye eat neither fat nor blood."* We will discuss this topic in more detail later, but let's close for now with a message from the Book of **I Timothy 4:3** *"Forbidding to marry and commanding to abstain from meats, which God hath created to be received with thanksgiving of them which believe and know the truth. 4. For every creature of God is good and nothing to be refused, if it be received with thanksgiving."* The vast majority of Bible readers and even preachers will say, "See I told you, as long as we bless it, we can eat anything we want." If I did not go to a little effort and rightly divide the word, I would agree with that statement. Look carefully: *"to abstain from meats, which God hath created to be received."* Let me ask you did God create scavengers to be eaten? If we read **Leviticus 11** we know God did not want us to eat scavengers. Did Jesus dying on the cross change our bodies to be different than when the food laws were given? Absolutely not! Have you ever wondered why we have so many unhealthy church going people? I can tell you, they have never been taught or learned for themselves that we are what we eat. But the advertizing people make bacon look so good and it taste so good. Hey, if you want to squeal like a pig running to the doctor, have a good trip. More later.

33. MYTH: Rape is not a capital offense.

FACT: According to God it is. **Deuteronomy 22:25** *"But if a man find a betrothed damsel in the field and the man force her and lie with her: then the man only that lay with her shall die."* There are some situations where it is not. **Deuteronomy 22:28** *"If a man find a damsel that is a virgin, which is not betrothed and lay hold on her and lie with her and they be found; 29. Then the man that lay with her shall give unto the damsel's father fifty shekels of silver and she shall be his wife; because he hath humbled her, he may not put her away all his days."* (He can not divorce her)

34. MYTH: It pleased God for preachers to always preach a salvation message.

FACT: Hebrews 6:6 *"If they shall fall away, to renew them again unto repentance, seeing they crucify to themselves the Son of God afresh and put him to an open shame."* When they preach a salvation message to people who are already saved they put Jesus to an open shame. In reality they are saying, He did not do it right the first time. It is a shame that too many pastors don't teach the entire Word of God, chapter by chapter and verse by verse. When this is done, the congregation is hearing about God and His ways and not the traditions of men.

35. MYTH: Divorced people should not be allowed to teach Sunday School or hold any church leadership role.

FACT: Divorce is not the unforgivable sin. Did you know that God got a divorce? **Jeremiah 3:8 "And I saw, when for all the causes whereby backsliding Israel committed adultery I had put her away and given her a bill of divorce:"** God is speaking here in accordance with the law that He gave as set forth in **Deuteronomy 21:1.** He gave Israel a bill of divorce. The reason that adultery is such an offense to God, is He likens adultery to idolatry because they both deal with unfaithfulness. So this is not a light thing with God and should not be with man, but it is not unforgivable. Many times too many church leaders try to play God by attaching a guilt trip on people by making them feel like second class citizens. They won't allow for an otherwise qualified person to teach Sunday School, etc. if they have been divorced. They will, however, let them contribute money. If God forgives them, the Preacher needs to grow up and mature.

36. MYTH: God will only save those that come from the seed line of Adam.

FACT: The Bible tells us they are saved from every nation, kindred and tongue. **Revelation 5:9** *"And they sung a new song, saying, 'Thou art worthy to take the book and to open the seals thereof: for Thou was slain and hast redeemed us to God by Thy blood out of every kindred and tongue and people and nation."*

37. MYTH: A curse can be placed upon a family for many generations.

FACT: This teaching is not only poor scholarship, but it has greatly hurt many families over the years. If the children continue to break God's laws they will suffer the same consequences as their parents. The Bible tells us that a dad eating a green plum does not set his child's teeth on edge. **Jeremiah 31:29** *"In those days they shall say no more, The fathers have eaten a sour grape and the children's teeth are set on edge. 30. But every one shall die for his own iniquity, every man that eateth the sour grape, his teeth shall be set on edge."* If the children of one who has displeased God and suffered God's cursing, turns and begins pleasing God, they will receive the blessings of God.

38. MYTH: God's original intention was for us to have an earthly king.

FACT: False, God always wanted us to want Him to be our King. As it is written, God will write His laws on our hearts and He will be our God and we will be His people. **Jeremiah 31:33** *"After those days, saith the Lord, I will put My law in their inward parts and write it in their hearts; and will be their God and they shall be My people."* **I Samuel 8:7** *"And the LORD said unto Samuel,* *the people have not rejected thee, but they have rejected Me, that I should not reign over them."*

39. MYTH: We must be perfect for God to accept us.

FACT: Many people actually believe this and use this as their reason not to accept and follow God. This probably has its origin in verses like **Matthew 5:48** *"Be ye therefore perfect, even as your Father which is in heaven is perfect."* This is another case where just studying in English causes a problem. The word perfect as used many times is better translated "mature." Paul said in **Romans 7:15 "For that which I do I allow not: for what I would, that do I not; but what I hate, that do I."** The truth is if you are going to live in these flesh bodies, you will mess up again and again. When we accept Jesus as our Lord and Master and keep His teachings and repent when we fall short, God will forgive us, love us and accept us. Our righteousness is as filthy rags. God, in the authority of Jesus name cleans and makes us whole again. The key is believing in Jesus and using the name of Jesus, because that gives us credentials to have God recognize we believe. You see the world says, **"Show me and I will believe." God says, "Believe and I will show you."** There is no other name on the face of the earth, that commands that kind of relationship with the Creator of the universe. All other originators of the many religions were born of a woman with an earthly father, they lived and died and they are still dead. Jesus was supernaturally born of a virgin with the Holy Spirit of God causing the conception. He lived a life without sin was put to death on a Roman cross and then resurrected and lives eternally and is returning at the end of this Fig Tree Generation. When we talk about the time in history before the birth of Christ, we say the year followed by BC. We don't say BB, before Buddha or BM, before Mohammad. All the world uses BC. Some ignorant people are ashamed of Jesus and now say BCE or before the common era. Is there "In God We Trust" on all U.S. Currency in spite of the opposition from the God and Jesus haters in this country? Yes!

40. MYTH: In this country an English language Bible is all you need to understand God's plan.

FACT and OPINION: At the front of the 1611 King James Bible the many interpreters instruct the reader that **"We did the best we could, but you need to check it out for yourselves."** The Bible

70

admonishes us *to* study to show ourselves approved that we might not be ashamed. **II Timothy 2:15** *"Study to shew thyself approved unto God, a workman that needeth not to be ashamed, rightly dividing the word of truth."* Did He say only clergy study? No! He said a workman which is the Greek word "ergates" with the meaning: a toiler, a teacher, laborer, worker. Your preacher will not stand with you before God at judgment. You and you alone will stand and be judged and pass the test and receive your eternal rewards or because you did not rightly divide the word and understand God and His ways, you will be ashamed and suffer the consequences. It is also this writer's observation and belief that some of the new versions of the Bible have been tampered with and key concepts are not taught. You say, "How could that happen and why? It has been going on for a long time. We find in **I Chronicles 2:55** *"And the families of the scribes which dwelt at Jabez; the Tirathites, the Shimeathites and Suchathites. These are the Kenites that came of Hemath, the father of the house of Rechab."* This was written about 990 BC. Did you notice that the scribes were Kenites? Scribe is the Greek word "caphar" with the meaning: to inscribe and enumerate, to recount, declare, speak, talk tell, writer. You see when you have sons of Cain (Kenites) acting as your keeper of the record, they can slant the record with a little different twist. Not too much because it would be noticed, but just enough to hide the devil's identity and purpose from God's people. Let me give you an example of this still going on today. The New Revised KJ Bible has been messed with. We discussed **Ezekiel 28:13 in MYTH 18.** This had to do with God being against those who taught His people to fly to save their souls. Well in some of the newer versions they have changed the meaning to "birds flying." Was this an accident? I don't think so because it hides one of the biggest con jobs pulled off by the devil. Just as all the world believes that the Christian Bible tells us that the first sin was a snake giving a woman an apple to eat. This completely distorts what really happened as we found in the first part of the Book of Genesis.

41. MYTH: December 25ᵗʰ is the birthday of Jesus.

FACT: Careful study of the Book of Luke tells exactly when the conception of John took place and when Elizabeth was six months pregnant with John. Using this information we find that December

25th was the conception of Jesus and that He was born on the first day of the Feast of Tabernacles, September 29th the following year. We also know that shepherds are not abiding in the fields in winter. Even today this is not so. The key to the date is the course of Abia in **Luke 1:5** Further study will show this would have been June 13-19 of that year. Zacharias finished his duties on the 19th. He was 30 miles from home and was an old man. He would have taken a few days to walk and recuperate from his journey and explain to his wife, Elizabeth, what had happened when the angel appeared to him. He would have been with his wife around the 24th or 25th of June. We find in Luke that Mary, the mother of Jesus, made haste to go see Elizabeth the same day she had conceived. This would have been December 25th and the reason God has allowed Christmas to be celebrated by the entire world. The date is correct, what happened on that date was conception not birth.

42. MYTH: The people marching around a prison demonstrating and saying the Bible says, "Thou shall not kill," when a convicted murderer is going to be executed are pleasing God.

FACT and OPINION: These misguided people, usually carrying a Bible, don't have a clue what the manuscripts say about murder. In the first place, the word kill as given in the ten commandants is a poor translation. For all those who will only accept what Jesus says, let's turn to the New Testament where Jesus was asked by a man, which of the commandants should I keep? **Matthew 19:18** Jesus said, *"Thou shalt do no murder, Thou shalt not commit adultery, Thou shalt not steal, Thou shalt not bear false witness."* Jesus is listing the commandments and you notice He did not say thou shalt not kill, He said, *"Thou shalt do no murder."* **I John 3:15** *"Whosoever hateth his brother is a murderer: and ye know that no murderer hath eternal life abiding in him."* This is the only place in the Bible that suggests that there is no forgiveness in this flesh life for murder. Now let us go to **Numbers 35**, to see a few examples of what murder is. **Verse 16** *"And if he smite him with an instrument of iron, so that he die, he is a murderer: the murderer shall surely be put to death. 17. And if he smite him with throwing a stone, wherewith he may die and he die, he is a murderer: the murderer shall surely be put to death. 18. Or if he smite him with an hand weapon of wood, wherewith he may die and he die, he is a murderer: the murderer* *shall surely be put to death. 19. The revenger of blood* (closest blood relative) *himself shall slay the murderer: when he meeteth him, he shall slay him. 20. But if he thrust him of hatred or hurl at him by laying in wait, that he die; 21. Or in enmity smite him with his hand, that he die; he that smote him shall surely be put to death; for he is a murderer: the revenger of blood shall slay the murderer, when he meeteth him."* the avenger or revenger of blood is the closest living relative of the victim. God always uses common sense. Careful study reveals that God is saying if they are not fit to live in an orderly society, execute them and send them to Me. Under God's law, it is not only the right, but the responsibility of the relative of the victim to execute the murderer. In today's society we bring them to trial where if they are convicted and there is no doubt, they should be executed. So the people marching around a prison when there is a mass murderer or cold blooded killer condemned to death, may mean well, but they are wrong. If the murderer's lawyer is slick enough to get him off and he is set free, he still has a problem because he has not had his real trial until he stands before God; his victim will also be there.

43. MYTH: The Bible says there is never a good reason to kill.

FACT: Solomon tell us in **Ecclesiastes 3:1** *"To every thing there is a season and a time to every purpose under the heaven." 3. "A time to kill and a time to heal; a time to break down and a time to build up."* **Deuteronomy 32:29** *"I kill and I make alive."* For those in the military in time of war, the Bible takes all the guilt from those who shed the blood of the enemy. **Psalms 144:1** *"Blessed be the LORD my strength, which teacheth my hands to war, and my fingers to fight: 2. My goodness and my fortress; My high tower and my deliverer, My shield and He in whom I trust; Who subdueth my People under me."* When a law officer in doing his duty protecting all citizens from those unfit to live in an orderly society, it is sometime necessary to take a life, but this is not murder. When a person is defending their home or business and his or her life is threatened and the person takes a life, this is not murder. The Constitution of this nation was taken for the most part from common law from England which was based on the Bible and was written by men who believed in God. There is nothing in our Constitution that prohibits us from defending ourselves. God has used war all the way through the Bible. God has sent the death angel to kill literately thousands of people for disobeying Him. So the reply to those who say the Bible says there is never a good reason to kill are wrong and really are not that familiar with our Father's word.

44. MYTH: God is love and would never hate anybody or anything.

FACT: Proverbs: 6:16 *"These six things doth the LORD hate: Yea, seven are an abomination unto Him: 17. A proud look, a lying tongue and hands that shed innocent blood. 18. An heart that deviseth wicked imaginations, Feet that be swift in running to mischief, 19. A false witness that speaketh lies, and he that soweth discord among brethren."* **Malachi 1:2** *"Was not Esau Jacob's brother? Saith the LORD: yet I loved Jacob, 3. And I hated Esau."* God created us in His likeness. He has emotions very similar to our own. He is slow to anger, but He does have a boiling point. Anyone who thinks or says that God never could hate does not know their Bible very well. There is a time to turn the other cheek and there are times that require righteous indignation, which is the right to get mad and take action.

45. MYTH: We really don't need anything but the New Testament to learn from.

FACT: Nothing could be further from the truth. If you don't understand Genesis and what took place at the beginning of this earth age, you will never understand God's plan or the New Testament. Much of the New Testament is spent quoting the Old Testament. Jesus said, *"I did not come to change one jot or tittle of the law."* One of the greatest Bible scholars, E.W. Bullinger stated: "The Bible can be thought of as a belt, with Genesis the buckle and Revelations the end. These two books are key to holding the belt together or understanding the entire Bible." When asked a question, many times Jesus answered the question with another question; *"It is written, have ye not read?"* What was He referring to, if not the Old Testament, for the New Testament had not been written. You can claim to be a Christian, but if you don't rightly divide all the Word of God, you won't ever reach your full potential or understand what true peace and happiness is. For a person to make the statement that we only need the New Testament is going to spend most of their time on a salvation message and never really grow and mature. Remember, salvation is very important and is the first step, but this is what Jesus did for you. For you to really please God, you must put on the whole armor of God and you can not do this without in-depth knowledge of the entire Bible. It is not too late to get started, it is up to you.

46. MYTH: God now approves of homosexual behavior as some churches teach and the Supreme Court has sanctioned.

FACT: If Sodom and Gomorrah had a Supreme Court, I'm sure they approved of this kind of perversion. I'm also sure, their entire cities were destroyed by God. If everyone practiced this kind of life style, it would be the end of the human race. There are no homosexual dogs, cats, cows etc. because they use the plumbing they were born with as intended and have not gone against God's plans for being here. In almost fifty years of counseling, the Lord has allowed me to help turn two homosexual men around and see that they had bought into a phoney lifestyle. They both thought and said that they were "born that way" and could not help it. I ask them if their last physical revealed that they had a uterine cervix? Every person I have asked that question over the many years of counseling always answers the same way. "What do you mean?" I reply, if you were born with female parts, then you were indeed born that way and I cannot help you, but if you have all the correct plumbing, you have bought into a lie. And not only that, God tells us if you want to go down that road, He will help you believe that lie. If you are living this life-style, I do not judge you, that is your choice, but just so you will know that when you stand before God, who will judge you, I want you to be aware of how He feels; regardless of how some foolish men vote or some misguided churches practice this lifestyle and have homosexual pastors. **Romans 1:18** *"For the wrath of God is revealed from heaven against all ungodliness and unrighteousness of men, who hold the truth in unrighteousness;* (they call wrong, right and right, wrong) *19. Because that which may be known of God is manifest in them; for God hath shewed it unto them. 20. For the invisible things of Him from the creation of the world are clearly seen, being understood by the things that are made, even His eternal power and Godhead; so that they are without excuse: 21. Because that when they knew God, they glorified Him not as God, neither were thankful; but became vain in their imaginations and their foolish heart was darkened. 22. Professing themselves to be wise, they became fools,*

75

(many including the Supreme Court) *23. And changed the glory of the uncorruptible God into an image, made like to corruptible man and to birds and four footed beast and creeping things. 24. Wherefore* (because of this) *God also gave them up to uncleanness through the lusts of their own hearts,* (minds) *to dishonor their own bodies between themselves: 25. Who changed the truth of God into a lie and worshiped and served the creature more than the Creator, Who is blessed for ever, Amen. (*Now listen up and pay close attention) *26. For this cause God gave them up unto vile affections: for even their women did change the natural use into that which is against nature: 27. And likewise also the men, leaving the natural use of the woman, burned in their lust one toward another; men with men working that which is unseemly and receiving in themselves that recompense* (retribution) *of their error which was meet.* (despised) In the Old Testament, this type of behavior was not tolerated and the participants were stoned to death. Let's read another witness so there is no doubt how God feels about this. **II Thessalonians 2:10** *"And with all deceivableness of unrighteousness in them that perish; because they received not the love of the truth, that they might be saved. 11. For this cause God shall send them strong delusion, that they should believe a lie. 12. That they all might be damned who believed not the truth, but had pleasure in unrighteousness."* Now don't shoot the messenger, I just think you should know how God feels about people who make these kinds of choices. Let me ask you a question, if this is so right, why do most people that go down this road have to get drunk or do drugs when they first get into this. Why, at least at one time did you feel deep down inside that this is wrong? The Bible is very clear, in spite of what some Bible thumpers say, there will be no homosexuals in heaven. So if you don't know this or know and don't care, then enjoy your road to hell. Remember, God loves all His children, but He does not love some of the things they do. This is not the unforgivable sin and only you can make the choice to change your ways, repent and be forgiven. The ball is in your court.

47. MYTH: Once saved always saved.

FACT: Many churches teach this and Jesus always does His part "if" we keep up our end. **Galatians 6:7** *"Be not deceived; God is not mocked: for whatsoever a man soweth, that shall he also reap.*

8. For he that soweth to his flesh shall of the flesh reap corruption: but he that soweth to the Spirit shall of the Spirit reap life everlasting. 9. And let us not be weary in well doing: for in due season we shall reap, if we faint not." Let's get another witness in **Ezekiel 18:20** *"The soul that sinneth, it shall die. The son shall not bear the iniquity of the father, neither shall the father bear the iniquity of the son: the righteousness of the righteous shall be upon him and the wickedness of the wicked shall be upon him. 21. But if the wicked will turn from all his sins that he hath committed and keep all My statutes and do that which is lawful and right, he shall surely live, he shall not die. 22. All his transgressions that he hath committed, they shall not be mentioned unto him: in his righteousness that he hath done he shall live. 23. Have I any pleasure at all that the wicked should die? Saith the LORD GOD: and not that he should return from his ways, and live? 24. But when the righteous turneth away from his righteousness and committeth iniquity and doeth according to all the abominations that the wicked man doeth, shall he live? All his righteousness that he hath done shall not be mentioned: in his trespass that he hath trespassed and in his sin that he hath sinned, in them he shall die. 25. Yet ye say, 'The way of the LORD is not equal.' Hear now, O house of Israel;* (If you are a Christian, you have become spiritual Israel) *Is not My way equal? Are your ways unequal? 26. When a righteous man turneth away from his righteousness and committeth iniquity and dieth in them; for his iniquity that he hath done shall he die. 27. Again, when the wicked man turneth away from his wickedness that he hath committed and doeth that which is lawful and right, he shall save his soul alive."* **II Peter 2:20** *"For if after they have escaped the pollutions of the world through the knowledge of the Lord and Savior Jesus Christ, they are again entangled therein and overcome, the latter end is worse with them than the beginning. 21. For it had been better for them not to have known the way of righteousness, than, after they have known it, to turn from the holy commandment delivered unto them. 22. But it is happened unto them according to the true proverb, 'The dog is turned to his own vomit again'; and the sow that was washed to her wallowing in the mire."* When a Christian slips and sins and then repents and ask for forgiveness, God hears and wipes the slate clean. If a Christian slips again and again and does not repent and does not ask God to forgive them, those sins are in the book of your life and if you die and the sins are great enough, you can loose your salvation. This is your fault because you did not do what God requires to keep in good standing with Him.

48. MYTH: Both white horse riders in the book of Revelation are Jesus returning.

FACT: The first rider in **Revelation 6** is anti-Christ or as the Greek says **"Instead of Christ."** He is coming to deceive those who do not know God's word in depth. In other words those who don't have the seal of God in their forehead. (minds) Anti-Christ is going to tell all the world that "I've come to fly you out of here." Most all religions of the world, including most Christians will believe and follow him. He will be very convincing and do many miracles. He will hold the biggest revival the world has ever witnessed. This rider appears at the sixth seal, the sixth trump and sixth vile. Christ does not appear until the seventh trump. It is amazing how many preachers can not count, seven always has and always will come after six. Jesus comes after the deceiver. **Revelation 19:11** *"And I saw heaven opened and behold, a white horse; and He that sat upon him was called Faithful and true and in righteousness He doth judge and make war. 12. His eyes were as a flame of fire and on His head were many crowns; and He had a name written, that no man knew, but He Himself. 13. And He was clothed with a vesture dipped in blood: and His name is called The Word of God. 14. And the armies which were in heaven followed Him upon white horses, clothed in fine linen, white and clean. 15. And out of His mouth goeth a sharp sword, that with it He should smite the nations: and He shall rule them with a rod of iron: and He treadeth the winepress of the fierceness and wrath of Almighty God. 16. And He hath on His vesture and on His thigh a name written, KING OF KINGS AND LORD OF LORDS."*

49. MYTH: Women are not allowed to wear men's pants.

FACT: Deuteronomy 22:5 *"The woman shall not wear that which pertaineth unto a man, neither shall a man put on a woman's garment: for all that do so are abomination unto the LORD thy God."* In the first place when this was written men wore skirts so the modern day church that has dress codes needs to take a good look at this before condemning a persons attire. Deeper study reveals that a man is not to take the place of a woman in a sexual act and a woman is not to take the place of a man. God uses figures of speech and metaphors to get His message across to the enlightened student. Wearing a man's garment would not be an abomination to God. "A Figure of Speech" is a designed and legitimate departure from the laws of language, in order to emphasize what is said. This peculiar form or unusual manner may not be true, or so true, to the literal meaning of the words; but is more true to their real sense and truer to truth. Figures are never used but for the sake of emphasis. They should never be ignored. Ignorance of Figures of speech has led to the grossest errors, which have been caused either from taking literally what is figurative or from taking figuratively what is literal. "The above scripture is a "figure of speech." Do you really believe a woman putting on a pair of jeans would be an abomination to God? He does tell us homosexuality is an abomination to Him.

50. MYTH: God is opposed to anyone buying or selling a dog.

FACT: Deuteronomy 23:17 *"There shall be no whore of the daughters of Israel, nor a sodomite of the sons of Israel. 18. Thou shalt not bring the hire of a whore or the price of a dog, into the house of the LORD thy God for any vow: for even both these are abomination unto the LORD thy God."* **Verse 17** is the subject and describes what is being discussed. The price of a dog is another figure of speech and is describing the manner in which the sodomite engages in his perverted sexual behavior. This is really a no-brainer for anyone who is really looking for the truth. If you think there is a sin involved in buying or selling a dog, you are way off base. God loves his animals and has always had them with Him. He had animals in the first earth age, they are here now and they will be in the third age. They were in physical bodies in the first age and this age, but they will be in spiritual bodies in the third age. Read **Isaiah 11** to find out more about God's animals.

51. MYTH: God is pleased no matter how much scripture is used when a preacher rambles on for an hour with his own sad/funny stories?

FACT: God gives directions to teach His Word line upon line, chapter by chapter and verse by verse. Let's ask the Bible how God wants His people to learn His teachings. You will notice the following instructions are addressed to those who are weaned from milk. In other words, those who have accepted their Savior and find they need to go on to perfection. **Isaiah 28:9** *"Whom shall He teach knowledge? And whom shall He make to understand doctrine? Them that are weaned from the milk and drawn from the breast. 10. For precept must be upon precept, precept upon precept;* (double for emphasis) *line upon line, line upon line, here a little and there a little."* Remember Paul fussing at those who were still on milk and teaching the basics. You have to be weaned from the milk bottle before you can go on to the deeper truths of our Father. Salvation is wonderful and the necessary first step, but if you want to grow and be useful to your Father, you must put on the whole armor of God. Now let's look at how God feels about pastors who are playing church. **Jeremiah 23:1** *"Woe be unto the pastors that destroy and scatter the sheep of My pasture! 2. Therefore thus saith the LORD God of Israel.* (believers are spiritual Israel) *against the pastors that feed My people; ye have scattered My flock and driven them away and have not visited them: behold, I will visit upon you the evil of your doings saith the LORD."* As you can see God is not happy with these pastors who teach half truths and teach the same thing over and over and drive His people away. How many people do you know that say, "I just don't get anything out of church;" and before long they stop going. When a pastor places more importance on their words than God's word, it does not please God. When you look around the world today and see that most church going people are starving for the Word of God to be taught instead of philosophy and psychology and sermons with their seven or ten points of light. There is a place for these things, but teaching the Bible is not one of them.

52. MYTH: The Bible doesn't say anything about us keeping our conversation clean?

FACT: That may be what some teach, but let's see what the Bible really says. **Ephesians 4:29** *"Let no corrupt communication proceed out of your mouth, but that which is good to the use of edifying, that it may minister grace unto the hearers."*

53. MYTH: Jesus' main purpose was to make salvation available to all that believe.

FACT: Salvation is certainly very important and the corner-stone of Christianity. We find in the Book of **Hebrews 2:14** *"For as much then as the children are partakers of flesh and blood, He also Himself likewise took part of the same; that through death He might destroy him that had the power of death, that is the devil."* The coming of Jesus in the flesh fulfilled all the prophecies written about Him in the Bible.

54. MYTH: Satan does not really have a plan?

FACT: The Book of Job is one of the oldest books in the Bible and Satan's earlier plan is found in **Job 1:7** *"And the LORD said unto Satan, Whence comest thou? Then Satan answered the LORD and said, From going to and fro in the earth and from walking up and down in it."* Let's look at a few more examples found in the Bible. **Daniel 11:36** *"And the king shall do according to his will; and he shall exalt himself and magnify himself above every GOD and shall speak marvelous things against the GOD of gods and shall prosper till the indignation be accomplished for that is determined shall be done. 37. Neither shall he regard the God of his fathers, nor the desire of women, nor regard any GOD: for he shall magnify himself above all. 38. But in his estate shall he honor the god of forces; and a god whom his fathers knew not shall he honor with gold and silver and with precious stones and pleasant things."* **II Thessalonians 2:4** *"Who opposeth and exalteth himself above all that is called God, or that is worshiped; so that he as God sitteth in the Temple of God shewing himself that he is God."* God's people need to wake up and be aware of what this guy is up to. If you want to remain willingly ignorant and bury your head in the sand, anti-Christ will have you for lunch. **Revelation 17:8** *"The beast that thou sawest was and is not; and shall ascend out of the bottomless pit and go into perdition: and they that dwell on the earth shall wonder, whose names were not written in the book of life from the foundation of the world, when they behold the beast that was and is not and yet is."* Let's read further so there is no doubt that Satan has a plan. **Revelation 12:3** *"And there appeared another wonder in heaven; and behold, a great red dragon, having seven heads and ten horns and seven crowns upon his heads. 4. And his tail drew the third part of the stars of heaven and did cast them to the earth: and the dragon stood before the woman which was ready to be delivered, for to devour her child as soon as it was born.* **Revelation**

13:1 *"And I stood upon the sand of the sea and saw a beast rise up out of the sea,* (=people **Revelation 17:15**) *having seven heads and ten crowns and upon his heads the name of blasphemy. 2. And the beast which I saw was like unto a leopard and his feet were as the feet of a bear and his mouth as the mouth of a lion: and the dragon gave him his power and his seat and great authority. 3. And I saw one of his heads as it were wounded to death; and his deadly wound was healed: and all the world wondered after the beast. 4. And they worshiped the dragon which gave power unto the beast: and they worshiped the beast, saying, "Who is like unto the beast? Who is able to make war with him?"* Go to verse *13. "And he doeth great wonders, so that he maketh fire come down from heaven on the earth in the sight of men. 14. And deceiveth them that dwell on the earth by the means of those miracles which he had power to do."* Let's go to **Daniel 11:21** *"And in his estate shall stand up a vile person, to whom they shall not give the honor of the kingdom: but he shall come in peaceable and obtain the kingdom by flatteries.* Vile person is one of the twelve or more titles given to the anti-Christ. He is not another successional world leader, but a totally different and unique personage. He comes in by "flatteries." He comes in peaceable or unexpectedly in a time of careless security, to a world abundant in idleness. So the answer to the question is yes, Satan has many plans, the question you must ask yourself, is do I know enough Bible to know what is going on and when will these things take place. His main objective is to deceive all the people he can in hopes of thwarting the death sentence that God has already placed on him.

55. MYTH: If a person can quote the Bible, they are saved and approved by God.

FACT: Some are: *"Ever learning and never able to come to the knowledge of the truth."* **II Timothy 3:7.** Satan is a scripture lawyer and can quote the Bible better than most Christians. In Mexico, they have a saying, "Beware of a Mexican smoking a big cigar and a white man carrying a Bible." Test everyone's fruit, no matter who they are.

56. MYTH: God shares all His secrets with those He loves.

FACT: God has some secrets He keeps to Himself. **Deuteronomy29:29.** *"The secret things belong unto the LORD our God: but those things which are revealed belong unto us and to our children for ever, that we may do all the words of the law."*

57. MYTH: God would never call anyone stupid.

FACT: Jeremiah 4:22 *"For My people is foolish, they have not known Me; they are sottish children and they have none understanding: they are wise to do evil, but to do good they have no knowledge."* The word sottish in Hebrew is stupid.

58. MYTH: We don't know if there will be animals in heaven.

FACT: God has always loved His animals and they have, are and will be in all three heaven and earth ages. **Isaiah 11:6** *"The wolf also shall dwell with the lamb and the leopard shall lie down with the kid; and the calf and the young lion and the fatling together; and a little child shall lead them."* We know that all flesh shall be changed to spiritual bodies at the last trump. The animals that will be in heaven will have changed bodies just like humans.

59. MYTH: We may not recognize our family in heaven.

FACT: We will not only recognize our family, but God's elect will be able to go to the ones who did not make it and teach them. **Ezekiel 44:25** *"And they shall come at no dead (spiritual dead) person to defile themselves: but* (except) *for father or for mother or for son or for daughter, for brother or for sister that hath had no husband, they may defile themselves. 26. And after he is cleansed, they shall reckon unto him seven days."*

60. MYTH: Kidnapping is not a capital offense.

FACT: Exodus 21:16 *"And he that stealeth a man and selleth him or if he be found in his hand, he shall surely be put to death."* The bleeding hearts can't handle this, but these are God's rules if you want to have a worthwhile society. We have the chaos today because we don't follow God's advice. Too many people blame God, but they really need to look in the mirror.

61. MYTH: God talks to some people and even tells them where to park their car.

OPINION: In most cases no. If a person doesn't have sense enough to know where to park, they won't be of much use to our Father. I have observed that if you are pleasing God, parking places do show up.

62. MYTH: God is not really concerned about the number of stars.

FACT: False, God not only made the stars in **Genesis 1:16, He numbers them and calls them by their names. Psalms 147:4** *"He*

telleth the number of the stars; He calleth them all by their names."
When a person gets to thinking they are pretty big stuff, they should go out and view the night sky and see how really small they are.

63. MYTH: God is really impressed with some people.

FACT: He takes no pleasure in man unless they revere God and hope in His mercy. **Psalms 147:10 *"He delighteth not in the strength of the horse: He taketh not pleasure in the legs of a man. 11. The LORD taketh pleasure in them that fear* (revear) *Him, In those that hope in His mercy."***

64. MYTH: Religion makes it easy for us to understand the plan of God.

OPINION: There was a time when God made it easy for man to have fellowship with Him. After being disappointed in man over and over again, God has allowed Satan to use man's traditions to pull us away from understanding God. He no longer makes it easy, but rather will only share His secrets with those who study and learn it for themselves. God must be important enough to you to first recognize the obstacles that are presented by our educational, religious, political and monetary systems to keep you distracted. Enough not to blindly accept what someone else says or is teaching. We must check out the so-called man of God. Test his or her fruit to see if it checks out with God's word. If it does not, it does not matter who the person is, they are probably not only deceiving others, but many time themselves. We must live in this world and learn to do things God's way. When we please God He allows us to beat Satan at his own game and become successful, happy and blessed. Let's go over this again to be sure this is understood. **Man's traditions are used to keep you away from the things of God.** They are used to keep you from finding out about God's plan. It is your spiritual understanding that brings about the wisdom of God to free you from the power of the devil. Recognizing this is half the battle. The other half is getting in your Father's Word with understanding.

65. MYTH: Following God will always make you popular.

OPINION: When we truly follow God we will upset many people who can't understand why we can follow a way of life that is contrary to the ways of man. (This includes church traditions) I have counseled with people for many years and deal with the mental, physical and spiritual aspects of life. Most counselors only deal with the Psyche and Soma or mind and body. The spiritual part is usually not given much time, yet the spirit is the part of us that is in need of the most attention. Unless we get our relationship with God in order, we will usually have trouble in all three areas. A person who does not have a good relationship with their Heavenly father will never know what real joy or peace of mind is. If you follow God you will always be popular with a Him.

66. MYTH: Jesus came through the seed line of David's son, Solomon.

FACT: The regal legal line came through Solomon. The natural legal line *"The seed of the woman"* came through David, but through his his son Nathan. If we study the third chapter of **Luke 3**, we find the line of Joseph through Solomon, but Joseph had nothing to do with the birth of Jesus. Mary on the other hand was on her mother's side of the tribe of Levi, the Priest Line and Judah, the King line, on her dad's side. So in *"The seed of the woman,"* who is Jesus, we have both the Priest line and the King line in one.

67. MYTH: The parable of the fig tree, taught by Jesus does not have much significance for us today.

FACT: In **Matthew 24:32-51** Jesus said learn the parable of the fig tree. If Jesus said *"Learn it"* we better take notice and learn it. He also let us know that if we could not understand this parable we could not understand any of the parables or His overall plan. The fig tree is first mentioned early in Genesis. You also notice in the parable of the wheat and tares, the tares were taken first and the wheat or faithful believers remained. This ties in with the parable of the fig tree and you notice who was taken first, the tares. This is just another example where the misguided people pushing the rapture doctrine use a scripture and don't even know what they are talking about. "Don't confuse me with facts, I've made up my mind." I've heard more than a few preachers, say, "I want to be the first one taken." They better start studying or they will get their wish.

68. MYTH: The fig tree generation has not started yet, so the end of this earth age is still along way off.

OPINION: The generation of the fig tree began May 15, 1948 when Israel became a nation. Jesus said those that were alive and remaining when and after this happened stood as candidates to be alive

85

and remaining at His second coming. As of this writing, that was 67 years ago.

69. MYTH: God does not use covert activity to carry out His plans.

FACT: Let's define covert: concealed, hidden, disguised. Using that definition as found in a Webster's Dictionary allows us to know that God has used covert activity many times in the Bible. One example that leaves no doubt is found in **II Kings 10:18** *"And Jehu gathered all the People together and said unto them, 'Ahab served Baal a little; but Jehu shall serve him much. 19. Now therefore call unto me all the prophets of Baal, all his servants and all his priest; let none be wanting: for I have a great sacrifice to do to Baal; whosoever shall be wanting, he shall not live.' but Jehu did it in subtility, to the intent that he might destroy the worshipers of Baal. 20. And Jehu said 'Proclaim a solemn assembly for Baal." And they proclaimed it. 21. And Jehu sent through all Israel: and all the worshipers of Baal came, so that there was not a man left that came not. And they came into the house of Baal; and the house of Baal was full from one end to another. 22. And he said unto him that was over the vestry, 'Bring forth vestments for all the worshipers of Baal.' And he brought them forth vestments. 23. And Jehu went and Jehonadab the son of Rechab, into the house of Baal and said unto the worshipers of Baal, 'search and look that there be here with you none of the servants of the LORD, but the worshipers of Baal only.' 24. And when they went in to offer sacrifices and burnt offerings, Jehu appointed fourscore men without and said, 'If any of the men whom I have brought into your hands escape, he that letteth him go, his life shall be for the life of him.' 25. And it came to pass, as soon as he had made an end of offering the burnt offering, that Jehu said to the guard and to the captains, 'go in and slay them; let none come forth.; and they smote them with the edge of the sword; and the guard and the captains cast them out and went to the city of the house of Baal, 26. And they brought forth the images out of the house of Baal and burned them. 27. And they brake down the image of Baal and brake down the house of Baal and made it a draught house until this day. 28. Thus Jehu destroyed Baal out of Israel. 30. And the LORD said unto Jehu, 'Because thou hast done well in executing that which is right in Mine eyes and hast done unto the* *house of Ahab according to all that was in Mine heart, thy children of the fourth generation shall sit on the throne of Israel."* This politically correct world we live in today could never understand what was just said and believe that God had not only sanctioned it, but was well pleased and rewarded this covert action. If you have friends or family that are worshiping other gods, you might let them know that if they don't change their ways, when the time comes, they won't like what happens to them. You can believe it or not believe it, but it won't change the facts of what is written in the Word of God.

70. MYTH: The Bible talks about a tribulation period at the end of this age.

PARTLY FACT: Actually careful study of the Bible tells us there will be two tribulation periods. The first will be Satan's tribulation where he deceives the majority of the people on earth into thinking that he is Jesus coming again. Contrary to what is being taught about wars and destruction, this period begins peaceable and prosperously. Anti-Christ will not be able to fool those that are grounded in God's word and know God's plan. The second tribulation will be God taking out His wrath on those that are not sealed with His truth in their minds. The power displayed by God will be so awesome and complete that every knee shall bow and every tongue shall confess that He is God. Those whose relationship with God is real don't have anything to be concerned about. Those who have been playing church will have a big problem. Dr. Arnold Murray on Shepherd's Chapel TV Broadcast expressed, "There will be trials in Jerusalem seen on world wide TV showing people brought before this false Christ." The Greek is clear this "anti-Christ" should be translated "Instead of Christ." This will give opportunity for God's elect to allow the Holy Spirit to speak through them as found in **Mark 13:11** *"But when they shall lead you and deliver you up, take no thought beforehand what ye shall speak, neither do ye premeditate: but whatsoever shall be given you in that hour, that speak ye: for it is not ye that speak, but the Holy Ghost."*

This can also be found in **Matthew 24 and Luke 21.**

71. MYTH: We must attend church in order to be saved.

FACT: John 3:16 makes it clear what is required to be saved. The Bible does say remember the Sabbath. The word Sabbath means rest. Jesus became our Sabbath, our rest. He tells us in **Matthew**

18:20 *"For where two or three are gathered together in My name, there am I in the midst of them."* Paul tell us in **Galatians 4:10** *"Ye observe days and months and times and years. 11. I am afraid of you, lest I have bestowed upon you labor in vain."* Every day is a holy day unto God. If you have a church in your area where you are taught the word of God and not the words and traditions of man, you are blessed.

72. MYTH: Believing is all that matters, works don't count with God.

FACT: James **2:20** *"But wilt thou know, O vain man, that faith without works is dead?* Verse **26.** *"For as the body without the spirit is dead, so faith without works is dead also."* **Matthew 16:27** *"For the Son of man shall come in the glory of His Father with His angels; and then He shall reward every man according to his works."* **Acts 9:36** *"Now there was at Joppa a certain disciple named Tabitha, which by interpretation is called Dorcas: this woman was full or good works and almsdeeds which she did."* Lets look at another situation that God also takes notice of. **II Timothy 4:14** *"Alexander the copper smith did me much evil: the LORD reward him according to his works."* There are over a hundred scriptures that deal with works in the New Testament alone. We will go to the Book of James and leave no doubt how God feels about works. **James 2:14** *" What doth it profit, my brethren, though a man say he hath faith and have not works: can faith save him? 17. Even so faith, if it hath not works, is dead, being alone. 19. Thou believest that there is one God; thou doest well: the devils also believe and tremble. 20. But wilt thou know, O vain man, that faith without works is dead? 21. Was not Abraham our father justified by works, when he had offered Isaac his son upon the alter? 22. Seest thou how faith wrought with his works and by works was faith made perfect? 23. And the Scripture was fulfilled which saith, Abraham believed God and it was imputed unto him for righteousness: and he was called the friend of God. 24. Ye see then how that by works a man is justified and not by faith only. 26. For as the body without the spirit is dead, so faith without works is dead."* **Revelation 14:13** *"And I heard a voice from heaven saying unto me, Write, Blessed are the dead which die in the LORD from henceforth: Yea, saith the Spirit, that they may rest from their labors; and their works do* *follow them.* " Now we can see how faith and works lead to righteousness, which make up the clothes we will wear in heaven. **Revelation 19:8** *"And to her was granted that she should be arrayed in fine linen, clean and white: for the fine linen is the righteousness of saints. 14. And the armies which were in heaven followed Him upon white horses, clothed in fine linen, white and clean. "*

73: MYTH: All Christians have to do is believe and pray and every problem will be solved.

REALITY: God is our heart know-er. Heart is better translated "mind" in most cases. He knows our thoughts. Many baby Christians (immature) pray the problem and tell everyone in sight what their problem is. Once we verbalize the situation, Satan knows exactly how to attack. He always attacks our weakness. If you are not a strong mature Christian, that knows how to put the devil on the run, you might be better served praying to your Heavenly Father silently in order to keep the enemy from knowing all about it. Satan can and does introduce thoughts into our minds (if we let him) and then observes us to see how we will react. He can tell by our reaction if he is getting through. If we get upset or react in a negative way he will keep it up. If we don't give away our position, he will go on to an easier victim. **Note:** His spirit is still going to and fro in the earth seeking whom he may devour. Once God becomes first in your life and you become strong in His word you will find Satan is afraid of you and has to run when you team up with God in Jesus name.

74. MYTH: I'm not important enough to have God concerned about me.

FACT: God does not have anyone like you, that is the reason He created you. God is your closest living relative. He may not like some of the things you do, but He loves you. When you start putting Him first and pleasing Him, He will start blessing you. Remember no one else has your fingerprints, your laugh, your walk or your talk. Only you can do best some of the things God wants done. If you don't do it, God will move someone else to take your place to do a job that was intended for you. It's up to you.

75. MYTH: Satan wears a red suit and carries a pitchfork.

FACT: Ezekiel 28 tells us Satan was one of the most beautiful of God's creation. God created him the full pattern and he was the guarding cherub over the mercy seat. Satan was created good, but with a free will, and pride was found in him. Satan decided he was smart enough to take over God's throne in the first earth age. **Genesis 1:1** *"In the beginning God created the heaven and the earth."* Did you notice the punctuation mark, the period... at the end of earth? Did it say six thousand years ago? No! Is it possible, with all the evidence we now have, that it was millions of years ago? Yes! Just a side note to remind us of the different earth ages. Same heaven and earth, different ages. Now continue with our subject. The devil persuaded one third of God's children into following him. We have previously read **Revelation 12:4** that confirms this treason by one third of the children of the Living God. God, in his mercy said, they are still My children and I will not destroy them without giving them another chance. God destroyed the first earth age including the heaven on earth atmosphere that existed at that time. This included the dinosaurs and other prehistoric birds and animals. We find in **Jeremiah** this was not Noah's flood. The first heaven and earth age was created perfectly and because of His children following the devil, we find God destroyed it. **Jeremiah 4:23** *"I beheld the earth and lo it was without form and void; and the heavens and they had no light. 24. I beheld the mountains and lo they trembled and all the hills moved lightly. 25. I beheld and lo, there was no man and all the birds of the heavens were fled. 26. I beheld and lo, the fruitful place was a wilderness and all the cities thereof were broken down at the presence of the LORD, and His fierce anger. 27. For thus hath the LORD said, 'The whole land shall be desolate; yet will I not make a full end."* We are not told how long God waited to start over with this earth age. Did you notice that all cities were destroyed? Does that help you better understand the "City of Atlantis?" Or Stonehenge or many of the things that don't fit into a six thousand year old earth? We said all that to give evidence that Satan will not be carrying a pitchfork or wearing a red suit. He will be one of the most handsome, charismatic beings that this world has ever witnessed. He fooled one third of God's children in the first age and will deceive even more of the people in this age. This anti-Christ will completely fool the vast majority of all peoples living on earth when he arrives. We repeat again, he will come in peacefully and prosperously, which is completely opposite from what most churches are teaching. The world has some turmoil to endure at the end of this final generation, but this will perfectly set the stage for "ole pretty boy" to come and fix everything, thus making it only fitting and natural and proving that he is the Messiah. **NOT!**

76. MYTH: Satan is uncomfortable to enter most churches today.

OPINION: Satan is a skilled scripture lawyer and knows more scriptures than most Christians. If you recall, quoting what God told Adam and Eve, in the Garden of Eden, is how he convinced them it was to their benefit to get involved with him. The only problem is that he quoted what God had said, but then twisted it. There was enough truth in what he told them for them to believe him, but the twist is where he crossed the line. He quoted scripture again when tempting Christ and again twisted it for his own benefit. There are four hidden dynasties discussed in the Bible that can only be uncovered by careful study. For now we will list them because they are controlled by the descendant's of Cain for Satan's benefit in this earth age. They are Political, Economic, Educational and Religious. If you look at the top of these national and international organizations, you will find greed and corruption. Look at government today. Look at the money world today. Look at the educational world today and finally look at the religious arena. Sad to say most churches today play right into Satan's hands by not teaching The Word of God. Knowing your Father's Word allows one to be able to use these areas for their advantage and not be fooled by Satan's deception. The question is, do you know the Word well enough to know when anti-Christ twists our Father's Word. You need to realize your very life will depend on this. When the whole world is following anti-Christ, it is the destiny of God's elect to allow themselves to be used by the Holy Spirit to testify against this total phoney anti-Christ.

77. MYTH: The Minor Prophets of the Bible are called "Minor" because they are of minor importance.

FACT: For the most part the twelve Minor Prophets are called minor because of their length. They are all reasonably short with Obadiah having only one chapter. These wonderful books are very important and have as much or more to say about this end time and "The Lord's Day" as any place in the Bible.

78. MYTH: The genealogy of Cain in **Genesis 4** is the same as the genealogy of Adam in **Genesis 5.**

FACT: This is false, if they were both listing the same genealogy there would be no need to devote two chapters to the same family

91

clan. How close do you investigate the written word? Careful study will show that there is good reason to have both off-spring listed. If you casually read, you will miss the fact that Cain is not listed in Adam's genealogy because he was not Adam's son. He was the son of Satan that old serpent in the garden. Also, some of the names are spelled the same and/or almost the same, just to throw you off if you don't read with focused attention. This is just one of the early attempts by the devil to confuse the reader. He has been successful with the majority of churches because they teach that a snake gave an apple to Eve and that is what caused all of our problems. If this were not so serious, it would be laughable.

79. MYTH: There are some things in God's Word we are not suppose to know.

FACT: Let's look at **II Timothy 3:16** *"All scripture is given by inspiration of God and is profitable for doctrine, for reproof, for correction, for instruction in righteousness: 17. That the man of God may be perfect, thoroughly furnished unto all good works."* Not all, but too many churches say it is alright not to know because they are too lazy to check it out. Others are ashamed of what it says or that it might embarrass their denominational point of view. I know this sounds harsh, but it is too late to continue to play church.

80. MYTH: God winks when pastors rely on tradition and humorous/sad stories and don't teach all of His Word in depth.

FACT: Jeremiah 23:1 *"Woe be unto the pastors that destroy and scatter the sheep of My pasture! Saith the Lord."* Many churches today are struggling to stay alive. They have raffles and bake sales, bingo games and send out buses to try to improve their attendance. The one thing they are not doing is teaching God's Word in depth. At our ranch when we go out and feed the cattle, they always come a running when they see or hear the feed truck, because they know they are going to be fed. If we started going out in the feed truck, but did not feed them it would not be long before they stopped coming. It is the same way with God's people. When they come to church time after time and don't get fed or hear the same message over and over, they lose interest and sooner or later they stop coming. **Amos 8:11** *"Behold, the days come, saith the Lord God, that I will send a famine in the land, not a famine of bread, nor a thirst for water, but for hearing the words of the LORD: 12. And they shall wonder* *from sea to sea and from the north even to the east, they shall run to and fro to seek the word of the LORD and shall not find it."* Here is an example of the Minor Prophets giving us valuable information about the times we are living in right now. People all over this world are starving for the Word of God. If God's Word is being taught, the people are just like those cattle when they are fed, they always show up. They wait with eager anticipation for the next time. We are made in God's image and it is only natural that we have a built in hunger to know all we can about the things of God. If God's well meaning pastors would do it God's way and not man's way, they would always have to look for a bigger place, not look at empty seats.

81. MYTH: Some churches believe it is OK with God for their pastor to get up and talk using their own thoughts, without much study and research into the manuscripts.

FACT: There are some people that are great orators. They can cause chill bumps to run up your spine with great or humorous stories. There are even some large congregations that are held together by a charismatic pastor. I can tell you first hand from counseling with church going folks that if God's Word is not being taught, the people will not learn and grow. There will come a time in every person's life when inspiring stories will not get them through the problem. They have not matured by knowing God's instructions for their life. If you are content to sit in a church and have your conscience appeased and never go the the effort to learn your Father's Word, you will be ashamed when you stand before Him. When you say, "I didn't know that," He will say **"It is written, have you not read?"**

82. MYTH: The only way to be happy in this life is to have a lot of money and the only way to have a lot of money is to "Do It" to the other guy before he does it to you.

OPINION: While it is true you can gain wealth by illegal or unethical means, you will never know what it is to have lasting peace and joy in your life. If you really want to be good to yourself, learn to bring pleasure to God. The reason God created all things, including you, was and is for His pleasure. **Revelation 4:11** *"Thou art worthy, O LORD, to receive glory and honor and power: for Thou hast created all things and for Thy pleasure they are and were created."* His promise to you is that when you learn to do things His way and please

Him, He will pour out His blessings upon you. Not only in this life, but in the world to come.

83. MYTH: A real friend will never do or say anything to upset you.

FACT: Proverbs 27:5 *"Open rebuke is better than secret love. 6. Faithful are the wounds of a friend; but the kisses of an enemy are deceitful."* If it is important to your long term well being, a real friend will tell you the truth even when no one else will. The reason real friends are so rare, is they always have your back, no matter what happens. Fair weather friends are a dime a dozen; most people are fortunate to have one true friend. When people tell me they are so alone, I remind them that they are never alone. *Hebrews 13:5 "Let your conversation be without covetousness; and be content with such things as ye have: for He hath said, 'I will never leave thee, nor forsake thee. 6. So that we may boldly say, 'The LORD is my Helper and I will not fear what man shall do unto me."* For this to become reality, you must establish a walking talking relationship with the Creator of your soul. If you are not there yet, don't give up, don't quit. When you get serious with God, He will get serious with you. That is a guaranteed promise. To say otherwise, would be calling God a liar.

84. MYTH: Heaven is in outer space somewhere.

FACT: Revelation 21:10 *"And he carried me away in the spirit to a great and high mountain and shewed me that great city, the holy Jerusalem, descending out of heaven from God. 11. Having the glory of God: and her light was like unto a stone most precious, even like a jasper stone, clear as crystal."* Heaven is where God is. This earth is where the Bible says we will be when this heaven and earth age is finished. The present earth age is out of line about ninety miles form true north. The atmosphere that was here in the first earth age will be restored and there will be no more jet streams and turbulent weather. The harmful rays from the sun will be filtered by the firmament of the heavens. For the serious student, we realize that God will not allow this earth to be destroyed by war. All of these warmongers trying to scare people into subscribing to their newsletters or merchandise are not familiar with God's Word.

85. MYTH: The Bible does not talk about the United States of America.

FACT: Isaiah 18:1 *"Woe to the land shadowing with wings, which is beyond the rivers of Ethiopia: 2. That sendeth ambassadors by the sea, even in vessels of bulrushes upon the waters, saying, 'Go, ye swift messengers, to a nation scattered and peeled, to a people terrible from their beginning hitherto; a nation meted out and trodden sown, whose land the rivers have spoiled! 3. All ye inhabitants of the world and dwellers on the earth, see ye, when He lifteth up an ensign on the mountains; and when He bloweth a trumpet, hear ye. 4. for so the LORD said unto me, 'I will take My rest and I will consider in My dwelling place like a clear heat upon herbs and like a cloud of dew in the heat of harvest. 5. For afore the harvest, when the bud is perfect and the sour grape is ripening in the flower, he shall both cut off the sprigs with pruning hooks and take away and cut down the branches."*

OPINION: The scriptures quoted above, is in this writer's opinion, describes the United States of America. A land shadowing with wings is used to describe this land. The Wright brothers started the wings of the airplane and no other nation has used the air as much as the U.S. It talks of people that are scattered and peeled. The word scattered in the manuscripts is tall and the word peeled is clean shaven. **In verse 2,** it describes a people that was terrible from their beginning or a people that have never been defeated. So we have a tall, clean shaven people that have never lost a war. **Verse 2** continues. A land the rivers have spoiled; spoiled is better translated here, divided. We are a nation divided by rivers. Every thing east or west of the Mississippi is a common comment. Here in Texas we say south of the Red River or west of the Rio Grand, etc. If we continue to read with understanding we find a land that produces food. This nation has produced more food than any nation in history. We have fed the world over the years. It talks about our ensign or flag that is lifted high on the mountains. (nations) Old Glory has flown with honor around the world of free nations. To be born in this country is to be blessed when compared with the rest of the world. **Genesis 26:2** *"And the LORD appeared unto him and said, Go not down into Egypt; dwell in the land which I shall tell thee of: 4. And I will make thy seed to multiply as the stars of heaven and will give unto thy seed all these countries; and in thy seed shall all the nations of the earth be blessed."*

For the serious student, what other nation has blessed the rest of the world like the United States. (From a lecture by Dr. Arnold Murray)

86. MYTH: God is pleased when we always turn the other cheek.

FACT: If you overwhelm someone with too much deeper truth and you offend them and they slap you, turn the other cheek. You did not use wisdom in sharing something the person was not mature enough to handle. If on the other hand someone tries to break in your home or threaten you or your family, you not only have the right, but the responsibility to use whatever means necessary to handle the situation. **Psalms 18:25 *"With the merciful Thou wilt shew Thyself merciful; With an upright man Thou wilt shew Thyself upright; 26. with the pure Thou wilt shew thyself pure; And with the froward Thou wilt shew Thyself froward."*** The word froward is taken from the Hebrew word "Iqqesh" which means: crooked, distorted, false. God's people are not second class citizens and don't have to put up with bullies. If you are dealing with an honest person who is forthright and honest in their dealings with you, treat them the same way. If you are dealing with a rascal, you act carefully and protect yourself. Jesus demonstrated how to handle a situation that is contrary to what most churches teach. Upon entering the Temple, He found money changers and merchants selling mite infested doves for people to use for their offering to God. This infuriated Jesus and He wove a cat of nine tails and turned over their unlawful tables and put the whip to their backs. He drove them out of the Temple. Did He turn the other cheek? **No!** Did He ignore the situation, so He would not have to get involved? **No!** Was He worried about what the other church people would think? **No!** Were the Priests flabbergasted? **Yes!** Had any of God's people acted that way since Elijah made fun of and killed the priest of Baal? **Probably not.** Did He show by His example there are times when we are not to turn the other cheek? **Yes!** There are times when Christians need to grow a backbone and do what is right, not only regarding church matters, but in everyday life. We have too many people not wanting to hurt someone's feelings or trying to be politically correct when an obvious wrong is being done. Many times the short term gain that we feel was accomplished by not rocking the boat, results in long term pain for everyone.

87. MYTH: After Satan's rebellion, God did not replace him as the Cherubim that protected the Mercy Seat.

FACT: This is interesting because God promoted the devil (who had free will and was called the king of Tyer) to the position of Cherubim with free will. As we read **Ezekiel 28** the devil took advantage of this and tried to take over God's office. The throne is now guarded by the four beast and I believe the Mercy Seat is as well. These beast are known in the Greek as the zoa and in Hebrew as zoon. They are mentioned in the manuscripts over twenty times usually by the name of beasts. **Revelation 4:6** *"And before the throne there was a sea of glass like unto crystal: and in the midst of the throne and round about the throne, were four beasts full of eyes before and behind."* The interesting thing is these zoa or zoon don't have free will and answer only to God. You might say God learned His lesson about not trusting this important position to anyone with free will.

88. MYTH: Some believe God is not concerned with our everyday lives and doesn't really care what happens to us.

OPINION: You are your Father's creation and He does care about you. He will allow things to happen (that we usually bring on ourselves) to help get us back on track. God does not use hocus-pocus, but rather the circumstances and situations of life. Circumstances are God's way of removing the wrong, imparting the right and giving us a willing heart. A person who thinks God does not care is listening to man and does not know God.

89: MYTH: Jesus changed the Ten Commandants to two.

FACT: Matthew 22:35 *"Then one of them, which was a lawyer, asked Him a question, tempting Him and saying, 36. Master, which is the great commandment in the law? 37. Jesus said unto him. "thou shalt love the Lord thy God with all thy heart and with all they soul and with all they mind. 38. This is the first and great commandment."* This truly is the first and greatest as it includes all of man's duty to God. How is it possible for a person to love God with all their heart, soul and mind without keeping the first four commandments? *39. "And the second is like unto it, Thou shalt love thy neighbor as thyself."* How can anyone love his neighbor as himself without meeting all the requirements of the last six commandments? What Jesus did was to summarize the principles of the ten commandments in two divisions: the first and greatest being the state of man's mind and heart in relation to God. The second pertaining to man's obligation to his neighbor. In these two divisions Jesus embodied the spirit of the whole law as seen with the conclusion, **"On these two commandments hang all the law and the prophets."** Dr. E.W. Bullinger, The Companion Bible.

90. MYTH: I'm not a Greek or Hebrew scholar and there is no way I can ever understand what the Bible is really saying if the English does not reveal all needed information.

MISCONCEPTION: Anyone can obtain an original Strong's Exhaustive Concordance of the Bible. This one tool and a King James Bible will make it possible for you to look up any word in the Bible and trace it back to the original root Hebrew or Greek meaning as used in the manuscripts. Then and only then does the Bible begin to really make sense. All those verses you have always wondered about come alive with new meaning when proper translation is done. When Eve used the word **"beguiled"** in Genesis you will never get what happened until you find the word means **"wholly seduced."** When God said don't touch the tree of the knowledge of good and evil, you won't understand until you find **"touch"** means to **"lie with a woman."** When you look up the word Easter, you will find it is not even in the manuscripts. When you do an in depth study of **Genesis 1:1,** you will find there were millions of years before **Verse 2** happened. You will not understand these and many other things in the Bible if you are depending on just the English translation. I could never understand, as a little Baptist boy growing up, why God would tell His people to go into a land and kill all the men, women and children. How could a loving God do such a thing? It just did not make sense at the time. Now, after finding out what really took place in the Garden of Eden with the devil being Cain's father, God was telling His people if you don't destroy all of Cain's descendents they will pollute your people and you will end up worshiping Satan rather than God. When we really understand God's Word, we understand why many of God's people are in such poor health because of their diet. Many falsely believe that the food laws given in the Old Testament were done away with by Jesus. Careful study will show He did not change those food laws, they are still in effect today. It does not matter if you believe Jesus died for you, if you abuse your body by eating things that the Bible says not to. You will pay the price of poor health sooner or later. Stop and think for yourself; is your body different from those bodies thirty-five hundred years ago when the food laws were given. Does the wrong kind of fat clog our arteries today the same as then? If we eat scavengers today, are our bodies different from when the instructions were given by God not to eat them? If medical science has all the modern answers, why is the average age for a medical doctor to die in this country only 58 years old? Why are there so many overweight unhealthy preachers? The main reason is many rely on the English only and listen to man's traditions rather than looking until they find the real truth hidden in the manuscripts. God is not telling us not to eat certain foods to prove we love Him. He is showing His love to us by saying, "Look, I made certain animals, birds and fish to cleanse the earth and they are not healthy for you to eat. In fact if you keep on eating them you will not be healthy and feel as good as you could if you didn't eat them. You will find the "Food Laws" in the eleventh chapter of the Book of Leviticus.

91. MYTH: A real Christian should never read anything from another religion or secular media.

OPINION: We have to live in this world and be strong enough in our knowledge of God's word that we have the ability to eat the grapes and spit out the seeds. A mature Christian is well founded in their Father's Word and will recognize false teaching when they hear it; no matter where it comes from. It is the same with you bringing up your children. They will be exposed to all the world sooner or later. How they handle it depends on how well they have learned the lessons you have taught them. You have been teaching them, right…?

92. MYTH: A church is there to tell you how and what you should believe.

FACT: False, the purpose of a church should be to provide a place of learning God's Word. A place where every member of your family should be allowed to grow and mature in the ways of God. The Kingdom of God is always expanding and causing you to grow. Just as a parent has different rules for a baby who is leaning to walk, there are different rules for an older child who is learning to drive a car. God is the same yesterday, today and forever. He also changes His method of dealing with us as we grow and mature. As you become familiar with your Father and His "Instruction Book," your maturity level will determine how your closest living Relative relates to you. The more you learn, the more He is able to use you for His purposes. When the light comes on in your head and you begin to realize that you are here to be about your Father's business, your whole life will change for the better. I'm not saying you will no longer have problems. I am telling you that your attitude will change and you will be at peace with yourself, because you will know that God is in charge. When we become willing clay in the Potter's hands, we will no longer sweat the small stuff and the big stuff does not overwhelm us like it use to. If your church is telling you what to believe, you are probably involved in a cult. A cult is building "A" kingdom, but not "The" Kingdom of God. You won't be welcomed in this kind of group if you want to think for yourself, unless you keep your mouth shut. Surprisingly, there are more than a few denominational churches that fulfill the definition of a cult.

93. MYTH: It pleases God to feed anyone who is hungry.

FACT: II Thessalonians 3:10 *"For even when we were with you, this we commanded you, that if any would not work, neither should he eat. 11. For we hear that there are some which walk among you, disorderly, working not at all, but are busy bodies."* That is pretty clear, but just in case you missed it, God, through His servant Paul, just told us not to feed lazy people. We are not talking about handicap people, we are talking about anyone who is capable of working, but is too lazy to work. God considers a lazy person to be like a door with hinges, except the person is the door and is hinged to the bed and just flips from one side of the bed to the other. No one really cares for them because they don't really like themselves. They always put it off till tomorrow, but tomorrow never comes. They always have an excuse; its too hot, its too cold, the people I tried to work for don't understand me, they are always making me do jobs that are beneath me. **Proverbs 26:13** *"The slothful man saith, "There is a lion in the way; A lion in the streets.: 14. As the door turneth upon his hinges, So does the slothful upon his bed. 15. the slothful hideth his hand in his bosom; It grieveth him to bring it again to his mouth. 16. The sluggard is wiser in his own conceit that seven men that can render a reason."* So yes, contrary to what most churches teach, there are some we are not to feed. You ask, why?, is that not being mean and unchristian like? No, that is tough love and causes the person to deal with his way of life. If he gets hungry enough, he will figure out he needs to change his ways. Unfortunately, today our government encourages people to not be productive and rewards them for being lazy. They have no self esteem and think the government owes them a living. It is one way to gain votes at election time. My personal belief is that it is a conflict of interest to have someone who is being paid to not work, then be able to vote. We will all pay for this kind of foolishness sooner than later.

94. MYTH: Some people think they can wait until late in life to give their soul to God.

FACT: God already has their soul. **Ezekiel 18:4** *"Behold all souls are Mine; as the soul of the father, so also the soul of the son in mine: the soul that sinneth, it shall die."* This scripture demonstrates the emotions of God. Listen as He shows His feelings in verse **23.** *"Have I any pleasure at all that the wicked should die? Saith the Lord God and not that he should return from his ways and live?"* God created your soul and He already has your soul. What we do, determines what He will do with your soul. Live for Him and follow His rules and live. Live for yourself and die. This is your choice, God wants all of His children to live. Sadly, many will not.

95. MYTH: The people that lived before Jesus did not have a chance to believe on Him.

FACT: I Peter 3:18 *"For Christ also hath once suffered for sins, the Just for the unjust, that He might bring us to God being put to death in the flesh, but quickened by the Spirit: 19. By which also He went and preached unto the spirits in prison."* Jesus did go to Paradise and preach to those on the bad side of the Gulf. Let's find another witness in **Isaiah 61:1** *"The Spirit of the LORD GOD is upon Me; because the LORD hath anointed Me to preach good tidings unto the meek; He hath sent Me to bind up the broken hearted, to proclaim liberty to the captives and the opening of the prison to them that are bound:* **Psalms 68:18** *"Thou hast ascended on high, thou hast led captivity captive: Thou hast received gifts for men; Yea for the rebellious also, that The Lord God might dwell among them."* God is always fair and gave those on the wrong side of the Gulf a chance and led many out.

96. MYTH: We can hate our brother and still love God.

FACT: I John 4:20 *"If a man say, I love God and hateth his brother, he is a liar: for he that loveth not his brother whom he hath seen, how can he love God whom he hath not seen?"*

97. MYTH: The Bible does not tell us much about what Jesus was really like.

FACT: If you will read these following verses slowly and let them sink in, you will gain insight into the life of Jesus while on earth. This was written about six hundred years before He was born in the flesh. **Isaiah 53:1** *"Who hath believed our report? And to whom is the arm of the LORD revealed: 2. For He shall grow up before Him as a tender plant and as a root out of a dry ground: He hath no form nor comeliness; and when we shall see Him there is no beauty that we should desire Him.* (while on the cross) *3. He is despised and rejected of men; a man of sorrows and acquainted with grief: and we hid as it were our faces from Him; He was despised and we esteemed Him not. 4. Surely He hath borne our griefs and carried our sorrows: yet we did esteem Him stricken, smitten of God and afflicted. 5. But He was wounded for our transgressions, He was bruised for our iniquities: the chastisement of our peace was upon Him; and with His stripes we are healed. 6. All we like sheep have gone astray; we have turned every one to his own way; and the LORD hath laid on Him the iniquity of us all. 7. He was oppressed and He was afflicted, yet He opened not His mouth: He is brought as a lamb to the slaughter and a sheep before her shearers is dumb, so He openeth not His mouth. 8. He was taken from prison and from judgment: and who shall declare His generation? For He was cut off out of the land of the living: for the transgression of My people was He stircken. 9. And he made His grave with the wicked and with the rich in His death: because He had done no violence, neither was any deceit in His mouth. 10. Yet it pleased the LORD to bruise Him; He hath put Him to grief: when thou shalt make His soul an offering for sin, He shall see His seed, He shall prolong His days and the pleasure of the LORD shall prosper in His hand. 11. He shall see of the travail of His soul and shall be satisfied: by His knowledge shall My righteous Servant justify many; for He shall bear their iniquities. 12. Therefore will I divide Him a portion with the great and He shall divide the spoil with the strong; because He hath poured out His soul unto death: and He was numbered with the transgressors; and He bare the sin of many and made intercession for the transgressors."* Jesus did not waver from His responsibility at any time. He was the perfect lamb of God that was sacrificed once and for all time for everyone who will believe on Him.

98. MYTH: God never gets weary of someone not seeking Him.

FACT: The Bible is clear, He gets upset enough that He sends delusions that they may believe a lie. **II Thessalonians 2:10** *"And with all deceivableness of unrighteousness in them that perish; because they received not the love of the truth* (GOD'S WORD) *that they might be saved. 11. And for this cause God shall send them strong delusion, that they should believe a lie. 12. That they all might be damned who believed not the truth, but had pleasure in unrighteousness."* You want to continue to ignore God in your life, which is so short compared to all of eternity, have a good trip.

99. MYTH: The Bible does not really discuss the sons of Cain.

FACT: False, Jesus talks about them in **John 8:44** *"Ye are of your father the devil and the lusts of your father ye will do. He was murderer from the beginning and abode not in the truth because there is no truth in him when he speaketh a lie, he speaketh of his own for he is a liar and the father of it."* The off-spring of Cain are called Kenites. We find them in **Numbers 24:22** *"Nevertheless Kenite shall be wasted."* These are just two places in both the Old and New Testaments. For the genealogy of Cain, read **Genesis Chapter 4**. Adam's genealogy is found in **Genesis Chapter 5.** If Adam was Cain's father, both genealogies should be the same; they are not. God made sure both are listed so that people who take the time to search out God's truth would easily find it. Unfortunately we have too many people who depend on someone else to tell them what the Bible says.

100. MYTH: We don't have to do anything but believe and have faith and God will take care of us when the devil attacks.

FACT: We had a similar topic earlier, but will try to expand on it further. The Book of **Ephesians 6:10** *"Finally, my brethren, be strong in the Lord and in the power of His might. 11. Put on the whole armor of God, that ye may be able to stand against the wiles of the devil. 12. For we wrestle not against flesh and blood, but against principalities, against powers, against the rulers of the darkness of this world, against spiritual wickedness in high places. 13. Wherefore take unto you the whole armor of God, that ye may be able to withstand in the evil day and having done all to stand, 14. Stand therefore, having*

*your loins gird about with truth and having on the breastplate of righ-
teousness: 15. And your feet shod with the preparation of the gospel
of peace. 16. Above all, taking the shield of faith wherewith ye shall
be able to quench all the fiery darts of the wicked. 17. And take the
helmet of salvation and the sword of the spirit, which is the word of
God: 18. Praying always with all prayer and supplication in the spirit
and watching there unto with all perseverance and supplication for
all saints."* God always does His part. If you are sitting in your rocking
chair waiting for Jesus to come back and get you, you are in for a big
shock. It is up to you to do your part. **"The evil day"** is anti-Christ's
tribulation. **Now, listen up and pay close attention:** You notice we
read in **verse 11.** *"Put on the whole armor of God, that ye may be able
to stand against the wiles of the devil."* This will not be a normal battle
with guns or bombs. You notice we are to put on the whole armor of
God to stand against the **"wiles"** of the devil. **"Wiles"** as defined by
Webster's Dictionary: magic, divination, Witch, a sly trick, deceitful
artifice, a beguiling trick, craftiness, lure, confusion. Now do you know
what he will be using to trick you? Most people don't, so I am going to
tell you; it will be Scriptures from the Bible, but with a twist that only
he can put on it. At first what he says will be ninety percent accurate so
that most church going people will accept anything he says, but the ten
percent twist will undermine and counter the ninety percent. Are you
beginning to see the reason the whole world will be fooled is because
anti-Christ in not going to be mean or ugly, but sweet and nice and
quoting scriptures from the Bible. How could anything be wrong with
that? This is why God's elect will be so despised during their time of
witnessing. These sweet, nice church going folks, that are unlearned,
will not be able to understand how anyone could speak ill of their savior. That is the reason that friends and family will betray God's true
servants, thinking they are doing the right thing. So let me close this
Myth by telling you that if you think God is going to do your part, you
will be easy pickings for "ole pretty boy."

101. MYTH: God is love and He would not have us to be a part
of traditions. The Bible does not warn us to beware of the traditions
of men.

FACT: Colossians 2:8 *"Beware lest any man spoil you through
philosophy and vain deceit, after the traditions of men, after the ru-
diments of the world and not after Christ."* Jesus warned us several

time to beware the traditions of men. Many traditions of men are very hard to go against until they are found to be based on non-truth. Even then, the majority of people will continue to follow tradition, especially if the tradition is hundreds of years old. Having counseled with people for many years, I can tell you traditions are like habits that once formed are almost impossible to break. In fact, in my humble opinion, unlearning something is more difficult than learning something new. To end on a positive note, not all traditions are bad, in fact many are healthy and should be observed or participated in.

102. MYTH: There is no power that can hinder people from believing God's word.

FACT: False, the Bible tells us in **Colossians 1:13** *"Who hath delivered us from the power of darkness and hath translated us into the kingdom of His dear Son. 14. In whom we have redemption through His blood, even the forgiveness of sins."* Life itself can keep you away from God's word. The *"power of darkness"* that the devil uses are made of of the four hidden dynasties listed in Zechariah. Satan is involved in education, politics, money and religion in order to keep people from choosing to follow God. Most people are so busy trying to make a living and pay their bills, feed their families and raise their kids, they have little time to think about God or at least that is the "rat race" that most people are caught up in. If you want to learn about God and His ways, it will be a conscious decision on your part. No one else can do this for you. Others can help, but you have to be motivated within yourself to find the time and do it.

103. MYTH: The laws on the books can now keep students from praying in school.

FACT: Men can pass all the laws they want to in an attempt to keep God out of school. The truth for a true believer is they can pray to God anywhere, anytime. They can pray right in front of the politicians that passed the laws or the school officials that are foolishly trying to administer this unconstitutional act. **I Chronicles 28:9** *"For the LORD searcheth all hearts,* (better translated minds) *and understandeth all the imaginations of the thoughts: if thou seek Him, He will be found of thee, but if thou forsake Him He will cast* **thee out for forever."** **Matthew 6:6** *"When thou prayest, enter into thy closet and when thou hast shut thy door, pray to the Father which is in secret and thy Father which seeth in secret shall reward thee* *openly."* No judge, no teacher, no Superintendent or foolish law can ever keep a student or teacher or anyone else from praying to "The Most High God." We just pray silently and our Creator understands every thought we direct to Him in prayer. How is any law or anyone going to keep you from praying silently. They won't even know you are praying unless you tell them. Let's look at another scripture for a better understanding of how much God knows about us. **Psalm 139:1** *"O LORD, Thou hast searched me and known me. 2. Thou knowest my down sitting and mine uprising, Thou understandest my thought afar off. 3. Thou compassest my path and my lying down and are acquainted with all my ways. 4. For there is not a word in my tongue, but lo, O LORD, Thou knowest it altogether. 5. Thou hast beset me behind and before and laid Thine hand upon me. 6. Such knowledge is too wonderful for me, It is high, I cannot attain unto it."* Foolish man can not comprehend the greatness of God. And anyone foolish enough to think they can legislate the ability of one of God's children to pray, borders on stupidity and they will answer for it when they stand before their Maker. Because they don't really believe there is a God, they will learn the hard way.

104. MYTH: There is no such thing as "Playing Church."

FACT: Isaiah 29:13 *"Wherefore The LORD said, for as much as this people draw near me with their mouth and with their lips do honor me, but have removed their heart far from me and their fear,* (reverence) *toward Me is taught by the precept of men. 14. Therefore, for this cause, the wisdom of their wise men shall perish and the understanding of their prudent men shall be his. 15. Woe unto them that seek deep to hide their counsel from the LORD and their works are in the dark and they say, who seeth us? And who knoweth us: 16. Surely your turning of things upside down shall be esteemed as the potter's clay, for shall the work say of Him that made it, He made me not? Or shall the thing framed say of Him that framed it, He had no understanding?"* **II Thessalonians 2:10** *"And with all deceivableness of unrighteousness in them that perish; because they received not the love of the truth, that they might be saved. 11. And for this cause God shall send them strong delusion, that they should believe a lie: 12. That they all might be dammed who believed not the truth, but had pleasure in unrighteousness."* When men continue to play church on Sunday and mock

God with the way they conduct their everyday lives and treat their fellow man, they shall pay a terrible price. Unless they repent and change their ways they will be dammed. We just read that God will even help them believe lies when they will not seek Him until they find Him. God is always fair, you get serious with Him and He will get serious with you. You want to play games, play on and reap what you sow. Now, lets bring this home, if you have a son or daughter or employee that never wants to grow up and does not take your advice seriously, what do you do? If you are a parent or employer worth your salt, you will take steps to educate and discipline your child or employee so that they may have the possibility to become all they can be. You give them the opportunity, what they do with it is up to them. Your Heavenly Father left you a long letter of instructions. Have you ever read it with understanding? Have you ever placed the same importance in getting to know about God as you do in learning about business or the stock market or sports or anything you want to know about? Have you always known there had to be more to God than you have been told? Be honest with yourself, have you just shrugged your shoulders, and thought, I guess there are some things we are not supposed to know. God does not share His secrets with someone who is not willing to at least try to give their best effort. God will not use "Hot House Lilies" for His important business. The first time the going gets rough, they fade and die on the vine. They can not withstand a little heat. You may have everything or you may have very little of this world's pleasures, but if you don't really know God you do not know what real peace of mind and true joy is. Paul gives us a glimpse into his life after he learned to put God first. **Philippians 4:11** *"Not that I speak in respect of want; for I have learned, in whatsoever state I am, therewith to be content. 12. I know both how to be abased and I know how to abound: every where and to all things I am instructed both to be full and to be hungry, both to abound and to suffer need. 13. I can do all things through Christ which strengtheneth me."* Your health and or wealth can be lost and regained and lost again. True happiness and peace of mind is having a real relationship with your closest living relative, your Heavenly Father, the One who created your soul. When this relationship is real, it can never be lost, no matter what is happening on the outside. This kind of relationship with your Father is teachable, learn-able and doable; anything less is playing church. The beautiful thing is that God is waiting on you to choose. Just as He will send strong delusion to those who choose not to follow Him, He will send opportunity after opportunity to help those who do want to find Him.

105. MYTH: There is a contradiction in what the Bible says. In the Lord's Prayer, it says to *"lead us not into temptation"* and in the Book of **James** it says *"count it all joy when you fall into divers temptations."* They both can't be correct.

FACT: Both are indeed correct. We have a loving Father, who will not allow anything to happen to us that we can not handle as long as we use common sense. When we were in school and the teacher said, OK, today we are going to have a pop quiz. Those who knew the lesson and had done their homework did not get excited or upset because they knew their stuff. Those who had not studied and did not know the material did not feel very good about it. In the Lord's prayer He is saying don't ask for the test. In James He is saying, be glad when the test comes because you know that you are ready for the test. It's not a good idea to go around and tell the Lord, OK Lord, test me. Let me prove I'm ready. Believe me the best thing you can do is to stay in His Word and get to know all you can about God and His ways. The test will come soon enough. Sometimes you will think you are not ready for the test at hand. Be assured, no matter how hard the circumstance or situation of life is, you can overcome the problem if you stay close to your Father. As we grow and mature in the Lord, He changes the way He deals with us. Just the way an earthly father changes the way he deals with his children. As the child grows he is given more responsibility and is held to a higher standard. The rules for a teenager or different than for a three year old. The problem today is we have too many Christians who accepted Christ years ago and are still on a milk bottle. They want all the benefits of being a Christian without accepting their responsibility to grow and mature. Now so we are clear on what James is telling us, let's listen to some more of **James 1:2** *"My brethren, count it all joy when ye fall into divers temptations; 3. Knowing this, that the trying of your faith worketh patience. 4. But let patience have her perfect work, that ye may be perfect and entire, wanting nothing."* The Bible is telling us that God does not punish us for something we did, rather He allows things to happen that we might grow and mature. We are no different than a tree or plant, we are either growing and changing or we are dying. There is no neutral position. Our prayer should always be, Father change me from what I am to what I ought to be. If you are going through a trial or testing, praise God for it is probably a sign that you are ready for more growth.

106. MYTH: The Bible does not talk about bad angels or fallen angels or angles that sinned.

FACT: False, lets read of "the angles that sinned" **II Peter 2:4** *"For if God spared not the angels that sinned, but cast them down to hell and delivered them into chains of darkness, to be reserved unto judgment."* The cause of their fall and the nature of their sins are particularly set forth by the Holy Spirit in **Jude 6** *"And the angels which kept not their first estate, but left their own habitation, He hath reserved in everlasting chains under darkness unto judgment of the great day."* The habitation they left is "oiketerion" in the Greek which occurs again only in **II Corinthians 5:2** where it is called our house (i.e. body) with which we earnestly long to be "clothed upon;" referring to the "change" which shall take place in resurrection. These angles departed heaven in their spiritual body or "oiketerion." They came directly to earth without being born of the water. (Water from a woman's womb that breaks at birth) It is difficult for man to understand this completely. **Hebrews 10:26** *"For if we sin willfully after that we have received the knowledge of the truth, there remaineth no more sacrifice for sins. 27. But a certain fearful looking for of judgment and fiery indignation which shall devour the adversaries."* Back to **Jude 6** *"And the angels which kept not their first estate,"* in which they were placed when they were created. The nature of their sin is clearly stated. **Jude 7.** *"Even as Sodom and Gomorrah and the cities about them, in like manner giving themselves over to fornication and going after strange flesh, are set forth for an example, suffering the vengeance of eternal fire."* Again, the nature of their sin is very clear. The sin of "Sodom and Gomorrah" is declared to be *"in like manner"* to that of the angels and what that sin was is described as *"giving themselves over to fornication and going after strange flesh"* (homosexuality) *are set forth for an example, suffering the vengeance of eternal* *fire. "* The Bible does indeed discuss the fallen angels and their sins, but most churches are too afraid they might offend someone rather that teach the Bible. Let me ask you pastor's that stay away from this subject, is it better to be silent and let the people involved in this life-style, go to hell or offend them with real love by telling them what God has to say so they at least have a choice? Preacher, their blood will be on your hands if you allow this to happen. I'm not saying you have to stand on the street corner, but when the opportunity is there, it is your responsibility to give the facts. If you call yourself a man or woman of God and you are afraid the Bible is going to offend someone, you better find something else to do, because God is not pleased with you. And no, I am not judging anyone, I don't have the right to judge, but God gives us spiritual discernment to try the spirits and check them out in light of God's Word.

107. MYTH: The Bible does not really tell us what happened to end the first earth age.

FACT: God tells us in **Jeremiah 4:22** that His people don't understand what is written. *"For My people is foolish, they have not known ME; they are "sottish" children and they have, none understanding. They are wise to do evil, but to do good they have no understanding.'"* Lets look at **Jeremiah 4:23** (which is taken from **Genesis 1**) and see what happened to the first earth age. *23. "I beheld the earth and lo it was without form and void; and the heavens and they had no light. 24. I beheld the mountains and lo they trembled and all the hills moved lightly. 25. I beheld and lo there was no man and all the birds of heavens were fled. 26. I beheld and lo the fruitful place was a wilderness and all the cities there of were broken down at the presence of the LORD and by His Fierce anger. 27. For thus hath the LORD said the whole land shall be desolate, yet will I not make a full end."* You notice there was no man, no birds and all the cities were destroyed. Careful study will result in the knowledge that this was long before the flood in Noah's time. We find the reason God destroyed the first earth age in **Revelation 12:4** *"And his tail drew the third part of the stars of heaven and did cast them to the earth: and the dragon stood before the woman which was ready to be delivered, for to devour her child as soon as it was born. "* We discussed this in an earlier Myth, but if you remember, this was when one third of God's children rebelled and follow the dragon, which is another of Satan's names.

This will conclude the Myth and Fact portion. We have talked about many areas of our Christian heritage that many times are based on traditions of men, rather than the Word of God. The scales really are coming from many eyes and God's plan is being revealed in these last days of this final generation. I hope you are making notes and writing down scriptures to go back and check after your first read.

BIBLE QUESTIONS
THAT HAVE COME UP
OVER THE YEARS

Having been a pastor for a few years and a counselor for forty-five years, many questions have come up that are addressed in this next section. Some of them seem simple, but to the person asking, they are many times life changing when the Word of God is applied. What myself or any other person thinks is really not important unless the information aligns itself with our Creator. Just like the Myths, we just covered, many times the myth or question addresses issues that you may have, yet never had the opportunity to have them discussed from the Bible point of view. What sets apart any pastor or counselor from the pack, is the strict adherence to the manuscripts. The answers reflect a lifetime of study and learning about God. They reflect direction from my mentors, personal experiences of life, family, friends, teachers, coaches, but mostly what the Bible says taken from the manuscripts. You see our traditions are so set in our unconscious minds, we are programmed to accept what our loved ones and teachers tell us. They certainly had our best interest at heart, but as we have seen, even though they were sincere, they were sincerely wrong in more that a few cases. Satan always counterfeits the major things of God. So most of the false traditions deal with our discipline that directly affects our belief system. You may find some of the things you have always wondered about among these questions.

QUESTIONS AND ANSWERS

1. QUESTION: Do numbers have any special significance in the Bible?

ANSWER: Many time numbers play a roll in understanding the Bible. We will list a few at this time.

- ⚔ One: denotes unity One God
- ⚔ Two: Difference: Opposites Cold, Hot: Up, Down: Short, Tall
- ⚔ Three: Spiritual completeness; Father, Son, Holy Spirit; Spirit, Soul, Body
- ⚔ Four: Creative Works, Earth: Spring, Summer, Fall, Winter: North, South, East, West.
- ⚔ Five: Grace: David's 5 stones; Pentagon five sided.
- ⚔ Six: The human number; also Satan's number 666
- ⚔ Seven: Spiritual Perfection
- ⚔ Eight: New Beginnings

⅄ Nine: Finality of Judgment
⅄ Ten: Ordinal Perfection
⅄ Eleven: Disorder
⅄ Twelve: Governmental Perfection

2. QUESTION: Is there any place in the Bible where God encourages us to remind Him of His promises?

ANSWER: This is surprising to most people. **Isaiah 43:26** *"Put Me in remembrance, Let us plead together: declare thou, that thou may-est be justified."* Does God need reminding? No! He wants to know if you know His word well enough to be able to recall what is written.

3. QUESTION: Does the Old Testament ever discuss God forgiving sin?

ANSWER: Isaiah 43:25 *"I even I, AM He that blotteth out thy transgressions for Mine own sake and will not remember thy sins:"* You notice God speaking twice for emphasis.

4. QUESTION: Could you discuss the Kenites in more detail" I really don't understand who they are and their significance. Did Jesus ever talk about them?

ANSWER: Kenite is a name given to the descendents of Cain. Let's go to the first book in the Bible to find where this began. **Genesis 3:13** *"And the LORD GOD said unto the woman, "What is this that thou hast done?" and the woman said, "The serpent beguiled* (Nasha in ancient Hebrew) *me and I did eat."* **II Corinthians 11:3** *"But I fear, lest by any means, as the serpent beguiled* (Esapatao in the Greek) *Eve through his subtitle, so your minds should be corrupted from the simplicity of Christ."* If we go to the manuscripts and look up the word beguiled and trace it to its root, we find **beguiled means wholly seduced.** Eve was seduced and impregnated by the serpent. Serpent is just one of the names Satan goes by as seen in **Revelation 12.** In other words Satan sowed his seed into Eve's womb and she had a son name Cain. Now let's document that from the mouth of Jesus in the parable of the sower. **Matthew 13:24** *"The Kingdom of heaven is likened unto a man which sowed good seed in his field: 25. But while men slept, his enemy came and sowed tares among the wheat and went his way. 26. But when the blade was sprung up and brought forth fruit, then appeared the tares* *also. 27. So the servants of the householder came and said unto him, sir, didst not thou sow good seed in thy field? From whence then hath it tares? 28. He said unto them, an enemy hath done this. The servants said unto him, wilt thou then that we go and gather them up? 29. But he said, nay, lest while ye gather up the tares, ye root up also the wheat with them. 30. Let both grow together until the harvest; and in the time of harvest I will say to the reapers, gather ye together first the tares and bind them in bundles to burn them, but gather the wheat into my barn."* This parable relates directly to the scripture in **Genesis 3** and **II Corinthians 11,** quoted above. Let's listen as Jesus explains the parable so that it is easy to understand for His disciples. **Matthew 13:36** *"Then Jesus sent the multitude away and went into the house and his disciples came unto Him saying "Declare unto us the parable of the tares of the field." 37. He answered and said unto them, "He that soweth the good see is the Son of man; 38. The field is the world, the good seed are the children of the Kingdom, but the tares are the children of the wicked one, 39. The enemy that sowed them is the devil, the harvest is the end of the world and the reapers are the angels. 40. As therefore the tares are gathered and burned in the fire, so shall it be in the end of this world."* If we look up the word "seed" as used here in a Strong's Concordance we find it refers to "male sperm." You notice He talks of children of the wicked one. Children are a result of sowing male sperm into a woman's body. Let's go to another witness and find Jesus talking to some of these descendants of Cain. **John 8:44** *"Ye are of your father the devil and the lusts of your father ye will do. He was a murderer from the beginning and abode not in the truth, because there is no truth in him. When he speaketh a lie, he speaketh of his own, for he is a liar and the father of it."* Who is the first recorded murderer in the Bible?" Cain! Careful study of **Revelations 2:9** and **3:9** tells us of those who are of the Synagogue of Satan which say they are Jews and are not, but are the off-spring of Satan through Cain. They claim to be Jewish priests, but are in reality they are Kenites, sons of Cain, disguised as Holy Men of God. It is a shame that most churches don't know, don't care and don't teach who the Kenites are. If you have read the scriptures above and understand what they said and you still don't understand, then it is probably not intended you understand at this time.

5. QUESTION: Does the Bible tell us to be humble?

ANSWER: James 4:10 *"Humble yourselves in the sight of the LORD and He will lift you up."* We are not to put anything or anybody above the Lord and that includes yourself.

6: QUESTION: I have developed contempt for some preachers. Is there any place where God shows His disdain for these preachers that get on TV and spend most of their time begging for money.

ANSWER: There are many places where God leaves no doubt. We find God's disgust with lazy, greedy teachers and preachers who pass themselves off as being His representative. Listen to these strong words. **Isaiah 56:11** *"Yea, they are greedy dogs which can never have enough and they are shepherds that cannot understand. They all look to their own way, every one for his gain, from his quarter."* For people on fixed incomes, especially seniors, this is most despicable. If a person is begging for money and claims to be a "man of God," he is lying to you. God does not and has never sent out His servants to beg for money. When Jesus sent out the seventy, His instructions were to take no purse or script with them. Stop and think for yourself, if the man or woman is sent by God, He will supply their needs. When you receive that letter in the mail, telling you that if you will send them $100. in seed money, you will be blessed by God and receive many times the amount you sent. Let's be reminded again how God feels about these people. *"Yea, they are greedy dogs which can never have enough and they are shepherds that cannot understand: they all look to their own way, every one for his gain, from his quarter."* God is telling you straight out, they are greedy and can never get enough. They also don't understand the word and ways of God. They are looking out for themselves, not you or God.

7. QUESTION: Is there any place where I can find what happens to a person when they die?

ANSWER: There are several places in the Bible that tell us what happens at death. We will begin in **Ecclesiastes 12:2** where we find a person that is up in years and looks at life differently than when they were young. *2. "While the sun or the light or the moon or the stars be not darkened nor the clouds return after the rain: 3. In the day when the keepers of the house shall tremble and the strong men shall bow themselves and the grinders cease because they are few and those that look out of the windows be darkened. 4. And the* *doors shall be shut in the streets, when the sound of the grinding is low and he shall rise up at the voice of the bird and all the daughters of music shall be brought low; 5. Also when they shall be afraid of that which is high and fears shall be in the way, and the almond tree shall flourish and the grasshopper shall be a burden and desire shall fail: (because man goeth to his long home and the mourners go about the streets:) 6. "Or ever the silver cord be loosed or the golden bowl be broken or the pitcher be broken at the fountain or the wheel broken at the cistern. 7. Then shall the dust return to the earth as it was: and the spirit shall return unto God Who gave it."* This needs a little help to be able to understand what was just said. In **verse 2** we begin a description of growing older. Let's look at some of these words and try to make them more understandable. In **verse 3,** we find the keepers of the house. The human body is often compared to a house. The word doors is used for the openings, our mouth and ears. We get a little hard of hearing and don't hear the birds as well. The grinders, our teeth, are not able to chew the hard nuts like we did when we were younger. The windows be darkened is used for our eyes don't see like they use to. We don't sleep as well and wake up early, getting up before the birds do. We grow afraid of lofty elevated heights as we age and we get a little queasy or light headed if we look down from up high. We have apprehensions of taking a trip or journeying a long way from home. Our desire shall fail. We are not as interested in sexual relations as when we were younger. The almond tree shall flourish: Grey hairs shall grow scanty. The grasshopper shall be a burden. We are not able to lift as much weight as we use to. Now as to some of the things that happen at the occasion of death itself. The silver cord is the spinal cord. The golden bowl is the head or skull. The pitcher be broken at the fountain is the failure of the heart. Dust is used for the body which is made of dust. The spirit or ruach in Hebrew returns to God for he is the God of the spirits of all flesh. **Numbers 27:16** *"Let the Lord, the God of the spirits of all flesh, set a man over the congregation."* Regardless if we are young or old when we die our flesh body returns to the earth and our spirit man returns to God who gave it. By the way it does not matter how the dead body returns to dust. Now we have another source that I personally accept. The Apocrypha was in the original King James 1611 Bible. Some of the books may be questionable, but **Esdras** is one of the books that brings great insight to this question. **II Esdras 7:75** *"If I have found favor in your sight, whether, after death as soon as each one of us gives up his soul, we shall be faithfully kept at rest until those times come when you begin to renew the creation, or shall be tortured at once." And he answered me and said, "I will show you that also, but you must not associate with those who have shown scorn, or count yourself among those who are tortured. For you have a treasure of works laid up with the Most High, but it will not be shown to you until the last times. For about death, the teaching is when the final sentence goes forth from the Most High that a man is to die, when the soul departs from the body to return again to Him who gave it, first of all it prays to the Glory of THE MOST HIGH, if it was one of those who scorned and did not observe the way of THE MOST HIGH and of those who have despised His law and of those who hate those who fear God, such spirits shall not enter dwellings but wander about thenceforth in torment, always grieving and sad, in seven ways. The first way is that they have scorned the law of THE MOST HIGH. The second way is that they can no longer make a good repentance, so that they may live. The third way is that they will see reward destined for those who have believed the agreements of THE MOST HIGH. The fourth way is that they will consider the torment destined for them in the last days. The fifth way is that they will see that the dwelling places of the others are guarded by Angels in profound silence. The sixth way is that they will see that some of them will pass over to be tormented henceforth. The seventh way, which is worse than all the ways that have been mentioned, is that they will waste away in shame and be consumed in disgrace and wither with fear, at seeing the Glory of THE MOST HIGH before whom they sinned while they lived and before whom they are destined to be judged in the last times. 88. "But of those who have observed the ways of THE MOST HIGH, this is the order, when they shall be separated from this fragile jar. In the time when they lived in it, they carefully served THE MOST HIGH, though they were in danger ever hour, so as to keep the law of the lawgiver perfectly. Therefore this is the teaching about them. First of all, they see with great rapture the Glory of Him who takes them up, for they will rest in seven orders. The first order is that they have striven with much toil to conquer the wicked thought* *that was formed with them, so that it should not lead them away from life to death. The second order is that they see the labyrinth in which the souls of the ungodly wander and the punishment that awaits them. The third order is that they see the testimony that He who formed them has borne to them, because when they were alive they faithfully observed the law which was given them. The fourth order is that they understand the rest which they not enjoy, gathered in their chambers, in great quietness, watched over by angels and the glory that awaits them in the last days. The fifth order is that they exult that they have now escaped what is corruptible and will possess the future as their inheritance and besides perceive the narrowness and toilsome ness from which they have been freed and the spaciousness they are destined to receive and enjoy in immortality. The sixth order is that is is shown to them how their face is destined to shine like the sun and how they are to be made like the light of the stars and be incorruptible thenceforth. The seventh, which is greater than all those that have been mentioned, they will exult boldly and that they will trust confidently and rejoice fearlessly, for they hasten to see the face of Him whom they served in life and from whom they are to receive their reward when they are glorified. These are the orders of the souls of the upright, as henceforth proclaimed and the above ways of torture are those which those who would not give heed will henceforth suffer."* WOW! We could do a whole book on this information alone.

8. QUESTION: Does God really know our thoughts and hear our silent prayers? I have not been able to find any scriptures in the Bible.

ANSWER: Let's take a scripture from both the Old and New Testament. King David is talking to his son Solomon. **I Chronicles 28:9** *"And thou, Solomon my son, know thou the God of thy father and serve Him with a perfect heart and with a willing mind, for the LORD searcheth all hearts and understandeth all the imaginations, of the thoughts. If thou seek Him, He will be found of thee, but if thou forsake Him, He will cast thee off for ever."* We find further insight into how to pray and please our Father. **Matthew 6:5** *"And when thou prayest, thou shalt not be as the hypocrites are, for they love to pray standing in the synagogues and in the corners of the streets, that they may be seen of men. Verily I say* *unto you, they have their reward. 6. But thou, when thou prayest, enter into thy closed and when thou hast shut thy door, pray to thy Father which is in secret shall reward thee openly."* **Psalms 139:2** *"Thou understandeth my thought afar off."* Your being unable to find any scriptures in the Bible for this or any other subject is the very reason that every serious student should have a Strong's Exhaustive Concordance of the Bible. If you know one word in the scripture you are seeking, look up that word and will find every place in the Bible where that word is used. Invaluable tool.

9. QUESTION: How many Old Testament Prophet Books are there and over what period of time did they cover?

ANSWER: There are sixteen Prophet Books; four Major Books: **ISAIAH, JEREMIAH, DANIEL** and **EZEKIEL** so called because of the length of their writings. The Minor Prophet Books are so called because, for the most part, they are shorter in length. In my opinion this is another tradition that has come down through the ages. Some of the best information about the end of this world age is found in the Minor Prophets. The Prophet Books covered a period of about 350 years before Christ. We will list them in order of the time period they served; some of them prophesied for only one year.

1. JONAH: ....690 BC
2. AMOS: ....689 to 687 BC
3. HOSEA: ....689 to 611 BC
4. **ISAIAH:** ....649 to 588 BC
5. MICAH: ....632 to 603 BC
6. NAHUM: ....603 BC
7. **JEREMIAH:** ....518 to 477 BC
8. HABAKKUK: ....518 BC
9. ZEPHANIAH: ....518 BC
10. **DANIEL:** ....495 to 424 BC
11. JOEL: ....488 to 477? BC
12. **EZEKIEL:** ....484 to 465 BC
13. OBADIAH: ....482 or 472? BC
14. HAGGAI: ....410 BC
15. ZECHARIAH: ....410 to 407 BC
16. MALACHI: ....374 BC

Please note these were not the only prophets God utilized. Moses, David, John the Baptist and others were prophets, but did not have a prophetic book that carried their name.

10. QUESTION: I see many Christians compare themselves to others and measure themselves by the others standard or try to imitate them. Is this what the Bible teaches?

ANSWER: II Corinthians 10:12 *"For we dare not make ourselves of the number or compare ourselves with some that commend themselves, but they measuring themselves by themselves and comparing themselves among themselves are not wise."* Wisdom is comparing your behavior with what God's Word states your behavior should be. Fools commend themselves and measure themselves by their own behavior. God made you special for a reason, be yourself.

11. QUESTION: In your opinion at judgment, when people tell the Lord, "I didn't know." What will be His reply?

OPINION: There will be many situations that will come to light, but one of the main replies is found in **Isaiah 40:21** *"Have ye not known? Have ye not heard: Hath it not been told you from the beginning: Have ye not understood from the foundations of the earth?"* When Jesus was on earth He gave the same answer, *"Have ye not read?"*

12. QUESTON: What is God's attitude toward people who think they are smarter than God or really don't believe in God?

ANSWER: Isaiah 40:6 *"The voice said, Cry. And he said, "What shall I cry?" All flesh is grass and all the goodliness thereof is as the flower of the field: 7. The grass withereth, the flower fadeth: because the spirit of the Lord bloweth upon it: surely the people is grass; 8. The grass withereth, the flower fadeth: but the word of our God shall stand forever." 12. "Who hath measured the waters in the hollow of his hand and meted out heaven with the span and comprehended the dust of the earth in a measure and weighed the mountains in scales and the hills in a balance? 13. Who hath directed the Spirit of the Lord, or being His counselor hath taught Him? 14. With whom took He counsel and who instructed Him and taught Him knowledge and shewed Him the way of understanding? 15. Behold the nations are as a drop of a bucket and are counted as the small dust of the balance: behold, He taketh up the isles as a very little thing. 18. To whom then will ye liken GOD? Or what* *likeness will ye compare unto Him?" 22. "It is He that sitteth upon the circle of the earth and the inhabitants thereof are as grasshoppers; that stretcheth out the heavens as a curtain and spreadeth them out as a tent to dwell in: 23. That bringeth the princes to nothing; He maketh the judges of the earth as vanity. 24. Yea, they shall not be planted; yea, they shall not be sown: yea, their stock shall not take root in the earth: and He shall also blow upon them and they shall wither and the whirlwind shall take them away as stubble. 25. To whom then will ye liken Me, or shall I be equal: Saith the Holy One."* After reading this account, it makes one wonder how anyone, including the devil, could think they are smarter than God?

13. QUESTION: What is the significance of the veil of the Temple being torn when Jesus was crucified?

ANSWER: The significance of this event is monumental for Christians. Let's quote the verse and then comment. **Matthew 27:50** *"Jesus, when He had cried again with a loud voice, yielded up the ghost. 51 "And, behold, the veil of the Temple was rent in twain from the top to the bottom; and the earth did quake and the rocks rent."* Based on descriptions of this veil, this was no ordinary piece of cloth. It was very thick, approximately four inches, used for a barrier between the Holy place and the Holy of Holies where only the High Priest could go once a year. You notice it was rent from top to bottom, not from bottom to top. This happened at the time that Jesus yielded up His spirit. The time was Passover, the highest Holy day of the year. The day of week was Wednesday afternoon. The high priest, probably, Caiaphas, was appointed by Herod the king. There were two living at the time, the other being Annas. At three PM the high priest entered the Holy Place for this one time a year event to atone for the sins of the people. Jesus, being the Lamb of God, had just paid the ultimate price for all mankind by dying on the cross once and for all. Can you imagine the look on Caiaphas's face when he saw the veil torn from top to bottom with no longer a barrier to keep anyone from entering into the presence of God. The reason it was torn from top to bottom was God Himself tore it and opened the door for you and me and "Whosoever will" to communicate directly with the Creator of the universe. Until this very act was accomplished, only the high priest could enter and then only once a year. This act ushered in a completely new and different way to relate to God. The people no longer had to bring their sacrificial animals to be killed for their sins. The main thing that was accomplished is we no longer need a third person to act as a go-be-tween from us to God. We can go directly to Him in the name of Jesus and we do not have to wait for once a year, we can approach Him anytime. We can not only repent and ask for forgiveness of sins, but also pray about needs, health, wisdom and a closer relationship with Him. Let's close with **Hebrews 8:13** *"In that He saith, "A new covenant," He hath made the first old. Now that which decayeth and waxeth old is ready to vanish away."* So the answer to your question is that what happened when the veil was rent is one of the most significant acts in the history of man and the plan of God.

14. QUESTION: Is there any evidence that there was an earth age before this one?

ANSWER: Absolutely! There is no dispute in the scientific community or among genuine Bible scholars. Science tells us the earth is millions of years old and the Bible agrees. The real fact is the Bible tells us the earth is millions of years old and science has learned it. Carbon dating tells us that fossil remains are very old. We have what some call the city of Atlantis, Stonehenge and many other things that can not be explained or accounted for in a six thousand year old earth as some Bible "experts" would have us believe. The manuscripts and diligent study leaves no doubt that the earth is millions of years old. Even the King James English Bible has references in **II Peter 3:5-6** where it talks about "the heavens were of old" and "the world that then was." Many scholars believe there was a tremendous amount of time that took place at the end of **Genesis 1:1** and the beginning of **Genesis 1:2.** Again the manuscripts shed much more light on this than the English translations. *"In the beginning GOD created the heavens and earth."* The English does not say when this took place. This is "The World That Was," creation in eternity past, to which all "Fossil" and "Remains" belong. We learn more in **Revelation 12:4** that this was the time when the devil convinced one-third of God's children to follow him. God could not bring Himself to destroy these gullible traitors; they were still His children. Let's read of God's angry emotions where He destroyed the first earth age instead of His children. **Jeremiah 4:23** *"I beheld the earth and lo it was without form and void and the heavens and they had no light. 24. I beheld*

123

the mountains and lo they trembled and all the hills moved lightly.
25. I beheld and lo there was no man and all the birds of the heavens
were fled." Remember "Gabriel" in Hebrew means "Man of God," so
it is not unusual for the first age spirit bodies to be referred to as man.
We see there was no man found, so we know this is not Noah's flood.
This was long before Noah's flood. Have you ever wondered about
these things? *26. "I beheld and lo the fruitful place was a wilder-*
ness and all the cities thereof were broken down at the presence of
the LORD and by His fierce anger. 27. For thus hath the LORD
said the whole land shall be desolate, yet will I not make a full end.
28. For this shall the earth mourn and the heavens above be black,
because I have spoken it, I have purposed it and will not repent,
neither will back from it." God said I shook the earth, the mountains
and hills moved. This was when the Grand Canyon was formed and
the east coast of America was separated from the west coast of Africa.
This explains why there are hundreds of African type animals found
in Ash Fall, Nebraska. This was when the firmament was broken up
and the weather patterns became unstable. The jet streams came into
being and the perfect conditions to live on earth changed to what
we have today with wonderful weather suddenly changing to violent
weather including hurricanes and tornadoes. We are not told what
period of time it took after this terrible shaking took place before
God started this heaven and earth age in **Genesis 1:2.** Based on the
fossil remains and carbon dating, it was probably millions of years.
On our ranch in Texas, hundreds of miles from the ocean, we find
fossil remains of sea creatures. We know that Noah's flood did not
last long enough for this to happen. The katabole or overthrowing did
last long enough and covered the entire planet. Some of this answer
was included in another question, but it is worthy to confirm it to our
memory. Have you ever wondered what and when God was referring to when He was talking to Job? God was wanting Job to realize
that he did not remember when: *"the morning stars sang together*
and the sons of God shouted for joy." Guess what, you and I don't
remember it either. It was the first earth age and we have no memory
of that time because we were in spiritual bodies. God chose not to destroy the third that rebelled, but rather to destroy the age instead. By
doing this, God offered to give the rebellious children another chance
to choose God or Satan. Now we know the reason we are living in

124

these flesh bodies in this second heaven and earth. Just to be clear, we are talking about one heaven and one earth with three different time periods. Not three heavens and not three earths. We are now living at the end of the second age at the end of the fifth seal, at the last of the Fig Tree Generation.

15. QUESTION: What does it mean to "Repent?'"

ANSWER: It is the Greek word "Metanoeo" and means to change one's mind, always for the better and morally. Because of this it is often used in the imperative as in: **Matthew 3:2** *And saying, "Repent ye: for the kingdom of heaven is at hand." Matthew 4:17 "From that time Jesus began to preach and to say, "Repent: for the kingdom of heaven is at hand."* One more witness: **Acts 3:19** *"Repent ye therefore and be converted, that your sins may be blotted out, when the times of refreshing shall come from the presence of the LORD."* It is not merely to forsake sin, but to change one's apprehension regarding it. It also answers to the Latin "Resipisco" which is to recover one's senses, to come to one's self. Repentance is one of the things that separates Christianity from other religions. To live in these flesh bodies is to mess up from time to time, even if we are trying to live perfectly. God wisely included repentance with salvation, for without it, no one would make it. Repentance is a requirement of God in order to wipe our slate clean and make us acceptable to God again. You notice sins are blotted out when we meet the conditions and God remembers them no more.

16. QUESTION: Does God really hear our silent prayers?

ANSWER: One of the best examples the Bible clearly spells this out for us is where King David is giving instruction to his son, Solomon. This is found in the Book of **I Chronicles 28:9** *"For the LORD searcheth all hearts and understandeth all the imaginations of the thoughts. If thou seek Him, He will be found of thee, but if thou forsake Him, He will cast thee off forever."* This is unmistakeable, if we seek Him, He will be found. If we don't make the effort or even try to find Him, we will be unable to find Him for He will cast us off. Further study will show He answers our prayers when we seek Him with our whole heart. He also loves us enough not to answer a prayer that asks for something that is bad for us. Just as we would not give our child a rattlesnake for a pet, even though they ask for one. **Romans 8:27** *"And He that searcheth the hearts (mind) knoweth* *what is the mind of the Spirit, because He maketh intercession for the saints according to the will of God."*

17. QUESTION: Is there a difference between the Holy Ghost and the Holy Spirit?

ANSWER: The word Ghost as used in the Bible is a poor translation and gives the reader a wrong impression many times. God is not a ghost or spook. The Greek word "Pneuma" is where we get the word "pneumatic" tires. It is a current of air, superhuman, Christ's Spirit. Spirit is a much better translation. This is a good question, because it points out that paying attention to these small details we become aware of other words that refer to the three dimensional Godhead. E.W. Bullinger points out in the Companion Bible that when the word **"Behold"** is used, this is referring to the **"Holy Spirit."** When the word **"Yea"** is used, it is of the **"Father"** and when **"Verily"** is used, it is of the Son. These of course must be used in context.

18. QUESTION: Can a person really change their ways or are we destined to go down a particular path?

ANSWER: The Bible always has an answer if we are willing to spend the time to look. For a good place to begin, let's go to **Psalms 119:59** *"I thought on my ways and turned my feet unto Thy testimonies."* The Psalmist is saying I took a look at my life and didn't like what I saw, so I changed direction and started following the Lord. If we look further, we find that many times the reason a person changes is because of some situation or circumstance that gets their attention. **Verse 67** *"Before I was afflicted I went astray: but now have I kept Thy word." 71. "It is good for me that I have been afflicted; that I might learn Thy statutes."* Many times the very thing that seemed so terrible and really shook us up turned out to be a blessing. It may be a life threatening event or accident. A divorce or money problems can cause a person to examine their life and take inventory. Whatever it may be, if it changes your life and causes you to seek God until you find Him, it is worth it.

19. QUESTION: I hear people talk about the Apocrypha, why should we consider this work?

ANSWER: The 1611 King James Bible included The Apocrypha and it provides more detailed answers to many questions. One example would be in **II Esdras.** We covered this in an earlier question about what happens to a person when they die. One of the things that a person of God must do is overcome our unrighteous thoughts. The Apocrypha sheds light on this and talks about the first thing a person who is on the good side of the Gulf did while in the flesh body. **II Esdras 7:92** *"The first order is that they have striven with much toil to conquer the wicked thought that was formed with them, so that it should not lead them away from life to death."* This is one of the first places I have found that says our wicked impure thoughts that give us a hard time and sometimes lead us astray were formed with us when we were born. This certainly explains a lot and answers many questions. Where do all those dumb, stupid, impure, unrighteous and even evil thoughts come from? This verse tells us and we have to strive or work hard to conquer this area of our lives. And everyone said, **"Amen."**

20. QUESTION: Is everyone born with free will?

ANSWER: The Bible is clear on this and the answer is simple, but it is hard for most people to get their arms around, because it goes against tradition. No, not everyone is born with free will. Did Moses have free will? No! Did Jonah have free will? No! Did Jeremiah have free will? No, God chose him before he was in his mother's womb. Did Saul have free will? No! These are just a few examples where God chose the ultimate path these men would follow. Let's look at what the Bible has to say. **Ephesians 1:1** *"Paul, an Apostle of Jesus Christ by the will of God, to the saints."* Here we see Paul was an Apostle by the will of God. Paul's will was to persecute Christians. God's will over rode Paul's will and He had no choice. You also notice he is talking to the Saints or chosen ones. **4.** *"According as He hath chosen us in Him before the foundation of the world."* (Note the first earth age again) **5.** *"Having predestined us unto the adoption of children by Jesus Christ to Himself according to the good pleasure of His will."* Now to keep the record straight, in case you think this means that these chosen ones have a free ride and do not sin, listen to **Verse 7.** *"In Whom we have redemption through His blood, the forgiveness of sins."* The beauty of salvation is that we have forgiveness of sins when we repent. Now let's go to **II Timothy 1:9** *"Who hath saved us and called us with a holy calling, not according to our works, but according to His own purpose and grace, which was given us in Christ Jesus before the world began."* (Before this earth age world began) **Romans 11:28** *"But as touching the election, they*

127

are beloved for the Father's sakes." Now let's get down to the nit-
tie gritty, the real question is do **you** have free will? Or are you one
of God's elect? The answer is yes "if" you have the blinders off your
eyes and understand the whole plan of God, that is to say understand
the three heaven and earth ages, what really happened in the Garden
of Eden and most of what has been discussed in this work. The real
litmus test is do you see through the rapture doctrine and know the
first Christ on a white horse is anti-Christ? For you see only God's
elect will refuse to fall for this imposters lies. They will not fall down
and worship him. Instead they will allow the Holy Spirit to speak thru
them when they are brought before anti-Christ. They will know he is
a fake. The majority of religions and Christian churches will eagerly
jump on his band wagon when he does a few miracles and tells them
"I've come to fly you out of here." Ask yourself this question. Do
you know God's word well enough to notice when it is changed just
a little? Did you notice the little change he made in quoting scripture
while tempting Jesus? Did you notice the way Satan changed what
God had said in Genesis when he was seducing Eve? Satan, looking like what you think Jesus is suppose to look like and doing what
you think Jesus would do, will deceive the vast majority. **Revelation
13:13** *"And he doeth great wonders, so that he maketh fire come
down from heaven on the earth in the sight of men."* You think people go crazy over rock stars and sports heroes, you have not seen anything like what will take place when "old pretty boy" shows up. The
word tells us that even the elect would be fooled if God did not cut
the time short. **Mark 13:20** *"And except that the LORD had shortened those days, no flesh should be saved: but for the elect's sake,
whom He hath chosen, He hath shortened the days."* For the mature
student, we find the length of Satan's tribulation has been shortened
in: **Revelation 9:5** *"And to them it was given that they should not
kill them, but that they should be tormented five months."* 10. *"And
their power was to hurt them five months."*

21. QUESTION: I Thessalonians 4:17 says we will be caught
up together in the air, if that is not the rapture, then what is it?

ANSWER: What is the subject being discussed? In order to find
what is being talked about we must start in **I Thessalonians 4:13**
*"But I would not have you ignorant, brethren, concerning them
which are asleep, that you sorrow not, even as others which have no*

hope." Here is the subject being discussed, which is where the dead are. He is telling us, I want you to know and not be ignorant so you are not as the ones that have no hope, because they don't know the Lord as Savior. There is nothing more pitiful than attending a funeral where the family does not know the Lord. They have no hope and no rock to stand on in times of trouble. If we continue to read in verse **14.** *"For if we believe that Jesus died and rose again, even so them also which sleep in Jesus will God bring with Him. 15. For this we say unto you by the word of the Lord, that we which are alive and remain unto the coming of the Lord, shall not prevent* (precede) *them which are asleep.* (Because they are already gone) *16. "For the Lord Himself shall descend from heaven with a shout, with the voice of the archangel and with the trump of God: and the dead in Christ shall rise first:* Paul is telling them Jesus is going to bring all those who have passed on that were believers, with Him. He says we can not prevent these from coming because they are already with Him there. When He returns with them they are already changed into their spiritual bodies. (remember **Ecclesiastes 12:7** at the occasion of death the spirit returns to the Lord. Those who have died to this flesh go back to their spiritual bodies.) Then we who have not died and are remaining will change into our spiritual bodies. **I Thessalonians 4:17** *"Then we which are alive and remain, shall be caught up together with them in the clouds, to meet the Lord in the air: and so shall we ever be with the Lord.* " The word air in the Greek as used is not atmosphere. We are not going to fly up in the atmosphere and be with the Lord in these flesh bodies. The word in your Strong's Concordance is number 109 "Aer" to breathe unconsciously and change. At the last trump which is the seventh trump, we shall all be changed to our spiritual bodies. This is tied directly with **I Corinthians 15:52** *"In a moment, in the twinkling of an eye, at the last trump: for the trumpet shall sound and the dead shall be raised incorruptible and we shall be changed.* " You better get an understanding of what is being said. This is no pre-trib rapture. This is the last trump. Anti-Christ has already been here and you were either dead or you lived through it. What this information tells us is that we will be changed into our spiritual bodies and we will remain in these spiritual bodies from then on with the Lord. You are not going to float around in outer space. Again, this verse has caused much confusion among well meaning

129

people. Ask yourself, does it really sound like God to tell us to put on the whole armor of God and then when the going gets rough, take us out of here? I can tell you right now this would be against the nature of our Lord. He has never taken His people out of anything. He has kept them in the midst of the trouble. He kept Daniel in the lion's den. He kept the Hebrew children through the fiery furnace. He led His people through the Red sea. Today, if you will seek Him until you find Him, He will take you through your problem. He does not remove the problem, He guides us over, under or through it so that we overcome the problem and come out the other side a more mature person. We pass the test. The main purpose of this earth age is for people to have a choice of who they will chose, God or the devil. So you will be here; you will either be fooled by the Jesus look alike or you will know who he is and wait for the real Jesus to return. Don't be fooled by this rapture doctrine that was started in the year 1830 by a woman name Margaret Macdonald, in Scotland.

22. QUESTION: Where does the name Jew come from?

ANSWER: It is misused most of the time. Today most people refer to anyone that is a Hebrew as a Jew. This is simply not correct. Jacob had twelve sons. One of those sons was Judah; from Judah has come the term Jew. A person referred to as Jewish correctly used would be a person from the tribe of Judah or a resident of Judea.

23. QUESTION: What are some of the most mistranslated words that are the Bible?

ANSWER: Mistranslated words can be confusing if careful study is not done. "Heart" in many cases is better translated "mind." We think and reason with our mind not our heart. We feel with our heart (sometime used for our emotions.) "Fear God" should be "revere God" much of the time. "Poor" in many cases should be "humble." The word "love" in English is broken into at least four Greek words. For example, I love my wife, has a different meaning than I love to go out to eat; yet the same English word is used. "Holy Ghost" is a terrible translation and "Holy Spirit" should be used in most cases. The word ghost as used in the Greek is "pneuma" with the definition: a current of air, spirit, divine, God's spirit, spirit of life body etc. God is not a ghost or spook. When you look up spirit or ghost in the Greek, you are given the same 4151 number in the Greek Dictionary. You can say Holy Ghost if you want, I prefer Holy Spirit.

130

24. QUESTION: Is there a difference between laws and statutes?

ANSWER: Absolutely, statutes cover a wide range of legislation. Painting this with a broad brush, they may be listed in two sections:

1. National Laws.
2. Ecclesiastical Laws.

There are some overlapping of certain statutes. Some fall into the category of both national and ecclesiastical. An example would be the law of the Sabbath has national as well as religious significance. Jesus became our Sabbath, our rest, for those that are hung up on a particular day. Biblical statutory laws make no distinction between the secular and the sacred, because all things that have any bearing on the welfare and happiness of people are sacred in the eyes of God. Affairs of the state concern the Lord as much as affairs of the church. The nation is the Lords just as the church is His. National statutes cover as wide a range of interest as the requirements of life itself; business relations, property rights, economics, agriculture, crime, etc. The 10 Commandants or Laws are still very much in effect today. (Taken from C.R. Dickey in his book: One Man's Destiny) Jesus did away with the ordinance of blood once and for all time when He shed His blood for all of us.

25. QUESTION: Is Biblical tax law different from our tax laws today?

ANSWER: As different as day and night. C.R. Dickey gives a great answer to this question. "Politicians are taxing everything in sight. Homes and farms are taxed while intangible assets amounting to billions are tax free. There is only one sensible and just way to levy taxes and that is on the basis of income. Biblical law taxes income from the land, but not the land. It assesses a tax on rentals from an apartment but none on the inventory, fixtures and building. In this way the tax is always in proportion to one's ability to pay because it is determined by a persons actual increase and not by their holdings." This is fair for both rich and poor.

In a speech about the Constitution, Howard Rand said it best. "The laying of taxes today is limited only by the endurance of our citizens. The future has been mortgaged for generations to come. The industrious are penalized with ever increasing taxes. Reality, personal, sales, luxury, inheritance, automobile, fuel and income with registration taxes of all types and descriptions; and countless others in city, state and federal government. The citizens of this country can have no guarantee of the security of their homes or farms. They live in fear of a day when income shall cease and savings lost and the fruit of years of industry will be confiscated as the home or farm is taken to satisfy taxes. The selfishness and the greed of the politician render him incapable of even seeking a solution so long as he can put his hand into the pocket of every citizen. God gave our forefathers a perfect law of taxation. Under that law no levying was made on property, either personal or real. The home, the farm, the possessions of all descriptions were free from confiscation. Taxes were paid, but tax was based upon increase only. The government income bore a direct relation to the income of the people. For national leaders to increase governmental returns, it was necessary that they first increase the prosperity of every citizen. Would to God this was the requirement imposed upon every politician and officer holder today. If this was so, instead of our people forever pursuing a prosperity "just around the corner" it would be present with us. God has declared that under His system our people would live, not in fear of future destitution and want, but in the enjoyment of continued prosperity, of security and peace in their possessions. The return of these just principles of administration are as fundamental to the welfare of the nation as the moral code isn fundamental to the life of the individual." Well said, Mr. Rand.

26. QUESTION: What does the Bible say about the separation of church and state?

ANSWER: We will quote again from "One Man's Destiny." "Both church and state are under God's laws and are subject to Him. Neither is under the same human administration. The outline for matters of the state are found in **Exodus 18** where Moses and a cabinet of judges whom he appointed and trained in statesmanship executed all matters of state. This plan was used forty years in the wilderness as found in **Deuteronomy1:15-16** and **16: 18-20.** It was still in use during the reign of Jehoshaphat, who adopted it in its original form, unchanged from the days of Moses; **II Chronicles 19: 5-11.** Aaron and his sons had no jurisdiction in matters of state. No one man is permitted, under the statutes of God, to execute both national and ecclesiastical law. No dignitaries in the sanctuary are privileged to control government. No preacher, priest rabbi or bishop is exempt from obedience to the statutory laws of the nation. Government officials are not permitted to control the church as they do in totalitarian countries. The sanctuary must not be dominated by the state nor the state by the church. Mutual interest and cooperation should be enjoined as all wise people will love and support both the church and state. When Christ returns as King of the nations and Head of the church, then, for the first time, will the rights of both offices be vested perpetually in one person." This is Mr. Dickey's take on this question and I can't improve on it. I also believe this is also the Biblical answer as well.

27. QUESTION: What is the best advice for getting God to be on my side?

ANSWER: Deuteronomy 28 says it best. *"If you walk in my statutes and keep my commandments and do them, then blessings will follow you as the day follows night. But if you will not hearken unto Me and will not do all these commandments, the stars in their courses will fight against you."* Learn to be good to yourself by doing things God's way and He will pour out His blessings on you. Live life the way the so called "experts" tell you and you will struggle all your life. Up then down, poor then rich, then poor again. Happy then unhappy. Thin then fat, healthy then unhealthy. All the time never knowing what true peace and joy is. Never having an honest relationship with your closest living relative, your Heavenly Father. As as been stated by more than one, if you are still doing things the same way, you are still getting the same results. God's way is the best way and the only way you will reach your full potential. If God is on your side you will always be on the winning side. Even in times of trouble, you can still have peace of mind, knowing that He is in charge. He knows exactly how to handle any of life's problems and has shared the information already written, if you will make the effort to find it.

28. QUESTION: Can you help me understand that God has a way of giving us a willing heart?

OPINION: Whenever someone comes up with a new product, they first build a model or prototype of that product. The model is worked with until it is perfect. The product is then evaluated to see if there is sufficient demand and if it can be cost effectively produced. Once that is approved it is given to production to see if it can be mass produced and still maintain the quality. A production line is set up and the first material is started down the production line. As the product makes it's way down the line it begins to take shape. As the first item comes off the line it is compared to the prototype. If it does not come up to that standard, they turn up the heat and the pressure so that it will conform to the perfect model. (Information taken from a private conversation with the former head of Engineers for IBM) Jesus is our prototype. We are in God's production line and He has determined that He would prefer us to be all that we can be. We ask God to let us be more like Him, He allows the heat and pressures of life to mold us into His Image. You don't take your Ford to the Toyota Dealer or your lawn mower to the plumber if you want the best results and the correct parts to fix the problem. If you want the best advice for your life, take your problems to the Creator of your spirit, soul and body. Consult the One who made you and take His advice. He has all the parts and know how to fix and prepare you to be all you can be. The more you stay in His presence and study His Word, the more you come up to the standard that your Creator had in mind for you. The more we measure up to His standards, the more we please Him. The more we please Him, the happier and blessed we will be. If we never make the effort to get to know Him, we stumble around through life, never knowing there is a much better way to live.

29. QUESTION: If there is only one God, why are there so many different religions and denominations?

OPINION: Martin Luther said he would not take all the gold in the world for his knowledge of the Hebrew language. The vast majority of people don't think they have access to the manuscripts. The English and other translations, no matter how sincere, have been corrupted, sometimes by accident, most time on purpose. When God said one thing and the translation changes the meaning, there is confusion. The truth is still there for those who seek till they find. Most give up and accept what their religious leaders tell them. As you know, man can never agree on anything. While there is only the one true God, the devil has always tried to imitate God, because he wants to be God. We have religions in the world today that have been around a long time. If you look at their origins, you will usually find the devil lurking somewhere in the background. One of the dominant religions teaches its followers to kill anyone who does not agree with their teachings. The god they serve is so insecure that he can not handle anyone questioning his existence. As far as denominations go, the lack of understanding the importance of the manuscripts is one of the main reasons we have umpteen different ones. In many cases, if a person is not born into a Christian family, they have difficulty with the concept that there really is a God. Most men's egos won't allow them to admit that they can't always do it, or fix it or find it themselves. Having to ask a God they cannot see, to help them is not acceptable, especially since they are taught in school that they evolved from a monkey. Whether you know it or not, whether you accept it or not, there is a God shaped void in every soul and sometimes men spend their entire lifetime trying to fill that emptiness with other things. Some try to fill it with alcohol, drugs, sex, sports, travel, expensive toys and religion. The problem is you can't fill a God shaped void with something that looks like a god, nor some man made object whittled out of wood or chipped out of marble or hammered out of metal or fashioned out of clay; only God will fill that void. Because man can appease his soul with attempting to be good, he will accept a substitute god that looks and feels so good. Deep down inside, he knows this is not the real thing, but it is better than nothing. So he gets with others that are accepting this belief and they get themselves a preacher and build themselves a building and elect themselves a board of directors and they set up rules and regulations and they call it ABC church that is a member of the XYZ denomination. They meet two or three times a week and they marry and bury folks. They have stained glass windows and an organ and they appease their conscience so they can continue their lives believing they are serving God. You have come this far, so stay with me a while longer. These are not bad people, in fact, for the most part they are very good people. The problem is they don't know God's Word. They don't have a leader that has studied the manuscripts and teaches all the "Word of God." Many denominations teach in their seminaries that a pastor should not discuss anything that is controversial and that they should not teach above a fourth grade level. As a result, their church has no real rock base to handle the things that are happening in the world today. People are so set on being "Politically Correct," they completely ignore what the Bible says or even what common sense tells them is wrong. Folks, the Bible is very clear, there will be no drug dealers in heaven, there will be no homosexuals in heaven, there will be no liars or thieves or murderers in heaven. There will be no one who uses false balances in their business in heaven. There will be no gossipers and sowers of discord in heaven. The only way for any of us to spend eternity with our Creator is to repent of all these things and ask for forgiveness and change our life-style. Your standing with God in the eternity is dependent on your accepting Jesus Christ as your savior and the good works you do while here. Your money won't save you. Your church won't save you. Your denomination won't save you. Your preacher, or mother or dad or uncle or aunt or grandparents won't save you. If you cut my finger, I will bleed red blood, but none of the above people's blood will save you, only the blood of the Lamb of God has the power and authority to cleanse your sins and save your soul. The question was why do we have so many religions and only one God? The real answer is because man would not accept God as their King. **II Samuel 8:7** *"And the LORD said unto Samuel, the people have not rejected thee, but they have rejected Me, that I should not reign over them."* Man has been looking to man to supply their king and no one ever measures up to the task, not a priest, not a rabbi, not a prophet, not a political leader, not a rock star can fill the void. Anti-Christ will come on the scene and make all religions of the world believe he is the real deal. People who call themselves Christians will accept him because they have been taught by their well meaning pastors and family that this is the one that is coming to solve all their problems and fly them out of here while all the bad stuff is going on..

30. QUESTION: Did Jesus need an interpreter to speak to the different people of that day?

ANSWER: Chapter one verse one John tells us that: *"In the beginning was the Word and the Word was with God and the Word was God. 14. And the Word was made flesh and dwelt among us."* Jesus did not need an interpreter to speak to any person. God the Father, God the Son, God the Holy Spirit are one. The Holy Spirit is the Spirit of God. This same Spirit will speak through God's elect when they stand before anti-Christ and the language that is spoken will be understood by every man, woman and child on the face of the earth. All languages, all dialects will hear what is spoken like it was coming from a person raised in their county. This will cover many more languages than was spoken during Jesus' time on earth. There is no mention of Him ever using an interpreter for the four languages spoken in that area and time. There was Hebrew, spoken by Hebrews. There was Greek, which was spoken in Palestine by the educated classes generally. There was Latin, the language of the Romans, who then held possession of the land and there was Aramaic, the language of the common people. In the synagogue Jesus would speak Hebrew. To Pilate and other Roman officials, He would answer in Latin while to the common people He would doubtless speak Aramaic. This Word that became flesh was able to communicate to all flesh regardless of the language.

31. QUESTION: Why do many higher critics find fault with much of the New Testament?

ANSWER: It is generally assumed by many that since the New Testament comes to us in Greek that it ought to be classical Greek and it is condemned because it is not. Classical Greek was at its prime some centuries before and there were several reasons why the New Testament was not written in classical Greek. The writers were Hebrews and while the language is Greek, the thoughts and idioms are mostly Hebrew. If the Greek is regarded as an inspired translation from Hebrew or Aramaic originals, most of the various readings would be accounted for and understood. Remember Paul, who wrote most of the New Testament was Hebrew and he spoke several languages. The Greek he used was colloquial or street Greek not classical Greek. If we put this in modern context, it would be like using a common expression understood by the locals, but not understood by another culture or language student a thousand years from now. If I said, "that guy is tighter than the bark on a tree," most natural Texans would know I was describing a person that was very stingy with his money. Now if that saying was translated to another language, say Korean, the words would be translated word for word, but this would confusing to a Korean and would not convey the real message especially if it was thousands of years later. Likewise many things in the Bible are not understood because they are taken out of context. Add that to the fact that the manuscripts were written from an eastern mindset and the translators and readers were and are trying to understand with a western mindset. Also, many times critics try to make spiritual what is physical and made physical what is spiritual. In my opinion, higher critics of the Bible are usually pseudo intellectuals who claim to be doing a good Christian work, while all the time they make a living trying to disprove the Bible. Ever learning, never able to come to the knowledge of the truth.

32. QUESTION: Why do many feel that the Hebrew text is corrupted?

ANSWER: These "so called" higher critic scholars show their ignorance when they say the Hebrew manuscripts are corrupted. Dr. E.W. Bullinger points out some of the facts laid out by Dr. C.D Ginsburg regarding the Massorah.

1.   All the letters of the Hebrew text were counted so that the number of each letter in each book would be known to the scribe that he might easily check his work and ascertain whether one letter had escaped. He was informed how many Alephs (A) there should be, how many Beths (B) etc.

2.   In cases of spelling, where a certain word occurs with a slightly different spelling, where one was a short sound and another with a long or full sound, these are noted, numbered and thus safeguarded.

3.   Where a certain word or expression occurs more or less frequently in varying forms, these are all noted, numbered and distinguished.

So when someone claims to be an expert about the Bible and says the Hebrew text is corrupted, they are only showing how little they really know. When people say that have found corruption in the English translations, this can be true.

33. QUESTION: What is the Massorah?

ANSWER: All of the oldest and best manuscripts of the Hebrew Bible contain on every page, beside the text (arranged in two or more columns) a varying number of lines of smaller writing, distributed between the upper and lower margins. This writing is called the Massorah Magne or Great Massorah. The wrting on the sides and middle of the columns is call the Massorah Parve or Small Massorah. (Taken from The Companion Bible, Appendix Number 30.)

34. QUESTION: Where are the ten lost tribes of Israel?

ANSWER: First of all they are not lost to God. He knows exactly where they are. If you trace the word Caucasian you will find it refers to those who traveled north over the Caucasus mountains. These factions of Hebrew tribes traveled north over the Caucasus mountains in Russia, migrated into Europe, especially Scotland, Ireland, England and then to the Americas and Canada. Today, they are called Caucasians and most don't have any knowledge of their history. Since this has taken many generations and thousands of years, these tribes do not have a clue who they are. **Lamentations 2:9** *"Her kind and her princes are among the Gentiles; the law is no more; her prophets also find no vision from the LORD."* Today these descendants of Abraham call themselves Gentiles. What goes on in many churches today is disgraceful to God and man. Over the last few hundred years we have developed many forms and ceremonies, but for the most part have left God out. **Matthew 15:8** *"This people draweth nigh unto Me with their mouth and honoureth Me with their lips; but their heart is far from Me. 9. But in vain they do worship Me, teaching for doctrines the commandments of men."* So the answer to your question is that many people who believe they are Gentiles are in reality from the so called lost tribes of Israel. Remember, the word Jew is widely misused and not understood. A Jew is of the tribe of Judah, but there are twelve tribes that make up the Hebrew race. Have you ever heard the song "Ruben, Ruben I've been thinking? That comes from Holland. Many from the tribe of Ruben settled in Holland and Germany. Many of us call ourselves Anglo Saxons. This comes from being a descendant of Issac; "Issac's Sons." Did you know that every King and Queen of England, when they are crowned, swears an oath to be "The defender of the faith of Israel." This would be the king line of Judah, but still of Israel.

35. QUESTION: What is your opinion of what is happening in some of the churches today with regard to religious leaders involved in perversion and having sex with minor children?

OPINION: Unfortunately this has gone on for a long time. The two sons of Eli, who was the High Priest a thousand years before Christ, were involved in perverted sex. In their case the Bible does not indicate they were having sex with children, but they were still using their position in the church to engage in many things that were an abomination to God and man. The real problem is the men doing these things were not being led of God. They are people who have been educated by man. With their credentials, they are hired by church boards or are self appointed. Because they are not walking daily with their Creator, the flesh is weak and they fall. The real sad thing is that their church leaders either don't know what to do or in most cases try to cover it up and the predator continues and even more victims have their lives really messed up; some to the point of committing suicide. Anyone that preys on young children should be prosecuted and taken out of society. As far as I'm concerned the sentence for this type of crime should be the same as murder. The Bible says rape should have the same punishment as murder. God knows exactly what to do with them. There are no unsolved mysteries with our Father. Until this nation gets away from the law by precedent and returns to God's law, we will never be able to rid society of such behavior. This is another example of men "thinking themselves wise, they have become fools."

36. QUESTION: Why is there so much confusion about the Sabbath? Some say Saturday and other Sunday.

ANSWER: Let's get Paul's take on this subject found in **Galatians 4:10** *"Ye observe days and months and times and years. 11. I am afraid of you, lest I have bestowed upon you labor in vain."* **Mark 2:27** *"The Sabbath was made for man and not man for the Sabbath."* When we do an in depth study of the word Sabbath we find the meaning of the word is rest. If Jesus is our rest, then every day is a Holy day unto God. Jesus became our rest when He became our Passover. The last part of **I Corinthians 5:7** *"For even Christ our Passover is sacrificed for us."* In our modern times we have allowed the traditions of men to convince us that we are to worship only one day a week. A true believer knows that we are to have fellowship with and worship our Father everyday and bring God into all of our life. **Revelation 4:11** tells us that all things were created for His pleasure. That includes you and me. So, if we want to please our Father, rest in Him daily.

37. QUESTION: I have never understood the parable of the ten virgins. If they were all virgins, why were five of them not allowed to go into the Bridegroom?

ANSWER: This question requires a more lengthy answer. First, let us quote the scripture in which we find the parable. **Matthew 25:1** *"Then shall the kingdom of heaven be likened unto ten virgins, which took their lamps and went forth to meet the bridegroom. 2. And five of them were wise and five were foolish."* Jesus is telling us that half of the people who acted like Christians were wise and half foolish. The word foolish in our Strong's is Greek number 3474 moros which comes from the root 3466 musterion a secret or mystery (through the idea of silence imposed by initiation into religious rites) Following the root word for wise, we find 2525, 2524 and 4908 in the Greek with the meaning, understanding, mentally put together. By finding the meaning of these words we find the path to the deeper meaning Jesus is conveying with this parable. First, the oil is symbolic for truth. Half of them had truth in their minds and understood the Word of God. The wise ones were prepared through study of God's Word and had a real relationship with their Lord. The foolish were into religious rites that looked godly, but had no depth or substance. **Verse 3.** *"They that were foolish took their lamps and took no oil with them."* They looked the part, they called themselves Christians, they were there every time the church doors were open. The problem was they depended on their preacher or religious leader to tell them what to believe. They did not have the truth of God in their own minds. How many times do people say when asked a question about a deeper meaning in the Bible, "Oh, you will have to talk to my preacher about that." Now let's see what Jesus is telling another parable about this same subject. Here we find the reason why half of the people who call themselves Christians don't have oil in their vessels or truth in their minds. **Luke 14:16** *"Then said He (Jesus) unto him, "A certain man made a great supper and bade many."* Many are called to the marriage supper of The Lamb. *17. "And sent his servant at supper time to say to them that were bidden, Come; for all things are now ready. 18. And they all with one consent began to make excuse. The first said unto him, 'I have a bought a piece of ground and I must needs go and see it: I pray thee have me excused.' 19. And another said, 'I have brought five yoke of oxen and I go to prove them: I pray thee have me excused.' 20. And another said, ' I have married a wife and therefore I cannot come.' 21. So that servant came and shewed his lord these things."* If we read on we find the master of the house became very angry and invited others to come. He also in a manner of speaking closed the door on those who made excuse. **Verse 24.** *"For I say unto you, That none of those men which were bidden shall taste of my supper."* Now let's bring this up to date. If we must have understanding about God and His ways (Oil in our vessels) in order to go in with the Bridegroom, then we can't make excuses for not knowing. Many have been mislead by well meaning people that say we don't have to understand God's Word. We are told, "come join our group and listen to us and we will get you there." If you read carefully God is not saying you are not suppose to take care

141

of business. He is saying there is a time to work and earn a living, get married, take care of your families and enjoy life. There is also a time for you personally to gain knowledge so you will know God's truth. Let me ask you a question. Does anyone else make a living for you or do you do that yourself? Does anyone else pay your bills or do you have to pay them? Does another person bleed for you when you cut your finger or do you feel the pain and do that yourself? Can you rely on someone else's education and experience enough for you to make a living? The answer is a no-brain slam dunk, NO! You have to do all these things yourself. Then why are you content to depend on someone else to do your study of God's Word? The majority of Christians today have bought into the "so called" rapture doctrine. This will cause them to worship the first christ that comes on the scene. Most don't know that there will be two Christs show up in the last days. Those without oil in their vessel will believe the first is the real one and want to fly away with him. What does the Word tell us the real Christ will say to those that claim to be Christians? **Matthew 7:21** *"Not every one that saith unto Me, Lord, Lord, shall enter into the kingdom of heaven; but he that doeth the will of My Father which is in heaven. 22. Many will say to Me in that day, Lord, Lord, have we not prophesied in Thy name: and in Thy name have cast out devils? And in Thy name done many wonderful works? 23. And then will I profess unto them, 'I never knew you: depart from Me, ye that work iniquity."* We are supposed to be hearers and doers of the Word. Too many "do" with out hearing or understanding. They just do what they are told by their religious leaders. So Jesus, in the parable of the ten virgins, is telling us that we have to do more than look the part of a Christian. We must be able to truly be about our Father's business by first understanding what His business is. Otherwise the door will be shut and those without the oil or truth to light their path will not enter. Many talk the talk, if you want to please your Father, you must talk the talk and walk the walk.

38. QUESTION: Why do you believe that the devil will be able to fool the majority of people when he shows up after being kicked out of heaven by Michael?

ANSWER: What I believe is not worth much if it can't be backed up in God's Word. What is written in the Bible is what is important. **Revelation 12:9** *"And the great dragon was cast out, that* *old serpent, called the Devil and Satan, which DECEIVETH THE WHOLE WORLD: he was cast out into the earth and his angels were cast out with him."* How much of the world is he going to deceive? A small part? Just the bad people? All except the Christians? NO, you just read it, he will deceive the whole world. That is the reason the majority of even the churches will be deceived. People will be looking for a devil in a red suit, forked tail and very scarey. They will be totally taken in by a handsome, well spoken entity that will say he is Jesus Christ. He will come in peaceably and prosperously and have the largest revival the world has ever seen. He will snap his fingers and have lightning come down from heaven. **Revelation 13:13** *"And he doeth great wonders, so that he maketh fire come down from heaven on the earth in the sight of men."* He and his supernatural buddies will convince most people that they have come to fly everyone out before the tribulation comes. You see if he came back looking like the devil, he would fool no one. But, if he can convince you that he is the Christ, he will fool all but those who really know the Word of God; those who already know what to look for. Now, we go where Jesus is telling us some of the things that will happen. **Luke 12:52** *"For from henceforth there shall be five in one house divided, three against two and two against three. 53. The father shall be divided against the son and the son against the father; the mother against the daughter and the daughter against the mother; the mother-in-law against her daughter-in-law and the daughter-in-law against her mother-in-law."* Jesus is telling those who have ears that hear that many people will be so convinced that the devil is Christ that he will deceive and divide even members of a family. Those that believe he is Christ and those that know he is a fake. Listen up! Here is a difficult thing to understand if you let it. I want you to read and reread this until you understand what is being said. **Luke 12:58** *"When thou goest with thine adversary to the magistrate, as thou art in the way, give diligence that thou mayest be delivered from him; lest he hale thee to the judge and the judge deliver thee to the officer and the officer cast the into prison."* Jesus is giving us the method to use when you have someone come to you during this time and say, "do you believe in Jesus?" Instead of saying, that's not the real Jesus, you are to make them think you agree with them and reply, "Yes, Jesus is wonderful." Now why would Jesus want us to do this at that time?

It is very simple. During the time of anti-Christ on the earth, God's elect are to allow the Holy Spirit to speak through them when they are brought before anti-Christ. If you have been thrown in prison over a minor skirmish with an underling, you won't be available when the Father needs you. Now, let's be sure everyone understands this. If you are required to worship anti-Christ, in order to buy or sell or to exchange your funds for his new currency, you refuse and take the consequences. In other words, you stay free and behind the scenes as long a possible until you are forced into agreeing to worship him, then you refuse and take the aftermath. This will cause you to be put in a different category and will eventually lead to you testifying against anti-Christ by allowing the Holy Spirit to speak through you. As this time approaches remember **Matthew 24:11** *"And many false prophets shall rise and shall deceive many. 12. And because iniquity shall abound, the love of many shall wax cold. 13. But he that shall endure unto the end, the same shall be saved." 22. "And except those days should be shortened, there should no flesh be saved: but for the elect's sake those days shall be shortened. 23. Then if any man shall say unto you, Lo, here is Christ, or there: believe it not. 24. For there shall arise false Christs and false prophets and shall shew great signs and wonders; insomuch that, if it were possible, they shall deceive the very elect.* Sidebar: Know for a fact the spirit of anti-Christ has been in the earth since the time of Jesus resurrection. Before that, the devil was here in person, just as he was in the days of **Job 1:6** *"Now there was a day when the sons of God came to present themselves before the LORD and Satan came also among them. 7. And the LORD said unto Satan, 'whence comest thou?' Then Satan answered the LORD and said, 'From going to and fro in the earth and from walking up and down in it."* His spirit is still here today and he is the accuser of the brethren. Every time one of God's people messes up, Satan's spirit is there pointing out our faults to God. We point this out to illustrate there is a difference in the devil's spirit being here and the full entity being here. There are many false preachers telling those who will listen, that Christ is coming back to rapture them out of here while anti-Christ is here. **I John 2:22** *"Who is a liar but he that denieth that Jesus is the Christ? He is anti-Christ, that denieth the Father and the Son.* Don't worry or panic when these things start to happen. We must pray often and know the mind of God's Spirit. **Verse 28.** *"And now, little children, abide in Him; that, when He shall appear, we may have confidence and not be ashamed before Him at His coming."*

39. QUESTION: What about all these different names of God? Who is God?

ANSWER: When God appeared to Moses and instructed him to carry out His plans, Moses ask Him, **Exodus 3:13** *"And Moses said unto God. 'Behold, when I come unto the children of Israel and shall say unto them, 'The God of your fathers hath sent me unto you;' and they shall say to me, 'What is His name?' What shall I say unto them?" 14. And God said unto Moses, "I AM THAT I AM:" and He said, 'Thus shalt thou say unto the children of Israel, I AM hath sent me unto you."* In the Hebrew, *'Ehyeh 'Asher 'Ehyeh* I will be what I will be which is continuance in time present, which was continuance in time past; which is to come continuance forever. "The Eternal" is a better rendering than Lord, which = Master and Owner. What He will be is left to be filled up according to the needs of those with whom He is in covenant = He Who becometh Saviour, Redeemer, Deliverer, Strengthener, Comforter, Healer etc. The correct pronunciation, found in five hidden acrostics in the book of Esther, is YHVH pronounced phonetically: YA HA VEY. To be clear an acrostic is a hidden message imbedded within scripture. You will not find it, just reading the verse. For the deeper student that wants to dig deeper the acrostics are found as follows:

1. **Esther 1:20** YHVH is spelled backward because He was turning back and overruling the counsels of man.

2. **Esther 5:4** YHVH is spelled forward because He was causing Esther to act; and take the first step, which was to lead up to so great an end.

3. **Esther 5:13** YHVH is spelled backward because He was overruling Haman's gladness and turning back Haman's counsel.

4. **Esther 7:7** YHVH is spelled forward because He was ruling and bringing about the end He had determined.

5. **Esther 7:5** "I AM" is spelled backward. The great enemy of the Messiah-the living Word-was seeking to destroy all hope of His promised coming and make void the repeated promise of YHVH. This acrostic is in the final letters of his question "Who is he and where is he? Only the great "I Am that I Am could know that.

Other names found in the Bible: Jah; Jehovah-Jireh; Jehovah-Nissi; Jehovah-Shalom, Lord etc. One way to explain all the different names of God, is to identify them as different offices of God. If we bring this down to our level, in my lifetime I have been called son, husband, dad, friend, uncle, employee, boss, employer, CEO, Chairman, author and so on. I am still the same one person, but depending on the relationship that a person has with me determines what they call me. It is the same with all the different names of God. As you establish a closer walk with your Creator, you will become familiar with all His ways and names. The most important thing, in doing this, is He knows your name and that you will live forever with Him.

40. QUESTION: What is a figure of speech and are they used in the Bible?

ANSWER: A figure of speech as used in the Bible is never used except for the purpose of calling attention to, emphasizing and intensifying the reality of the literal sense and the truth of the historical facts; so that while the words employed may not be so strictly true to the letter, they are are all the more true to the truth conveyed by them and to the historical events connected with them. (Taken from The Companion Bible) A figure of speech has the ability to paint a word picture in our minds that helps us understand what is being said, usually in fewer words than required if it was not employed.

41. QUESTION: Who are the sons of God and who are the fallen angels? What is the purpose of the fallen angels?

ANSWER: It is only by the Divine specific act of creation that any created being can be called a "son of God." God is Spirit and that which is "born of the Spirit is spirit." **John 3:6 *"That which is born of the flesh is flesh; and that which is born of the Spirit is spirit."*** Adam is called a son of God in **Luke 3:38 *"Which was the son of Enos, which was the son of Seth, which was the son of Adam, which was the son of God." * II Corinthians 5:17 *"Therefore if any man be in Christ, he is a new creature: old things are passed away; behold, all things are become new." * Ephesians 2:10 *"For we are His workmanship, created in Christ Jesus unto good works, which God hath before ordained that we should walk in them." * John 1:13 *"Which were born, not of blood, nor of the will of the flesh, nor of the will of man, but of God." * Romans 8:14 *"For as many as are led by the***

Spirit of God, they are the sons of God." I John 3:1 *"Behold What manner of love the Father hath bestowed upon us, that we should be called the sons of God: therefore the world knoweth us not, because it knew Him not."* Let's find some places in the Bible where angels are called "sons of God." **Psalms 29:1** *"Give unto the LORD, O ye mighty, give unto the LORD glory and strength."* The word "mighty" in the Targum reads "angels."We find God addressing this subject while referring to the first heaven and earth age in **Job 38:7** *"When the morning stars sang together and all the sons of God shouted for joy?* We were all in angelic bodies and called the sons of God. **Psalms 89:6** *"For who in the heaven can be compared unto the LORD? Who among the sons of the mighty can be likened unto the LORD?"* There was a fall of some angels as is certain in **Jude 6.** *"And the angels which kept not their first estate, but left their own habitation, He hath reserved in everlasting chains under darkness unto the judgment of the great day."* The nature of their fall is clearly stated in **Jude 7** as the sins of Sodom and Gomorrah. The time of their fall is given as having taken place "in the days of Noah." Their progeny, called Nephilim (translated giants) were monsters of iniquity and being superhuman in size and character had to be destroyed. This is the one and only object of the flood. Noah and his family had preserved their pedigree pure from Adam. **Genesis 6:9** *"These are THE GENERATIONS OF NOAH: Noah was a just man and perfect in his generations and Noah walked with God."* All the rest had become "corrupt."

NOTE: While there were only eight Adamic souls saved in the Ark, Noah was instructed to take two of every flesh aboard, which included two of every race of people as well as the animals. This act by God illustrates how fair He is in dealing with all His creation. The only remedy was to destroy them. This irruption of fallen angels was Satan's second attempt to prevent the coming of the Seed of the woman foretold in **Genesis 3:15.** His first attempt was seducing Eve in an attempt to corrupt the seed line that would lead to Christ. If either of these or any of the other times were to succeed, God's Word would have failed and Satan's own doom would be averted. As soon as it was made known that the "Seed of the woman" was to come through Abraham, there was another irruption, as recorded in **Genesis 6:4** *"and also after that"* (After the days of Noah, more than 500 years after the second influx.) The aim of the enemy was to occupy Canaan in advance of Abraham and contest its occupation by his seed. This attempt is repeated over and over again throughout the Bible. In each case the human instrument had his own personal interest to serve, while Satan had his own great object in view. In every case we see God had to interfere and avert the evil and the danger of which His servants and people were ignorant. For more examples of the purpose of the fallen angles we will list some more:

⅄ The destruction of the chosen family by famine. **Genesis 50:20**

⅄ The destruction of the male line in Israel. **Exodus 1:10, 15 etc.**

⅄ David's line was singled out in **II Samuel 7** this was the next selected for assault.

⅄ Jehoram killed off all his brothers. **II Chronicles 21:4**

⅄ The Arabians slew all the seed line, except Ahaziah **II Chronicles 21:17**

⅄ When Ahaziah died, Athaliah's mother killed "all the seed royal." **II Chronicles 22:10** The babe Joash alone was rescued and for six years, the faithfulness of God's Word was at stake. **II Chronicles 22:11-12**

⅄ Hezekiah was childless when a double assault was made by the King of Assyria. **Isaiah 36:1 and 38:1**

⅄ Joseph's fear was worked on **Matthew 1:18** *"Now the birth of Jesus Christ was on this wise: When as His mother was espoused to Joseph, before they came together, she was found with child of the Holy Ghost. 19. Then Joseph her husband, being a just man and not willing to make her a public example, was minded to put her away privily. 20. But while he thought on these things, behold, the angel of the LORD appeared unto him in a dream, saying, 'Joseph, thou son of David, fear not to take unto thee Mary thy wife: for That Which is conceived in her is of the Holy Ghost."* Being a just man he did not wish to have Mary stoned to death, hence Joseph determined to divorce her, but God intervened: *"Fear not."*

⅄ Herod sought the young Child's life. **Matthew 2**

⅄ At the temptation *"Cast thyself down"* was Satan's temptation.

⅄ At length the cross was reached and the sepulcher closed; the watch set; and the stone sealed. But **"God raised Him from the dead."** And now like another Joash, He is seated and expecting. **Hebrews 10:12** *"But this Man, after He had offered one sacrifice for sins for ever, sat down on the right hand of God; 13. From henceforth expecting till His enemies be made His footstool."* Hidden in the house of God on High; and the members of: "the one body" are hidden there in Him.

Colossians: 3:1 *"If ye then be risen with Christ, seek those things which are above, where Christ sitteth on the right hand of God. 2. Set your affection on things above, not on things on the earth. 3. For ye are dead and your life is hid with Christ in God."* To summarize, the irruption of "The fallen angels" ("sons of God") was directed against the whole human race. When Abraham was called, then he and his seed were attacked. When David was enthroned, the royal line was assailed. And when "the Seed of the woman" Himself came, then the storm burst upon Him and is still going on today. (Note: Much of this answer was taken from Appendix 23 in The Companion Bible)

42. QUESTION: What can you tell me about the Muslim religion?They claim to be a peaceful religion, but they are always associated with horrible violent acts.

OPINION: I will answer part of this question by quoting author, Rick Mathes, a well known leader in prison ministry. "The Muslim religion is the fastest growing religion per capita in the United States, especially in the minority races. Last month I attended my annual training session that's required for maintaining my state prison security clearance. During the training session there was a presentation by three speakers representing the Roman Catholic, Protestant and Muslim faiths, who each explained their beliefs. I was particularly interested in what the Islamic Imam had to say. The Muslim gave a great presentation of the basics of Islam, complete with video. After the presentations, time was provided for questions and answers. When it was my turn, I directed my question to the Muslim and asked:

'Please, correct me if I'm wrong, but I understand that most Imams and clerics of Islam have declared a holy jihad (holy war) against the infidels of the world and that by killing an infidel, (which is a command to all Muslims) they are assured of a place in heaven. If that is the case, can you give me the definition of an infidel? There was no disagreement with my statements and without hesitation, he replied, "Non-believers." I responded, 'So, let me make sure I have this straight. All followers of Allah have been commanded to kill everyone who is not of your faith so they can have a place in heaven. Is that correct?' The expression on his face changed from one of authority and command to that of a little boy who had just been caught with his hand in the cookie jar.' I then stated, 'Well sir, I have a real problem trying to imagine the Pope commanding all Catholics to kill those of your faith or Dr. Charles Stanley ordering all Protestants to do the same in order to guarantee them a place in heaven.'

The Muslim was speechless.

I continued, 'I also have a problem with being your friend when you and your brother clerics are telling your followers to kill me! Let me ask you a question: Would you rather have your Allah, who tells you to kill me in order for you to go to heaven or my Jesus who tells me to love you because I am going to heaven and He wants you to be there with me?'

You could have heard a pin drop.

Needless to say, the organizers and promoters of the "Diversification" training seminar were not happy with my way of dealing with the Islamic Imam and exposing the truth about the Muslims' beliefs. In twenty years there will be enough Muslim voters in the U.S. to elect a President." If we go to **Genesis 16:1** *"Now Sarai Abram's Wife bare him no children: and she had an handmaid, an Egyptian, whose name was Hagar. 2. And Sarai said unto Abram, 'Behold now, I pray thee, go in unto my maid; it may be that I may obtain children by her. And Abram hearkened to the voice of Sarai."* We find that Sarai regretted doing this because Hagar was acting like she was better that her mistress. So Sarai ran her off into the desert. Now, lets pick it up in **Genesis 16:7** *"And the angel of the LORD found her by a fountain of water in the wilderness, by the fountain in the way to Shur. 8. And He said, "Hagar, Sarai's maid, whence camest thou? And whither wilt thou go? And she said 'I flee*

from the face of my mistress Sarai.' 9. And the angel of the LORD said unto her, 'Return to thy mistress and submit thyself under her hands.' 10. And the angel of the LORD said unto her, 'I will multiply thy seed exceedingly, that it shall not be numbered for multitude. 11. And he angel of the LORD said unto her, 'behold, thou art with child and shalt bear a son and shalt call his name Ishmael; because the LORD hath heard thy affliction. 12. And he will be a wild man; his hand will be against every man and every man's hand against him; and he shall dwell in the presence of all his brethren."
If you notice, Hagar was an Egyptian and the father of her son was Abram, later changed by God to Abraham with the meaning "father of many nations." Ishmael's off-spring developed into twelve tribes. This imitating the twelve tribes of Israel is another example of: **"for every positive there is a negative."** The Islam religion today are for the most part descendants of Hagar and Abraham. They play a vital role in this "Fig Tree Generation." They are called the locust army in several places in the Bible, both Old and New Testaments. In **Revelation 9:7** *"And the shapes of the locust were like unto horses prepared unto battle, and on their heads were as it were crowns of gold and their faces were the faces of men. 8. And they had hair as the hair of women and their teeth were as the teeth of lions."* Pay close attention, you notice they mask their appearance, but they had faces like men because they are men. You are told they are wearing crowns. One definition of the word crown is "to wrap," like a turban. What other religion wraps their heads with a turban that looks like a crown. The dictionary defines turban as: a cloth wound in folds about the head; turbante, tulbend, dulband; headdress of Moslem origin. The radical Taliban's name is taken from Turban. You also notice they had hair like women. They appear so gentle and peaceful and talk a very good game, just as the Imam did presenting his case to the prison officials above. You also notice they had teeth like lions. Now if you understand symbolism, you were just given a description of the locust army, what they look like, how they act. God is using them to fulfill His prophesies in these last days. So don't think you can wish them away or pray them to be gone. Just remember God is and always has been in complete control. Your job is not to fear what is going on, but to arrange the priorities in your life to line up with what your destiny is in God's plan. Both Isaac and Ishmael were sons

of Abraham. Isaac born from the free woman and seed of Adam that would lead to the line of Christ and Ishmael born of the bond woman Hagar with the promise that: *"And he will be a wild man; his hand will be against every man and every man's hand against him; and he shall dwell in the presence of all his brethren."* The god they serve is none other than the devil himself. Stop and think how any so called religion could order its followers to strap bombs on men, women and children and kill innocent people with the guarantee of going to heaven. They have made a bargain with the devil. **Satan, who is death, is so insecure** that he will not permit any opposition to his teachings. He will not allow anyone to question what is taught under penalty of death. Ask any follower of Allah if they know they are going to heaven? They will tell you they don't know. Their teaching is, if over half of their deeds please Allah they will go to heaven and if over half of their deeds don't please Allah, they will go to hell. Most people from the west can't get their arms around how anyone could be so gullible to believe this. The fact is, when a child is born and held up and dedicated to Allah and that teaching is drilled into their young minds everyday, they learn to accept this as fact. In their mind, anyone who is not a follower of Islam is an infidel and should be killed. The other way they are guaranteed to go to heaven is to kill infidels in a holy jihad. **Now listen up very close.** You see the evil way the followers of Allah are described and the inhuman deeds they commit is the way most Christians perceive that the devil will look and act. Mean, war-mongers, inhuman in appearance and that is why most of the world will be fooled when anti-Christ comes. In contrast to traditions taught in Christians churches, **instead-of-Christ** will be very handsome, polite, well dressed, well spoken and very charismatic. He will do many miracles, quote many scriptures and have the largest revival the world has ever seen. He will be shown on all the noon, six and ten-o'clock news. All media outlets and stations will be drawn to him. He will be the hottest news story they have ever covered. The religious and political leaders will sing his praises. He will end all poverty, stop all wars and pay off everyone's bills. Why in the world could anyone not love and worship this wonderful man. He will look and act exactly like your idea of what Christ will look like and he will be telling everyone, "I've come to take you out of here during the soon coming tribulation." So, go get all your friends and family;

152

encourage them to join me while we assemble the entire world of my followers and worshipers. During this short time we will have peace, peace, peace and in order to settle all the money problems, I will introduce a new world currency. (He is so vain, it will probably have his picture on it.) He will set up the rules for people to have this new currency by telling everyone: To ensure that we have only my followers, they must show their allegiance to me by worshiping me or by signing an agreement that they love and worship me. Of course this is conjecture on my part about the money, or exactly what will be done and said, but something along these lines will take place. The Muslim situation will only intensify from now on, so pray about it and follow the leading of the Holy Spirit. The path may not be the same for everyone. **Luke 21:17** *"And ye shall be hated of all men for My name's sake. 18. But there shall not an hair of your head perish. 19. In your patience possess ye your souls."* When all the world is raving about this wonderful charismatic man and you are being brow-beaten to accept him, remember, *"In your patience possess ye your souls."*

43. QUESTION: My son served in Iraq and had the same problem as I am having now. What do we say when we are talking to people who are coming here with completely different religious beliefs? They want to know why they should believe in Jesus Christ more than Buddha or Mohammed?

FACT and OPINION: That is an excellent question. First, let's look at some reasons that are factual and known by everyone today. When we talk about the calendar we do not say BB, before Buddha or BM, before Mohammed. We say BC, before Christ. In fact when we look up Buddha in the dictionary we find he lived and died 563-483 years BC. Doing the same with Mohammed we find he lived and died 600 years AD, or Anno Domini, in the year of the Lord of the Christian era. When we look up Jesus, the dictionary does not mention either of the other two. You can do the same with any other non-Christian religion. Both Buddha and Mohammed lived and died. Jesus was born of a virgin, lived, died for our sins, was buried and rose again on the third day. The other two just died. Now, let us consider the fact there are no authentic books telling us about Buddha or Mohammed thousands of years before they were born. In contrast, we are told about Jesus thousands of years before He was born by many different prophets, many of which can be confirmed by historical data other than the Bible. Let's take a little time and look at some of the writings in the Bible that tell us about the coming and life of Jesus before he was born. We will begin 4000 years before Jesus was born. This is also the first prophesy in the Bible. God is talking to the serpent who is the devil in **Genesis 3:15** *"And I will put enmity between thee and the woman and between thy seed and her seed; it shall bruise thy head and thou shalt bruise his heel."* Careful study will show this is speaking of Jesus on the cross having His feet bruised or nailed to the cross. It also shows Jesus overcoming death and dealing a death blow to the head of Satan at the Great White Throne Judgment. Referring to the Adamic seed line through which Christ would come we go to **Genesis 22:18** *"And in thy seed all the nations of the earth be blessed."* **Exodus 12** tells us of the sacrificial lamb which is symbolic of Jesus being our sacrificial lamb. **Numbers 24:17** was written 1450 years before Christ and refers to Him as a Star that shall come of of Jacob. Written 630 years before it happened declares **Isaiah 7:14** *"Therefore the Lord Himself shall give you a sign: Behold a virgin shall conceive and bear a son and shall call His name Immanuel."* Immanuel means God with us. Again in **Isaiah 9:6** *"For unto us a child is born, unto us a son is given: and the government shall be upon His shoulder: and His name shall be called Wonderful, Counselor, The Mighty God, The everlasting Father, The Prince of Peace. 7. Of the increase of His government and peace there shall be no end, upon the throne of David and upon His kingdom, to order it and to establish it with judgment and with justice from henceforth even for ever. The zeal of the LORD of hosts will perform this."* Another place written 600 years before it happened. **Isaiah 53:4** *"Surely He hath borne our grief's and carried our sorrows; yet we did esteem Him stricken, smitten of God and afflicted. 5. But He was wounded for our transgressions, He was bruised for our iniquities: the chastisement of our peace was upon Him: and with His stripes we are healed. 6. All we like sheep have gone astray; we have turned every one to his own way; and the LORD hath laid on Him the iniquity of us all."* 600 years before the fact we find in **Micah 5:2** *"But thou, Bethlehem Ephratah, though thou be little among the thousand of Judah, yet out of thee shall He come forth unto me That is to be ruler in Israel; Whose goings forth have been* *from of old, from everlasting."* **489** years BC we find in **Jeremiah 23:5** *"Behold, the days come, saith the LORD, that I will raise unto David a righteous Branch and a King shall reign and prosper and shall execute judgment and justice in the earth."* We find this same message beginning with **Jeremiah 33:17** written 477 years B.C. Written 410 years before it happened we find the Lord referred to as the BRANCH in **Zechariah 9:9** *"Rejoice greatly, O daughter of Zion; shout, O daughter of Jerusalem: behold, thy King cometh unto thee: He is just and having salvation: lowly and riding upon an ass and upon a colt the foal of an ass."* **Zechariah 12:10** tells of the one that was pierced. **13:7** refers to Him as the Shepherd that was smitten. **Malachi,** written 374 years beforehand tells about the messenger that will be sent before Him to prepare the way. Now let's go to where we find one of the most amazing pieces of evidence spoken by David 1000 years before it took place. These are the words of Jesus as He hung on the cross. I will quote the first and last verse and strongly suggest you turn to **Psalm 22** and study for yourself. **Verse 1** *"My God, my God, why hast thou forsaken me: Why art thou so far from me and from the words of my roaring?"* In **verse 6** we see where He is despised and laughed at. In **verse 14** we find that His bones are pulled out of joint from hanging on the cross. In **verse 16** it is written that His hands and feet are pierced. In **verse 18** we see the solders casting lots for His vesture. **In verse 31** which is the last verse we see the words in English, *"That He hath done this."* If we go to the Greek we find the meaning to be *"It is finished."* The first and last verses are quoted in the Bible as Jesus having spoken them. However, careful study will indicate He quoted the entire chapter and is proof positive that Jesus is the Son of God. Now only God could arrange for these things to be told of thousands of years before they happened, even as to what the Roman solders would say and have them come to pass exactly as written. Only God could arrange for our dating system to be BC or AD. So the answer to your question is there is much evidence to support that Jesus is the Son of God and your believing and accepting Him is not only a matter of faith, but also of fact. All others are a poor substitute to place your future upon.

44. QUESTION: It seems every Christian religion says they got their beliefs from the Bible. How can you know for sure?

ANSWER: The Bible was not originally written in English. It was translated from Hebrew and Greek. Consequently, there is much content lost by honest mistakes and even more lost through deliberate changes by unholy hands and heads repeating the same mistakes over and over. Through the years, good sincere people obey the traditions of their church or family rather than following the Word of God. In these last days, God is removing the scales from the eyes of His people so they will be able to see the hidden truths that have been in plain sight all the time. We are living in the days that the Bible calls the Fig Tree Generation. Jesus told us to learn the parable of the fig tree. This is that generation you are living in right now. What I am saying is that your relationship with your Father, now and in the future, is dependent upon you taking responsibility for yourself. If you study with understanding, you will learn the hidden mysteries that are there for those who make the effort to dig it out. Blindly accepting what someone else tells you is not advisable without checking it out in the manuscripts. Your soul is too important. If what you have been taught is true, then it will line up with the manuscripts. If it does not agree with the manuscripts, you have bought into the traditions of men and the blessings of God will not follow you. How can you really know what is really true? The answer is very simple, go to the manuscripts and check it out for yourself. By doing this consistently you will find many things that our Father would have us know about living up to our full potential.

45. QUESTION: Aren't Christians supposed to forgive everybody, no matter what they do to you?

ANSWER: I'm glad you asked. Many Christians and non-Christians wrongly believe that a Christian has to forgive no matter what the circumstances. Now before you get upset with the messenger, let's look at what the Bible has to say for it does not matter what you or I think is true, if it is not in our Father's word. If we go to the first book of the New Testament we find Jesus telling His disciples about forgiveness. **Matthew 18:21** *"Then came Peter to Him and said, Lord, how oft shall my brother sin against me and I forgive him? Till seven times? 22. Jesus saith unto him, I say not unto the, seven times: but, Until seventy times seven."* After reading this, most would say "see I told you so." Now if that was all the information we had, I would agree with you. Before we decide too quickly, let's go to **Luke 17:3** *"Take heed to yourselves: 'If thy brother trespass against thee, rebuke him and if he repent, forgive him. 4. And if he trespass against thee seven times in a day and seven times in a day turn again to thee, saying, I repent; thou salt for give him."* Here we see the forgiveness has a condition attached to it. Jesus is saying *"Rebuke him and if he repent forgive him."* Now, if you want to forgive him no matter what, that is up to you. God's way is to rebuke him. In other words use tough love in order that you might really help him by causing him to see the error of his ways. Webster's Dictionary gives the definition of rebuke as: to blame or scold in a sharp way; reprimand. The Greek Dictionary gives the word rebuke as "epitimao" which means censure or admonish; forbid. So we see you are not obligated to forgive a wrong done unless the person is sorry for what they have done and ask for forgiveness. Now, to take this a step further let's go to the last part of the verse in **I John 3:15** *"And ye know that no murderer hath eternal life abiding in him."* Careful study will show that murder in not even forgiven by God in this flesh life. The murderer is to be executed and sent to the real Judge, who is God. As far as I can tell, if someone murders your friend or loved one, you are not obligated to forgive him in this life. I know that most don't teach this, but that's the way it is. Let me ask you, is a person that had done you wrong helped more by forgiving him no matter what or by bringing them up short and making them think about what they have done? We have too many Christians believing they are doing God's will by acting like door mats when someone runs over them. Christians are supposed to be salty. What does salt do when added to food? It changes the flavor for the better. It makes a difference. Christians are not supposed to be milk toast weaklings. Stand up for what is right and make a difference. Christians are not second or third class citizens. They are not doormats to be walked on by abusive people as some churches teach. If you are a Christ man, a Christian, you are a child of the Most High God. So act like it and conduct your life as though you are.

46. QUESTION: What is the unforgivable sin?

ANSWER: This question has been asked many times. To hear many religious leaders, you would think it was divorce, murder or speaking against Jesus. This subject is discussed in several places. We will begin in **Luke 12:8** *"Also I say unto you, Whosoever shall* *confess Me before men, him shall the Son of man also confess before the angels of God: 9. But he that denieth Me before men shall be denied before the angels of God. 11. And when they bring you unto the synagogues and unto magistrates and powers, take ye no thought how or what thing ye shall answer or what ye shall say. 12. For the Holy Spirit shall teach you in the same hour what ye ought to say."* Now let's look at when and where this will take place. **II Thessalonians 2:3** *"Let no man deceive you by any means: for that day shall not come, except there come a falling away first and that man of sin be revealed, the son of perdition. 4. Who opposeth and exalteth himself above all that is called God, or that is worshiped; so that he as God sitteth in the Temple of God, shewing himself that he is God."* Now where do we find the two church types that God was pleased with and the other five He was not pleased with? Speaking to the church of Smyrna: **Revelation 2:9** *"I know thy works and tribulation and poverty (but thou art rich) and I know the blasphemy of them which say they are Jews and are not but are the synagogue of Satan.* **Revelation 3:8** *"I know thy works: behold, I have set before thee an open door and no man can shut it: for thou hast a little strength and hast kept My word and has not denied My name."* So we see in these verses that this will take place when Satan is sitting in the temple of God pretending to be God. The elect of God will be brought before him and allow the Holy Spirit to speak through them. Most of the world will have bought into Satan's lies and worship him. The door that can not be shut or opened is speaking of those people who know God's word well enough that no one can take it away from them. Daniel is referred to in **Matthew 24:15** *"When ye therefore shall see the abomination of desolation, spoken of by Daniel the prophet, stand in the Holy place. (whoso readeth, let him understand:)* This would better read whoso understands what he reads. Moffett correctly translated desolation as desolator. (This changes the meaning from a condition to an entity) This gives us the more clear meaning. When we see the desolator, who is the devil, standing in the temple of God pretending to be God and having the majority of the world believe he is God, we know this is the time and place. Then the Holy Spirit will move on God's elect and they will speak the truth about this fake. When you see this taking place, shortly thereafter the two witnesses shall be killed and come back to life after three days.

When this happens Christ shall return and God's wrath shall come upon those who have worshiped the false Christ. So the answer to your question is quite simple. Only God's elect can commit the unforgivable sin and only at the time and place spoken of in the Bible. The sin is denying the Holy Spirit to speak through a person, who is one of God's elect, when they are brought before anti-Christ acting as though he were God. Now, I will ask you a question, does your church teach what the two church types of Smyrna and Philadelphia taught? If they don't, you will never reach your full potential.

47. QUESTION: Why is it that some people don't seem to be able to see some of the obvious truths in the Bible?

ANSWER: Isaiah 29:10 *"For the LORD hath poured out upon you the spirit of deep sleep and hath closed your eyes: the prophets and your rulers, the seers hath He covered." 11. And the vision of all is become unto you as the words of a book that is sealed, which men deliver to one that is learned, saying, "read this, I pray thee:" and he saith, "I cannot; for it is sealed:" 12. And the book is delivered to him that is not learned, saying, "Read this, I pray thee:" and he saith, "I cannot; for it is sealed:" 13. Wherefore the LORD said, "For as much as this people draw near Me with their mouth, and with their lips do honor Me, but have removed their heart* (mind) *far from Me and their fear* (reverence) *toward Me is taught by the precept of men:"* **Romans 11:8** *(According as it is written, "God hath given them the spirit of slumber, eyes that they should not see and ears that they should not hear") unto this day."* You notice even the preachers and wise men, as well as the unlearned did not understand what was written. Have you ever heard the pastor, of even a large church, tell his congregation, "You don't have to understand the book of Revelation, because you will be gone." Some even say, we are not supposed to understand the Bible. There is one thing about our LORD that always stands out. If you are honest with Him and try to do your part of understanding His Word, He will always help you. If you are more interested in the traditions of men and accept man's words instead of God's, He will help you be blind. This is especially true today. Let's look at **Revelation 3:5** *"He that overcometh, the same shall be clothed in white raiment; and I will not blot out his name out of the book of life, but I will confess his name before My Father and before His angels. 6. He that hath an ear, let him hear* *what the Spirit saith unto the churches. 7. And to the angel of the church in Philadelphia write; 'These things saith He That is Holy, He That is True, He That hath the key of David, He That openeth and no man shutteth and shutteth and no man openeth; 8. I know thy works: behold, I have set before thee an open door and no man can shut it:"* Now pay close attention, the key of David is the ability to see God's truths and have them in your mind or brain. Once you understand what this end time generation is all about, no man can take it from you. He has opened the door of your understanding and no one, not even the devil can take that from you. If you understand about the three heaven and earth ages and the off-spring of Cain living today, you will not be fooled when anti-Christ shows up. They can tattoo 666 all over your body and it will not change your relationship with your Creator. This teaching of a physical mark being put on your forehead or a microchip implanted under your skin is completely in error. I don't doubt that some will attempt to do this, but it has nothing to do with what the manuscripts tell us.

Another reason that some people can't see or hear spiritually, is because God sometimes winks at ignorance. If a person were to actually see and understand and then worship anti-Christ, they are without excuse. If they are blinded and don't really see, this blinding may give them a way of escape. When God's elect stand before anti-Christ and testify against him, those people who were given details by a friend or in a book, may change their minds. When they see it going down just as they were told, but dismissed at the time, the key of David may kick in and the light bulb of truth hits them and they repent and see anti-Christ for what he really is. If you still don't understand, put it on the back burner and let it simmer a while.

48. QUESTION: I am confused, I read in **Ecclesiastes Chapter 5** that the dead know not anything and in **Chapter 12** that the spirit returns to God. My church teaches we are suppose to stay in the grave until Christ returns and then we resurrect and meet Him.

ANSWER: Let's read the portion you mentioned in **Ecclesiastes 9:4** *"For to him that is joined to all the living there is hope: for a living dog is better that a dead lion. 5. For the living know that they shall die: but the dead know not any thing, neither have they any more a reward; for the memory of them is forgotten."* Remember the Book of Ecclesiastes was written to the man who walks under the sun. The man in the flesh body. The lion is king of the jungle when he is alive, but when he dies, a living dog is better. This flesh body is nothing but a piece of meat when the spirit departs. It returns to the dirt from which it came. **Ecclesiastes 12:7** *"Then shall the dust return to the earth as it was: and the spirit shall return unto God who gave it."* One more witness and then we will comment and try to put this together for you. **I Corinthians 15:35** *"But some man will say, "How are the dead raised up? And with what body do they come?" Verse 40. "There are also celestial* (heavenly spiritual) *bodies and bodies terrestrial:*(earthly flesh) *but the glory of the celestial is one and the glory of the terrestrial is another."* The celestial realm is in a different dimension. The Bible tells us we cannot see God and live. A better translation would be that anyone living in these flesh bodies is unable to see into the dimension of the the the spirit. A person who has passed from this life, immediately is taken in their spirit body into a dimension where they can see the things of the spirit, including God. All of us are made up of spirit, soul and body when we are born into this world. Your spirit being, which is the real you, stays within the physical body as long as your body is alive. The spirit is the intellect of the soul and they remain together. So the answer to your question is there are two different dimensions. Now let's go and find where God through Paul, does not want us to be ignorant regarding where the dead are. **I Thessalonians 4:13** *"But I would not have you to be ignorant, brethren, concerning them which are asleep, that ye sorrow not, even as others which have no hope."* I don't want you to be ignorant or fearful about your loved ones who have died. A funeral where the people don't know the Lord is a sad thing indeed, because they have no hope. *14. "For if we believe that Jesus died and rose again, even so them also which sleep in Jesus will God bring with Him."* For believers know that just as Jesus died and rose again, we will also return with God when He returns, because at the occasion of death we joined Him and will be with Him until that day. *15. "For this we say unto you by the word of the Lord, that we which are alive and remain unto the coming of the Lord, shall not prevent them which are asleep."* We, who have not died when the Lord returns can not keep those who have died from coming back with him, because they are already with Him. We can not prevent something from happening that has already happened. *16. "For the Lord Himself shall*

161

descend from heaven with a shout, with the voice of the archangel and with the trump of God and the dead in Christ shall rise first: 17. Then we which are alive and remain shall be caught up together with them in the clouds, to meet the Lord in the air: and so shall we ever be with the Lord." The Lord descends from heaven with the trump. Let's be sure which of the trumps He is talking about. **I Corinthians 15:52** *"In a moment, in the twinkling of an eye, at the last trump: for the trumpet shall sound and the dead shall be raised incorruptible and we shall be changed."* Now which trump did it say? How many trumps are there? There are seven trumps in the great Book of Revelation and the authentic Christ returns at the seventh and last trump. As discussed in an earlier question, the word air is not atmosphere, but your spirit life body. No one is going to go into outer space or float around in these flesh bodies for even a few seconds, much less forever. **I Corinthians 15:53** *"For this corruptible must put on in-corruption and this mortal shall have put on immortality, then shall be brought to pass the saying that is written, "Death is swallowed up in victory." 55. O death, where is thy sting: O grave, where is thy victory."* These mortal bodies are corruptible and in order to live forever with God, we must be changed into our in-corruptible spiritual bodies. Why would anyone want to hang on to these flesh bodies? They get sick, they wear out and get old and just won't last very long. Mortal means; liable to die or the ability to die. If we remain in our mortal flesh bodies, we always have the ability to die. If we put on immortality we will be able to live forever with our Lord in the third heaven and earth age. By the way, these verses in **I Thessalonians** are where the rapture believers base a lot of their doctrine. The problem is they skip **Verse 13** where we find the subject and object, which is where are the dead. Their favorite part is **Verse 17.** *"Then we which are alive and remain shall be caught up together with them in the clouds, to meet the Lord in the air: and so shall we ever be with the Lord."* The problem is "caught up" is from the root number 138 in the Strong's Concordance with the meaning: to take for oneself, to prefer, to choose. And the word air is number 109 aer with the meaning: to breathe unconsciously or our spirit life body. Since we are discussing the Lord's return, let's go to **II Thessalonians 2:3** *"Let no man deceive you by any means: for that day shall not come, except there come a falling away first* *and that man of sin be revealed, the son of perdition. 4. Who opposeth and exalteth himself above all that is called God, or that is worshiped; so that he as God sitteth in the Temple of God, shewing himself that he is God."* Did you notice that Christ will not return until after anti-Christ is here and exalting himself as God. Anti-Christ comes at the sixth seal, the sixth trump, and the sixth vial. When he is sitting in the Temple of God playing God, is the time and place when God's elect will be brought before him and allow the Holy Spirit to speak through them in that cloven tongue that everyone on the face of the earth will understand. Let's read again, **Verse 3.** *"Let no man deceive you by any means: for that day shall not come, except there come a falling away first and that man of sin be revealed, the son of perdition."* Have you been deceived into falling for this carefully orchestrated plot to fool the world? The Bible tells us in **Mark 13:23 "But take ye heed: behold, I have foretold you all things."** Did you catch that, "take heed," listen up, pay close attention, I have told you all you need to know. You don't need a modern day prophet to give you some final instructions. Don't be deceived by these slick preachers, passing themselves off as God's anointed that spend most of their time begging for money. Don't be deceived by well written books that play on people's fear of these end times. Don't be deceived by anyone taking scriptures out of context and telling you this is talking about the rapture. Don't foolishly take anyone's word who is not a scholar of the manuscripts, especially when what they have written about won't hold up under the light of the manuscripts. It does not matter if what they have written has sold millions of copies, it does not change the facts laid out in the Bible that totally disagree with this dangerous doctrine. Just because some people have scales on their eyes, does not mean you have to be blind. It is against my nature to be so blunt, but it is time to stop playing church and following unsound, false teaching.

49. QUESTION: In the book of Ezekiel there is a parable about dry bones. Can you tell me what that is about.

ANSWER: Let's go to **Ezekiel 37** and quote the scriptures that tell us in parable form where the world is today and what is needed to fix the problems. We will begin in **Verse 1** *"The hand of the LORD was upon me and carried me out in the spirit of the LORD and set me down in the midst of the valley which was full of bones. 2. And* *caused me to pass by them round about: and behold, there were very many in the open valley; and lo, they were very dry. 3. And He said unto me, Son of man, can these bones live? And I answered, O LORD GOD, Thou knowest."* Ezekiel is telling us God allowed him to see the condition of the world in the last days of this earth age. He saw many spiritually dead people. It appeared to him they were hopeless. *4. "Again He said unto me, Prophesy upon these bones and say unto them* (teach these spiritually dead people) *O ye dry bones, hear the word of the LORD."* Ezekiel is telling us that God told him to teach these spiritually dead people the truth about His Word. *Revelation 19:13 "And His name is called The Word of God"* Now back to *Ezekiel 37:5 "Thus saith the LORD GOD unto these bones; Behold I will cause breathe to enter into you and ye shall live."* (The LORD GOD said unto these spiritually dead, it is possible for you to live.) *6. "And I will lay sinews upon you and will bring up flesh upon you and cover you with skin and put breath in you and ye shall live and ye shall know that I am the LORD. 7. So I prophesied* (I taught) *as I was commanded; and as I prophesied,* (I taught) *there was a noise and behold a shaking and the bones came together, bone to his bone."* Ezekiel is telling us that even though it looked hopeless, I did as I was told to do. I started teaching these spiritually dead people about the powerful Word of God; and it caused a stirring within the people. This does not happen all at once, but a little at a time. Here a little, there a little, line upon line, precept upon precept. *8. And when I beheld, lo, the sinews and the flesh came up upon them and the skin covered them above: but there was no breath in them. 9. Then said He unto me, Prophesy unto the wind, prophesy, son of man and say to the wind, Thus saith the LORD GOD; Come from the four winds,* (so there is no doubt what generation this message is for, let's go to **Revelation 7:1** *"And after these things I (John) saw four angels standing on the four corners of the earth, holding the four winds of the earth."* John is in the spirit looking at the end of this age.) Now we return and finish the thought in **Ezekiel 37:9** *"O breath and breathe upon these slain, that they may live."* Now go to *James 1:21 "Receive with meekness the en-grafted word, which is able to save your souls. 22. But be ye doers of the word and not hearers only, deceiving your own selves."* Don't read over that! To just hear the Word is to squander the Word, to just hear the Word is to fritter the Word away. If you don't allow the Word to become one with you, you are deceiving yourself. James was talking to people who had already accepted Jesus and yet he is telling them you must become one with Jesus, who is the Word. Pay attention! Don't let that go in one ear and out the other. What does the great book of John tell us? **I John 1:1** *"In the beginning was the Word and the Word was with God and the Word was God. 14. And the Word became flesh and dwelt among us."* **Revelation 19:13** *"And His name is called The Word of God."* Christianity is not a religion it is a way of life. **Hosea 6:6** Tells us: *"For I desired mercy and not sacrifice; and the knowledge of God more than burnt offerings."* God is telling us; I want your love and for you to learn about Me and My ways; this is more important than your religious ceremonies. Christianity is your right of passage into God's Kingdom. Accepting Christ and growing in Him to where you are able to become of service to Him is what is pleasing to Him. He is telling us over and over again; don't be like the unwise virgins, don't be like the dry bones. He is telling those who will hear it, go on to perfection and go on to maturity by learning My Word. Jesus is the way, the light and the only truth for eternal life. Even if you have 20/20 vision and are in total darkness, you can not see. Even if your IQ runs off the charts and you don't get God involved in your life, you are of all men most miserable. If you only give God and His Word lip service, you are stumbling around in darkness. You are like the unwise virgins; you are like the dry bones. You only have a form of Godliness, you are playing church, you are still on milk and you are still a baby. Babies have to have everything done for them. God can not trust His important end time duties to babies. Every time an immature Christian stumps their toe, they cry "Lord, Why did you let this happen to me?" If you are still a babe, then it is time to grow up and take responsibility for yourself. If you know who you are in Christ, then you know God is on His Throne, His arm is not short and His ear is not deaf. There is no reason to whine and carry on like there is no hope. It is time you know that God is building an army in these last days. The question is, are you a part of His army? Or are you part of the problem? Do you know enough of God's Word that you are well aware of what time we are living in and that you have a destiny to help carry out your Father's plans? There is no sin in not knowing, the sin is staying that way by being willingly ignorant.

The ball is in your court, it is up to you, no one will or can do it for you. Stand up, shake yourself and get serious about your relationship with your Creator. Tell Him you love Him everyday; show Him you love Him by putting Him first in your life everyday. Study His Word everyday and you will begin to feel the scales come off your eyes and you will be renewed from the inside out. You will begin to feel the sinews come upon your spirit man, woman or child. You will be aware of your filling out your own spiritual skin. Every one of God's promises has a condition. There are no free rides. You must meet the conditions and do your part.

Let me close this answer with an observation. I probably don't know you personally and you may not know if the many people in your life fit into the category of the unwise virgin or the immature adult. Many are walking around like a bag of dry bones, knowing about salvation, but willingly ignorant of God's mysteries. Here is how you will know if the person sitting in your seat can pass God's litmus test.

- If you don't know about and have a good understanding of the three heaven and earth ages, you have a problem and will never understand the Bible until you do.
- If you don't know about Cain and his off-spring, who are a race of people called Kenites, you have a problem and will be easy prey for anti-Christ when he arrives.
- If you believe that all God requires of you is to remain a baby Christian, you will be very disappointed and never reach the potential God has planned for you.

I know this is blunt and seems to be without feelings toward you or anyone who is ignorant of these things, but time is short and playing church won't get the job done. You might say, "If I don't understand these things, what am I suppose to do? Let's go and see what Jesus says that might help you. **John 9:1** *" And as Jesus passed by, He saw a man which was blind from his birth. 2. And His disciples asked Him, saying, Master, who did sin, this man or his parents that he was born blind?"* This man is symbolic for those of you who have a destiny for God. Jesus is going to give him sight as God can give you eyes to see His truth. **Verse 3.** *Jesus answered, "Neither hath this man sinned, nor his parents: but that the works of God* *should be made manifest in him.*" This example was given to show that even though we may have been spiritually blind from birth, God can give us sight if we soak up His Word and become one with it. Ask the Father in Jesus name to remove the scales from your eyes that you might see. Only God can give sight. Only He can turn on the light, for He is the light. Remember the one with 20/20 vision in a dark place can not see. Have you ever turned on the light in a dark room and seen the roaches run for cover. Something else happens when the spiritual light is turned on. Not only do you begin understanding the deeper things of God, but Satan is exposed just like the critters of the dark. You will no longer be an easy mark for the devil to prey on. When the light is turned on you will be weaned from milk because you will see there is much more to dine on. You will no longer need someone to change your diapers. When the Word shines light for your path, you will not stumble in the dark. You will begin to see the bumps in the road of life and maneuver around them. You will no longer be fearful of the future, because you will know that God is in control. Your life will take on a new meaning with purpose of doing something useful for your Creator. A purpose in life that is bigger than yourself, more important than your job and more fulfilling than the rat race that seems so important to the rest of the world. If we continue to read in John, we find that Jesus took a little clay (from which Adam was formed) and spittle and anointed the blind man's eyes and told him to go wash and when he obeyed he received his sight. Some of you need to pay attention to this. Those who have a future to be of service to God should read with understanding. God is in control and will utilize you just as He made use of the blind man to accomplish His plan. If we read on we find the former blind man's neighbors, friends and especially the religious leaders had a problem with him being able to see. When you begin to see and understand the Word of God from the manuscripts, you may also have a problem with those around you. They may not be able to see what you see. They can not understand the things that have become so clear to you. Don't let this get you down. Don't complain about being able to be used of God. If you have to prepare in secret, so be it. The main thing is to prepare and be about your Father's business. Learn to move on. If you share with another and they reject it, move on, it's not their time. Continue to love and provide for your family. Do those things

167

to make a living that God has provided. Use your talents that He has given you. Be sensitive to His leading from His Word. We are told in **Mark 13:23** *"Behold, I have foretold you all things."* Foretold means He has already told us in His Word. You don't have to wait for a so called modern day prophet to tell you. Man usually gets it wrong anyway. You don't have to wonder what is going to happen; study His Word and you will know what is going to happen. You will know who the players are and what they are going to be doing. When you understand God's Word, it is like having not only your own playbook, but your opponent's playbook as well. You will not only know what you are supposed to do, but what anti-Christ is going to do. People are afraid of the unknown. When you know what "ole pretty boy" is up to before he does it, you no longer have to be afraid. Instead of dreading judgment you can look forward to it. Those who please God will receive rewards at judgment not punishment. Those who have righteous acts will be clothed in beautiful white garments. Those who follow man and his traditions will be deceived by anti-Christ and pray for mountains to fall on them. **Revelation 6:15** *"And the kings of the earth and the great men and the rich men and the chief captains and the mighty men and every bondman and free man, hid themselves in the dens and in the rocks of the mountains; 16. And said to the mountains and rocks, Fall on us and hide us from the face of Him That sitteth on the throne and from the wrath of the Lamb."* If you read carefully the scriptures in the book of Revelations, you will find many people who thought they were following Christ and learned too late they were like the unwise virgins and ended up worshiping Satan. You notice they were people from all walks of life; world leaders, rich men, chief captains of industry along with everyday people. Their social and economic standing had nothing to do with them being deceived. They were told by their religious leaders that they had nothing to worry about and all the while they were stumbling around in the dark of man's traditions. There has never been any doubt as to who wins the battle. God has always been in charge. In the first earth age God's children had never been tested and when they were put to the test of who to serve, many chose Satan. God destroyed that first age and started over with this present age. This time there will be no doubt in God's view as to who is faithful to Him. He has given plenty of opportunity to all of His children to follow Him. Those who allow themselves to be fooled again by Satan will be thrown into the lake of fire with their leader. They will not even be remembered by those who remain. The tried and true will live with the LORD forever.

50. QUESTION: Why is it so important for me to have a Concordance? My church teaches we should only read the Bible.

ANSWER: If you are articulate in the manuscript languages, you probably won't need a Concordance as much as most. But, even if a person is well versed in English, they still require the use of a dictionary from time to time. How many Christians do you know that are fluent in ancient Hebrew and Greek? Do you want to trust your soul to someone who does not know what the Bible really says. You need to be able to check them out for yourself. A wise person should double check everything when their eternal soul is at stake. Most people will investigate all the information available when making a major purchase. An automobile or home is certainly worth checking out before you spend your money. The most important thing you have is your yourself, your spirit, soul and body. I hope you will check everything written in this book for yourself to be sure this writer is not leading you astray. Sometimes the translators got it wrong as we have witnessed in several places corrected in this writing. The Strong's Exhaustive Concordance is the best, least expensive way for anyone to check out the words written in the King James Bible. It is a must for the serious student.

51. QUESTION: Where is the Ark of the Covenant? Many people think it is in this place or that. There was even a movie made showing it was found.

ANSWER: Like most things, we should go to the Bible to find the answer. **Revelation 11:19** *"And the Temple of God was opened in heaven and there was seen in His Temple the ark of His testament:"* Case closed, you either believe the Bible or you don't. What this question really exposes is the fact that people would rather believe a hyped-up movie production or show on the History Channel rather than believing the Word of God.

52. QUESTION: Where did the modern day "Altar Call" come from? I have not been able to find it in the Bible.

ANSWER: That is because it is not in the Bible. This is another of man's traditions that we accept as scriptural. There are denominations that measure their success on how many people come down the aisle after a sermon. Some pastors' income is based on their ability to get people out of their seats. There is nothing wrong with something that truly brings a person to accept Christ. Many people have come to the Lord after an Evangelist came to town. Salvation is an Evangelist's calling. A pastor on the other hand is there to feed the flock on a regular basis. When he or she preaches a salvation message week after week and relies on music and psychology, many times the experience is not real, in that the person returns to their old ways in a short time. There was no altar call when the thief on the cross, next to Jesus, observed what was taking place and ask that Jesus remember him. There was no altar call when Saul was struck blind on the road to Damascus. Jesus said, follow Me when He recruited His disciples. In this writers opinion, if the Word of God is taught Chapter by Chapter and verse by verse with understanding, by a God called servant of God, there would be more true conversions, healing, needs met and people growing up and maturing. Instead of the church having to have bingo games, to get people to come to church, they will have to build a bigger church when the congregation is fed the Word of God.

53. QUESTION: Is suicide unforgivable? I have a friend that took his own life and I have always wondered about this.

ANSWER: Only God can make that call. Only God knows all the facts in a person's life. The chemical imbalance we live with today can cause people to have all sorts of health issues and suicide could be one of them. Brain tumors putting pressure on the brain can be the cause for someone taking their own life. Marital problems, money problems can overwhelm some people to the point, they don't know what they are doing. In God's eyes suicide is murder and one place in the New Testament that addresses this is **I John 3:15** *"Whosoever hateth his brother is a murderer: and ye know that no murderer hath eternal life abiding in him."* It did not say this was unforgivable. Since the person took his own life, he is no longer living in his flesh body. *"To be absent from the body and to be present with the Lord."* **II Corinthians 5:8** David was guilty of first degree murder when he sent her husband to be killed, to cover up David's adultery with Bathsheba. Yet God forgave Him. We are told there is only one unforgivable sin. **Matthew 12:31** *"Wherefore I say unto you, All manner of sin and blasphemy shall be forgiven unto men: but the blasphemy against the Holy Ghost shall not be forgiven* *unto men. 32. And whosoever speaketh a word against the Son of man, it shall be forgiven him: but whosoever speaketh against the Holy Ghost, it shall not be forgiven Him, neither in this world, neither in the world to come."* If we look up blasphemy in either the Strong's Concordance or in Webster's Dictionary, we find pretty much the same definition: To Vilify: to use abusive or slanderous language about; revile defame to degrade. In this writer's opinion this can only happen at one time and place; and that is for one of God's elect to blaspheme the Holy Spirit when they stand before anti-Christ. This can only be done by someone who knows what is happening and at the last minute switches sides and vilifies the Holy Spirit with abusive, slanderous talk meant to defame and degrade God, trying to find favor with Satan. They will be switching to Satan's side, which will be like a slap in the face of God and this would not be forgivable. Now, do I think this is possible to happen? No way! I do not believe that one of God's elect would turn traitor and follow Satan. I guess we will have to wait and see.

54. QUESTION: Could you give me some examples of what you are talking about when you say some of our English words are used in error or have a different meaning than was translated?

ANSWER: This is a question that many people don't look into and as a result, their knowledge of God's plan is limited. This is why we need a Strong's Concordance. Listed below are some of the words that in many cases have been overlooked or poorly translated in your English Bible. The numbers used are taken from the original Strong's Exhaustive Concordance of the Bible. This work is like a dictionary that takes words back to their original meaning from the language in which they were written.

- **Luke 12:26 "hate"** Greek 3404 **love less**
- **Genesis 3:3 "touch"** Hebrew 5060 **"Naga" to lie with a woman.**
- **Genesis 3:13 "beguiled"** Hebrew 5377 **"nasha" wholly seduced**
- **Deuteronomy 5:17 Thou shalt not "kill" Matthew 19:18 Jesus speaking** Greek 5407 **"phoneuo" thou shalt do no murder**
- **Holy Ghost** should be **"Holy Spirit"**

- **Unicorn** Hebrew 7214 "rem" should be **"wild bull"**
- **Heart** in many cases should be **"Mind"**
- **Poor** in many cases should be **"Humble"**
- **Fear God** has two meanings **"revere God"** should be used in many cases.
- **Love** has at least five different Greek meanings.
- **Genesis 9:22** to uncover your father's nakedness is to have sexual relations with his wife **Leviticus 18**
- **"And"** as used 93 times in the first chapter of **Genesis** is used as a **Polysyndeton:** which means to bind together; each act is emphatic and is to be dwelt upon and considered; there is much more implied than written. 1. Large amount, 2. Much, many 3. More than usual, excessive 4. Many kinds or parts. This same "And" is used many times through the Bible to begin a sentence. You will find it continued to be used in the last and Great Book of Revelation.
- The word **Easter** is not found in the manuscripts.
- Some people use the first chapter of **Matthew** to prove that Joseph had something to do with the birth line of **Jesus.**
- The **Bible** uses **"Figures of Speech, Hebraisms, Symbolism** throughout.
- The **original manuscripts** were all **CAPITOL LETTERS.**
- There was **no punctuation** used in the **original manuscripts.**
- Even though the **New Testament** was **written in Greek** it was written with **a Hebrew mind set.** It was not written in **Classical Greek, but colloquial Greek or Street Greek** as Paul spoke.
- **II Peter 3:8 One day to God is 1000 years** to us.
- **Tree of Life, Rose of Sharon, Bright and Morning Star, Prince of Peace, Melchizedek, Emanuel, Savior, Messiah, Lion of the Tribe of Judah, Yeshua, First Begotten of the Father, Lamb of God, Beloved Son, The Second Adam, The Word of GOD** are some of the names Jesus is called in the Bible.
- Tree of knowledge of good and evil, serpent, dragon, devil, satan, prince of prince of Tyrus, king of Tyrus, morning star, death, lucifer, anointed cherub, adversary, ruler of demons,

fallen angel and others are names and offices used by the devil.

⅄ The **1611 King James Bible** contained **The Apocrypha.**

⅄ All the promises in the **Bible** are conditional, **there are no free rides.**

⅄ **"IF"** is the biggest little word in the **Bible. God always does His part, "if" we do our part.**

⅄ **Selah** occurs seventy-one times in the **Psalms** and three times in **Habakkuk.** Defined as: Pause, stop and reflect on the fact that something that has just been said will be connected to something that will be said.

⅄ **Grandchild:** There is no word for grandchildren in **Hebrew**. The reference is rendered **"son of"** even though there may be several generations between them.

⅄ **He, She, It, Her, Him, His, They, Them:** Greek 846; These are all the same word in Greek. How this word is used determines the translation. The same is true of Hebrew 1931, but more difficult to find.

These are just a few of the many words that can and do cause confusion in the mind of the English reader. As you study your way through the Bible, you will find many more.

55. QUESTION: I have heard you mention the word katabole, what does it mean?

ANSWER: We find the Hebrew term **"katabole"** is used to describe what happened in **Genesis 1:2.** and confirmed by **II Peter 3:6** *"Whereby the world that then was,* (1st age) *being overflowed with water, perished: 7. But the heavens and the earth which are now,* (2nd age) *by the same word are kept in store, reserved unto fire against the day* (3rd age) *of judgment and perdition of ungodly men."* The expression should be rendered **"the disruption or ruin of the world,"** that then was, clearly referring to the condition indicated in that verse. For the earth was not created **"tohu"** or void as we can clearly see in **Isaiah 45:18** *"For thus saith the LORD That created the heavens; God Himself That formed the earth and made it; He hath established it, He created it not in vain, He formed it to be inhabited: "I Am the LORD; and there is none else."* Since this always seems difficult for most people to get their arms around, I want to quote the second verse in **Genesis** again so you can compare the **Isaiah** scripture and the **Genesis** scripture back to back and leave no doubt that God did not create this earth void. **Genesis 1:2** *"And the earth was without form and void; and darkness was upon the face of the deep. And the Spirit of God moved upon the face of the waters."* Either the translators messed up, or more likely unholy hands slipped in and made a change. The change that was made is the Genesis verse was altered (by Kenites) to falsely indicate that God had made this world void and without form instead of showing that God caused **"the disruption or ruin of the first heaven and earth age or world."** People are always asking, "How do you get a first earth age out of **Genesis 1:1?** The answer is so simple a child that has learned to read could figure it out. *"In the beginning God created the heaven and the earth."* Now did that say, He created the earth six thousand years ago? No! There is no time at all indicated. Quite frankly, when an in depth study is done, you will find the earth itself is millions of years old. Rather than God destroying one third of His children, He caused **"the disruption or ruin of the first heaven and earth age or world."** God then created this second heaven and earth age and *"He created it not in vain, He formed it to be inhabited: "I Am the LORD;"* If you still don't get it, It is probably not your time, maybe later.

56. QUESTION: How many Hebrew and Greek words are there?

ANSWER: According to the Strong's Concordance there are 8674 Hebrew words and 5624 Greek words. One scholar noted that Hebrew is much more akin to English than any other language.

57. QUESTION: Are there any surprises coming our way, that the Bible does not tell us about?

ANSWER: Let's quote **Mark 13:23** *"But take ye heed: behold I have foretold you all things."* There are no surprises in truth. If you are surprised about anything, you have overlooked truth. We are talking about the important things at the end of this earth age. We are not talking about what man can come up with. I don't know about you, but I am no longer surprised at anything man does. I don't think they were born that way, they must have learned to be stupid.

58. QUESTION: Why doesn't the Bible talk about dinosaurs? This is one of the reasons some of my College Professors do not believe in God. They say it is obvious they were here and yet there is no mention of them in the Bible.

ANSWER: Job 40:16 *"Lo now, his strength is in his loins and his force is in the navel* (muscles) *of his belly. 17 He moveth his tail like a cedar: the sinews of his bones are as strong pieces of brass; his bones are like bars of iron."* What other creature has a tail as large as a cedar tree? This description fits only the dinosaurs. These huge creatures were in existence in the first earth age and their fossil remains are found in many places around the world. Your College Professors would receive an "F" in their knowledge of the Bible or using common sense.

59. QUESTION: Can you give me the approximate dates in time that the first five books of the Bible were written?

ANSWER: We will give the time period based on the research of E.W. Bullinger. You will note that since Moses was the author of the first five books of the Bible, two of them were written in a year or less. We will do a few more to show the span the Bible covers. The amount of time they cover can be thousands of years. The authorship coincides with the life of the writer.

- **Genesis** .... 4004 BC to 1689 BC
- **Exodus** .... 1635 BC to 1492 BC
- **Leviticus** .... 1490 BC
- **Numbers** .... 1490 BC to1452 BC
- **Deuteronomy** .... 1452 BC
- **Job** .... 1726 BC to 1516 BC
- **Psalms** .... 934 BC to 921 BC
- **Malachi** .... 374 BC
- **Matthew** .... AD 26 to AD 29
- **Revelation** .... AD 95 to AD 97

60. QUESTION: Does the Bible discuss UFO's? I have never heard a preacher talk about them when teaching the Bible. I also viewed a History Channel episode a few years ago and they made mention of using a Strong's Concordance in their research of the Bible.

ANSWER: I also saw the History Channel show. I was about to change the channel when there appeared on the screen a Strong's Concordance just like the one I use. To say the least, this got my attention. Isn't it amazing that Dr. Strong completed his work in 1890 and it has taken all these years and a subject like UFO's to bring attention to his work and the Bible? It must be amusing to our Father to see modern man, with all his knowledge, find more accurate information on this subject in the Bible than anyplace else. As far as I could tell, most of the scripture references used on the show were correct as to referring to what we call UFO's. They are not unidentified as far as God is concerned. He is very familiar with them and they are discussed many times in the Bible. While the so called experts on the show were familiar with some of the scriptures, many of the conclusions they reached were way off base. This subject is very difficult for most Christians to get their arms around. In order to do so, you will have to completely enlarge your vision as to the scope of our Father's universe. Once you make this breakthrough of just how wonderfully supreme God is, then and only then will these scriptures have the light of truth shined on them. When this happens, the same scriptures that confused you and caused doubt as to why they are in the Bible will all of a sudden begin to reinforce your faith. After all, unless you stick your head in the sand and ignore this part of our Father's Word, you will have to deal with it sooner or later. If you keep an open mind and follow the facts, this subject is no different than any other.

Let's look at some scriptures that are absolutely about this subject. The one that most people refer to is found in **Ezekiel 1:4** *"And I looked and behold, a whirlwind came out of the north, a great cloud and a fire infolding itself and a brightness was about it and out of the midst thereof as the color amber, out of the midst of the fire."* The key word is **"amber"** number **2830 "chashmal"** with the meaning **"bronze or polished spectrum metal."** in the Hebrew dictionary. If we look up spectrum in our Webster's Dictionary, we find one of the meanings to be: **"same as electromagnetic spectrum."** Wow! That's kind of space age sounding for something that was written about 484 BC. If you continue to read in Ezekiel, you find without too much difficulty, a pretty good description of what sounds like some of the sightings today. You notice words like : whirlwind, a great cloud and a fire enfolding itself. Keep these words in mind as we look at other places describing these flying objects. **Zechariah 6:1** *"And I turned and lifted up mine eyes and looked and behold there came four chariots out from between two mountains; and the mountains were mountains of brass."* Let's look at a few more before commenting. **II Kings 2:11** *"And it came to pass, as they still*

176

went on and talked, that, behold, there appeared a chariot of fire and horses of fire and parted them both sunder; and Elijah went up by a whirlwind into heaven." Here we have *"chariot of fire"* added to our evidence. Staying with **II Kings 6:17** *"And Elisha prayed and said, LORD, I pray thee, open his eyes, that he may see. And the LORD opened the eyes of the young man; and he saw: and behold, the mountain was full of horses and chariots of fire round about Elisha."* There are others, but that should be enough to make the point that when chariots of fire, horses of fire, whirlwinds, clouds etc. are mentioned in the right context, we must be talking about these vehicles. We must keep in mind that we profit today from seeing and talking about space age type travel. They did not in those days. The best they could do in trying to describe them was to compare them to something they were familiar with. Also, some translations of the language render the word chariot as any form of transportation. It was quite natural for someone living at that time to use words they were familiar with. There have been countless sightings today and all through the ages by too many different people to ignore them and act like they don't exist. The Bible goes into more description on these vehicles in the Great Book of Ezekiel than any other place. We also know the description beginning in **Ezekiel 1:24** is describing **THE LORD GOD HIMSELF. Verse 24.** *"And when they went, I heard the noise of their wings, like the noise of great waters, as the voice of THE ALMIGHTY, the voice of speech, as the noise of an host: when they stood, they let down their wings. 25. And there was a voice from the firmament that was over their heads, when they stood and had let down their wings. 26. And above the firmament that was over their heads was the likeness of a throne, as the appearance of sapphire stone: and upon the likeness of the throne was the likeness as the appearance of a man above it. 27. And I saw as the color of amber, as the appearance of fire round about within it, from the appearance of his loins even upward, and from the appearance of his loins even downward, I saw as it were the appearance of fire and it had brightness round about. 28. As the appearance of the bow that is in the cloud in the day of rain, so was the appearance of the brightness round about. This was the appearance of the likeness of the glory of the LORD. And when I saw it, I fell upon my face and heard a voice of one that spake."* If we continue to read in Chapter

177

2, we will find more evidence that God Himself was aboard this vehicle and He spoke directly with Daniel, instructing him what to do and say to this rebellious people. In **verse 6**. Daniel is told not to be afraid even though he is in the midst of scorpions. Be not afraid of their words, nor dismayed at their looks. In **verse 7.** he is told to speak God's words unto them, whether they will hear or whether they will forbear; for they are most rebellious. **In verse 8.** Daniel is instructed to open his mouth and eat what God gives him. In **verse 9.** It is a scroll that is written on both sides of the parchment. In **Chapter 3:1** *"MOREOVER He said unto me, Son of man, eat that thou findest; eat this roll* (scroll) *and go speak unto the house of Israel. 2. So I opened my mouth and he caused me to eat that roll. 3. And He said unto me, Son of man, cause thy belly to eat and fill thy bowels with this roll that I give thee. Then did I eat it; and it was in my mouth as honey for sweetness."*

Writer's OPINION: What we have here in my opinion is symbolic of what will shortly be happening at the end of this Fig Tree Generation. We know that Satan tries to counterfeit all the important things that God does. You notice, he came out of the north; God's throne is always on the sides of the north. Consequently, I am convinced that some of the sightings we see today are of Satan. The truth is that today no one understands all there is to know about these vehicles, but if you consider yourself a student of God's Word, then you will need to deal with this. It will not go away just because you don't understand it. You also have to know they are no surprise to the One who created them to begin with. We will find in the near future, this type of activity will increase more and more. Some of them in secret with more and more becoming visible. The verses in the first part of the Great Book of Daniel, are given to us to understand today, because we are being shown how we are being sealed with God's Word. We are to eat the book and absorb it into our very being. When we truly begin to see our Father's overall plan, His Word is like honey in our mouth. What did Jesus instruct us to do while He was on earth. **Mark 14:22** *"And as they did eat, Jesus took bread and blessed and brake it and gave to them and said, Take, eat: this is My body."* Remember, this is the one who was the Word that became flesh. What are we to eat?, His Word. How are we sealed in our forehead? By absorbing His Word until we become one with it. This is also a shadow and type of

178

Matthew 24, Mark 13 and Luke 21 which give the details of what will take place when anti-Christ is here. Let me quote something that sums up how the light of truth comes upon us. **"Our eyes are holden that we cannot see things that stare us in the face until the hour arrives when the mind in ripened, then we behold them and the time when we saw them not is like a dream."** Written by: Ralph Waldo Emerson. Don't ever quit. Don't ever stop your search to learn about your Creator. If you stump your toe, shake it off and continue. Don't listen to negative people that don't have a clue as to the time we are living in. You are living in the last generation and God's plans are right on schedule. The saints of old wanted to live at this time, so you make the most of your opportunity.

61. QUESTION: Is there any evidence that some of the "lost tribes" are now in the United States?

ANSWER: E. Raymond Capt, a Biblical Archeologist, in his book, "The Great Seal of The United States" addresses this question. "The theory (generally held in disrepute) that the Lost Tribes of Israel migrated west from the lands of their captivity to settle in western Europe, the Isles in the west and many on to America, the "land in the Wilderness," has in recent years been found by archaeologists to be factual. These amazing findings are based on Assyrian cuneiform tablets identifying the names changes of the Israelites till they became both the "Cimmerians" and the "Scythians. It is common knowledge the the Cimmerians and the Scythians became the Anglo-Saxon, Scadinavian, Germanic, Lombardic, Celtic and kindred peoples. This is the fulfillment of God's promise to Israel: **Jeremiah 31:10** *"Hear the word of the Lord, O ye nations and declare it in the isles afar off and say, He that scattered Israel will gather him and keep him, as a shepherd doth his flock."* Lost Israel being found fulfills yet another Bible prophecy concerning Israel. **II Samuel 7:10** *"Moreover, I will appoint a place for my people Israel and will plant them, that they may dwell in a place of their own and move no more, neither shall the children of wickedness afflict them any more, as before time."* Since the Israelites were then in Palestine, it follows that the "appointed place" had to be somewhere else. This must have been a strange saying to the Israelites, they had a place, they had the land of Palestine. They were established there in peace and power. Nothing seemed less probable than that they should ever move. Yet here was a plain declaration that Israel should be moved to a new place outside of Palestine, from which they should be moved no more.

Another characteristic "mark" whereby Israel could be identified in the latter days is its form of government. **Jeremiah 30:21** *"And their nobles shall be of themselves and their governor shall proceed from the midst of them."* What Jeremiah is prophesying is a nation, of the people, by the people and for the people, a nation in which the people are supreme, a Republic. **Hosea 1:26** *"And I will restore thy judges as at the first and thy counselors as at the beginning: afterward thou shalt be the city of righteousness, the faithful city."* Ancient Israel being a "theocratic" republic, the promise in the passage of Hosea is, that the officers necessary to constitute a republican form of government would be restored and the elective franchise would be free. The people would possess the sovereign right of choosing their own rulers and judges. The Divine right of kings finds no authority here, for the power invested in the people allows for the monarchy, limited or absolute.

Our Pilgrim Fathers called themselves the "Seed of Abraham," "God Servants," "Children of Jacob," "His Chosen;" they followed after the council of Moses, the lawgiver of Israel and in all their undertakings asked for guidance and the blessings of the God of Abraham, Isaac and Jacob. The evidence blazoned on the Great Seal of the United States is that the founders of this nation came from the tribe of Manasseh. The name Manasseh, means forgetfulness and if there has ever been a people forgetful of their past, it is the last, this thirteenth, this Manasseh-Israel people of the United States. However, America, as prophesied of Manasseh, did become the great nation "E. Pluribus Unum" (One Out of Many) and took her place in the appointed time in fulfillment of God's covenant with Abraham, Isaac, Jacob and Joseph." Dr. Arnold Murray has also led many documented archaeological trips and found many ancient Hebrew writings in rock shelters and caves. Dr. Murray interpreted the bat creek stone in Loudon County, Tennessee where the grave of nine Hebrew Priest was found along with two brass bracelets that were dated to the first century AD. This information gives pause to consider the theory that at least some of our Native American tribes are descendants of the tribes of Israel. There are more than a few of the Cherokee Nation that make this claim. There are others as well.

62. QUESTION: I still have a problem with the theory of Satan's seed. My church will not talk about Eve having sex with the devil. it just doesn't seem like a subject that should be discussed in church.

ANSWER: While your statement is not in the form of a question, it is never the less a question that the majority of church goers have either never heard of or they are embarrassed with. We discussed this earlier, but let me address it from a different angle. First of all, if your church is uncomfortable teaching or even talking about something that is in the Bible, I would suggest that your church is "too good" for God. If your church wishes to go on believing that a snake talked a woman into eating an apple, when this has nothing to do with what happened, I feel sorry for them. Let's go listen to God Himself talking: **Genesis 3:*14 "And the LORD God said unto the serpent, because thou hast done this, thou are cursed above all cattle and above every beast of the field; upon thy belly shalt thou go and dust shalt thou eat all the days of thy life. 15. And I will put enmity between thee and the woman; and thy seed and her seed; it shall bruise thy head and thou shalt bruise his heel. 16. Unto the woman he said, I will greatly multiply thy sorrow and thy conception; in sorrow thou shalt bring forth children; and thy desire shall be to thy husband and he shall rule over thee."* Did God just say thy seed? Referring to the serpent who is the devil. Seed refers to children and God is saying Eve's seed, children, off-spring shall bruise the devil's head and deal a death blow to the devil. This is referring to the Great White Throne Judgment and the lake of fire where Satan will be destroyed. God also stated that the serpent's seed, children, off-spring will bruise Eve's descendants, off-spring, Adamic line leading to Jesus. His feet were nailed to the cross. Did you also notice that **verse 16** is talking about conception and that Eve's desire would no longer be toward the serpent, but toward her husband, Adam. The serpent sweet talked Eve into having sex with him and Cain was conceived with the devil as the father.

Now let's look at another verse that nails the fact that Cain was of Satan's seed. **I John 3:8 *"He that committeth sin is of the devil; for the devil sinneth from the beginning. For this purpose the Son of God was manifested, that he might destroy the works of the devil. 10. In this the children of God are manifest and the children of the devil: whosoever doeth not righteousness is not of God, neither he*** *that loveth not his brother. 12. Not as Cain, who was of that wicked one and slew his brother. And wherefore slew he Him? Because his own works were evil and his brother's righteous."* You notice in **verse 10** it talks about the children of God and the children of the devil. In **verse 12** we find Cain named and who his father was. *"Not as Cain, who was of that wicked one and slew his brother."* If you will not allow yourself to accept *"of that wicked one"* being the devil, then you are kidding yourself and accepting man's traditions and denying the Word of God. Let's get another witness, where Jesus has just given the parable of the wheat and tares. His disciples came to Him later in private and ask for an explanation of the parable. **Matthew 13:36** *"Then Jesus sent the multitude away and went into the house and His disciples came unto Him, saying, Declare unto us the parable of the tares of the field. 37. He answered and said unto them, He that soweth the good seed is the Son of man; 38. The field is the world; the good seed are the children of the kingdom, but the tares are the children of the wicked one; 39. The enemy that sowed them is the devil; the harvest is the end of the world; and the reapers are the angels."* Again, did you notice that the tares are the result of the devil sowing his seed and producing children, his off-spring, that are in the earth today. I know it is difficult for many to have their beloved traditions not only questioned, but completely refuted right out of the same Bible that they have been taught from all their lives to believe what amounts to a fairy tale. In **verse 38,** we see that there are two kinds of seed, children, off-spring; those who are born of God and those whose father is the devil. This is a race of people the Bible calls Kenites. And no, I don't know all the reasons most churches are afraid to go down this road of truth, but it does not change the truth. God is opening spiritual eyes today of those who are diligently seeking Him. You have a choice, seek God with all your being or continue to play church. It is too late to play games.

63. QUESTION: I am unable to find the word Bible in the Bible, where does the word come from?

ANSWER: Here is another case of using just English and assuming there is no answer. When we go to the Greek Dictionary and review the word book, we find the numbers 974, 975, 976 Biblos: with the meaning: a scroll of writing; the inner bark of the papyrus plant. In the Hebrew Dictionary we find 5608, 5612 with the meaning: to mark, to inscribe, declare, scribe, shew forth, speak, talk, tell, writer. The word Bible was translated from the Greek Biblos. The Bible as we know it was not a hard bound book, but a series of papyrus scrolls. The original writings had no punctuation and all letters were capitalized. This is the reason that the English translations seem to have a chapter start or end at the wrong place. The punctuation was added to the original Greek and Hebrew and does not always match up with English. This is another reason that we are told to **"study to show ourselves approved."** We have to "rightly divide the Word."

64: QUESTION: Proverbs 31 talks about a king named Lemuel, can you tell me anything about him?

ANSWER: King Solomon was called by six names: Solomon, Jedidiah, Koheleth, Son of Jakeh, Agur and Lemuel. This is a very interesting Proverb. At first blush, it appears to be a mother instructing her son about different aspects of life. When we reach the tenth verse, we find in the manuscripts an acrostic with each letter of the Hebrew alphabet beginning each of the remaining verses. The first verse of the acrostic begins with what would be our A and the next B and C and all of the 22 letters of the Hebrew alphabet ending with the last letter of the Hebrew alphabet. The acrostic cannot be reproduced in English, because the letters of the two alphabets vary in their number, order and equivalents. This is to emphasis the great lessons King Solomon was to learn from his mother, Bathsheba. If we look at the meaning of the name Bathsheba we find: "daughter of the seven." For the deeper student we find this Proverb has a messianic connotation regarding Christ and His Bride. We find the "seven" are the seven thousand of God's elect. The virtuous woman whose price is above rubies whose husband doth safely trust in her is the bride of Christ. Just as King Solomon failed to heed his mother's advise and got mixed up with foreign women, most of the followers of Jesus get mixed up with the cares of this world and commit idolatry. The word virtuous as used in English is limited to one kind of excellence. The meaning of the Hebrew is wider: Hayil: with the meaning: strong in all moral qualities. We will endeavor to quote the entire remaining Proverb and comment from time to time. This writer's prayer is that the reader's spiritual eyes will have any hindering scales removed. If this is your time to understand, you will. **Proverbs 31:10** *"Who can find a virtuous woman? For her price is far above rubies."* Where can we look for one of God's elect? Their value to God is priceless. *11. "The heart of her husband doth safely trust in her, So that he shall have no need of spoil."* God knows He can trust His elect to carry out His plans. *12. "She will do him good and not evil All the days of her life."* They will not be fooled by the evil one and have known all their life that there was more to God's Word. *13. "She seeketh wool and flax and worketh willingly with her hands."* She is always looking for the wool from the Lamb of God and diligently works at earning her linen garments made up of her righteous acts. *14. "She is like the merchants' ships; She bringeth her food from afar."* The elect travel on the sea of people and feed them the Word of God wherever the Lord leads. *15. "She riseth also while it is yet night, And giveth meat to her household And a portion to her maidens."* She seeks God in the early morning and has communion with her Lord and then shares this spiritual food with all that she is led of the Holy Spirit to feed. Remember the famine in the last days is not for food or water, but for the Word of God. *16. "She considereth a field and buyeth it: with the fruit of her hands she planteth a vineyard."* Buy of Me gold tried in the fire is the command of our Lord. The field is the world and the good seed are of God. The fruit are the lives touched by her life. *17. "She girdeth her loins with strength And strengtheneth her arms"* We are commanded to put on the whole armor of God that we might be able to stand in that day of evil. *18. "She perceiveth that her merchandise is good: Her candle goeth not out by night."* She knows that her belief and standing with God are sufficient to make it through the darkest night. *19. "She layeth her hands to the spindle And her hands hold the distaff."* She holds on to Christ who causes her to prosper. *20. "She stretcheth out her hand to the poor; Yea, she reacheth forth her hands to the needy."* She is an extension of the life of Christ and shares the Word of Life to all that are in need. A rich man can be poor in spirit. *21. "She is not afraid of the snow for her household: for all her household are clothed with scarlet."* When the elect come into their own, they are prepared for any and all situations of life because they are clothed by the scarlet blood of the Lamb. *22. "She maketh herself coverings of tapestry: Her clothing is silk and purple."* By her faithful service, she is blessed in all areas of her life. *23. "Her husband is known in the gates, When he sitteth among the elders of the land."* Her Husband, who is Christ, will sit in the judgment seat with His elect and judge the world. *24. "She maketh fine linen and selleth it; And delivereth girdles unto the merchant."* She has enough righteous acts that make up the fine linen that will be worn by God's faithful, to share with even the business community in order that they can put on the armor of God in that day. *25. "Strength and honour are her clothing; And she shall rejoice in time to come."* The elect know in whom they believe and are *"persuaded that He is able to keep that which they have committed unto Him against that day."* The Hebrew even says she shall laugh and rejoice at that time. *26. "She openeth her mouth with wisdom; And in her tongue is the law of kindness."* True wisdom only comes from God and His tongue is a two edged sword, it cuts going in and heals coming out. His judgment is just and true and everyone gets what they deserve. This is the law of kindness. *27. "She looketh well to the ways of her household and eateth not the bread of idleness."* She is not taken with the cares of this life and knows full well where her strength lies. *28." "Her children arise up and call her blessed; Her husband also and he praiseth her."* The spiritual children she has brought to the Lord are thankful that she obeyed God when she ministered to them. Her Husband, who is God, is pleased as well. He created all things for His pleasure and she does please Him. *29. "Many daughters have done virtuously, but thou excellest them all."* The elect were chosen in the first earth age when they fought with God against the devil. They proved themselves then and will do so again when anti-Christ shows up. *30. "Favour is deceitful and beauty is vain: But a woman that feareth the LORD, she shall be praised."* She will not rely on the favor of men or her own beauty to get through life. She knows that only if she reveres God at all times shall she find favor in His eyes. *31. "Give her the fruit of her hands; And let her own works praise her in the gates."* By her faithful works and service that are written in the Book of Life, shall she reap what she has sown and rejoice in it. This Proverb is for the advanced student of God's Word. Age has nothing to do with it, if you have eyes that see. Also, remember the Bride of Christ are all true believers and doers, it has nothing to do with being a man or woman. Even though there are only a few of God's very elect, there will be many from all races, nationalities, positions in families and governments from all over the globe that will be a part of God's Kingdom. Some will have a higher position with Him and rule and reign with Him.

65. QUESTION: Why is Jesus able to die and take my place? Where did the idea of a substitute come from?

ANSWER: You bring up an important question that very few ask about. Let's go all the way back to Genesis, to Cain and Able. Let's begin with a little background regarding Adam. The Dispensation Adam found himself in Eden was very unique and there will be nothing like it until we come to the last Dispensation which will be after the Great White Throne Judgment. In both of these Dispensations there was and will be no sin in the presence of God. The Creator of the Universe, the Giver and Sustainer of all life, was Adam's teacher at first. God revealed Himself and Adam witnessed His ways and acts directly. God actually made Himself known at certain times to Adam. We do not know what all God did for Adam and what He would have done had not the fall taken place. Man to this day still blames Adam and Eve for all our problems. The real truth is, it is not only what Adam did, it is what mankind is. It is impossible to live in these flesh bodies and not fall short and sin. So don't blame Adam for all your problems, just look in the mirror. Up until the fall, man was under probation. At the time of the fall the probation ended. E.W. Bullinger says "man has been dealt with as lost, guilty, ruined, helpless, unclean and undone. All of this is because of what he had done. God gave man a way back to His favor right after the fall." The way was declared to be by substitution, sacrifice and blood. It was by faith that Able brought his substitution, the Sacrificial Lamb to suffer in his place. We know that faith comes only by hearing the Word of God. Able must have heard God's requirements and followed the rules. He then obtained the witness that he was righteous as spoken in **Hebrews 11.4** *"By faith Able offered unto God a more excellent sacrifice than Cain, by which he obtained witness that he was righteous, God testifying of his gifts: and by it he being dead yet speaketh."* God accepted Abel's sacrifice by consuming it with fire from heaven. We find examples of this in **Leviticus 9:24** *"And there came a fire out from before the LORD and consumed upon the Altar the burnt offering and the fat: which when all the people saw, they shouted and fell on their faces."* Other examples may be found in **Psalms 20:3; I Kings 18:38; Judges 6:21.** These are just a few scriptures that show God's acceptance was not by any fire

186

kindled by man on earth. So here we have evidence that God accepted Able's gift by fire from heaven. The fire fell on the substitute instead of the sinner. Neither Cain nor his gift was accepted because it was of the "fruit of the ground" which God had just cursed.**Genesis 3:17** *"cursed is the ground for thy sake."* So in these two, Able and Cain, we see two choices. The way back to God was opened by God and Able followed and obeyed. Cain followed his own way and suffered. There was God's way, which Able adopted; there was the devil's way which Cain fabricated. Bullinger puts it this way.

"One was God's and the other was mans.
One was by faith, the other by works.
One was Christ, the other was religion.
One was by God's grace; the other was by human merit."

So to answer your question, the idea of substitution came from God. Jesus is our sacrificial lamb that is accepted by God. He forgives our sins when we repent and ask for forgiveness. Only God has the power and authority to do this. That is the "why" He can and the "where" it came from. The reason God does this is because He loves His children, which are His creation. We are created in His image and are like Him in many ways. One of which is we would find it difficult to destroy our children. We would go to great lengths to avoid this, even to the point of dying in place of our children to save them. That is what salvation is all about. How foolish the person that turns it down. Yet there are many who do, how sad.

66. QUESTION: What is the significance of the man named Barabbas who the church leaders turned loose so they could crucify Jesus?

ANSWER: This answer will reflect only my opinion since it is difficult to find much information about this man. Having said that, once you understand God's overall plan, the following information should make sense to you. While many people have heard of Barabbas, most don't know what his name means. The name is Aramaic and means "son of a father." Now we know that Jesus is the Son of His Father, God. It is no accident that Barabbas was a son (descendent) of his father the devil. Names are very important, especially in the Bible. As we study the Word of God we find that to know the meaning of a person's name, many times will give insight as to their character. Since there is not a lot of information about Barabbas, we must read between the lines. For me it is not too much of a stretch to understand that this man was a descendant of Cain who was the first murderer. The innocent man, Jesus, was put to death by the church leaders. Barabbas, who was a robber and murderer was guilty and was set free. He was a murderer in a long line of murderers who have been responsible for murdering men of God all through the Bible. When we realize that the high priest and the other church leaders were not legitimate Levitical Priests at all, but descendants of Cain, it is not difficult to understand how Barabbas fit right in with their plan. Let's go to **Matthew 23** and see how the church leaders of that day were led by the off-spring of Cain. Keep in mind this is Jesus doing the scolding. **Verse 27** *"Woe unto you, scribes and Pharisees, hypocrites!"* Notice the exclamation point, Jesus is showing strong emotions as He speaks. In other words He was not whispering or being meek when He spoke. *"For ye are like unto whited sepulchers, which indeed appear beautiful outward, but are within full of dead men's bones, and of all uncleanness."* He is telling these so called church leaders, "you are spiritually dead. *28. "Even so ye also outwardly appear righteous unto men, but within ye are full of hypocrisy and iniquity. 29. Woe unto you, scribes and Pharisees, hypocrites! Because ye build the tombs of the prophets and garnish the sepulchers of the righteous, 30. And say, If we had been in the days of our fathers, we would not have been partakers with them in the blood of the prophets."* Now pay close attention to Jesus words. *31. "Wherefore ye be witnesses unto yourselves, that ye are the children of them which killed the prophets, 32. Fill ye up then the measure of your fathers, 33. Ye serpents, ye generation of vipers, how can ye escape the damnation of hell? 34. Wherefore, behold, I send unto you prophets and wise men and scribes: and some of them ye shall kill and crucify; and some of them shall ye scourge in your synagogues and persecute them from city to city; 35. That upon you may come all the righteous blood shed upon the earth, from the blood of righteous Able unto the blood of Zacharias son of Barachias, whom ye slew between the Temple and the alter."* Did you understand what Jesus just said? Jesus called them the children of them that killed the prophets. To be sure there is no misunderstanding, let's look up the word **"generation."** Going to Webster's, we find: **the act or process**

of producing offspring; procreation. He is telling us that He as God sent prophets all the way through the Bible to warn the people that they were slain by the sons of Cain. This began with Able. Did He say some of the righteous? No, He said all the righteous blood shed upon the earth. If we want to know who He is calling serpents and vipers, we can go to **Revelation 12** and find out these are other names that Satan goes by. In another chapter we discussed where Jesus told Caiaphas, *"you don't know me because you are not of My Father, but your father the devil."* This was the high priest of the church. He is also describing His own scourging and crucifixion that was to take place shortly. So when you look at all the information available and tie in the meaning of the name Barabbas, it is not difficult to assume that Barabbas was a son or descendent of his father, the first murderer. Like I said, the meaning of his name is a very strong clue.

67. QUESTION: In your opinion what is the most important thing a Christian can do to prepare for Christ's return?

OPINION: First, a believer must be well studied in our Father's Word. They must have a real relationship with the Father. These are people who study on a daily basis. They are not playing church once a week. They are not depending on a third person to do their study for them. For you see most people don't know there will be two Christ beings show up calling themselves Jesus. The first will fool the majority of the world into believing he is Jesus. This fraudulent con-man will do many miracles as though he were God. If you are not familiar enough with God's plan, you along with the rest of the world will worship this fake. **Revelation 12:9.** If you do know your Father's plan, you will not be fooled and you will have an opportunity to witness against this "instead of Jesus." This will not be a time for the faint hearted. Friends and family who are convinced this con artist is Jesus will turn against anyone who does not accept him. As the Bible states, father against son, mother against daughter. Those who are fooled by this false Jesus will be ashamed when the true Christ comes on the scene five months after the imposter. This is found in **Revelation 9.**

We can know if the one calling himself Jesus is real or fake by knowing what the prophets have told us. Jesus comes at the seventh or last trump and everyone will know He is LORD. He won't have to tell anyone who He is. Anti-Christ comes at the sixth trump. All of the people that are pushing the rapture theory are using things that happen at the fifth and sixth trump as their reason that the real Jesus is here. Millions of books have been sold proclaiming believers will be taken out when Satan's tribulation is upon the earth. Many pastors are telling their congregation, "You don't have to understand the Bible or the book of Revelation, because you won't be here." While their intentions may be sincere, they are sincerely wrong about one of the most important things in a believer's life. This rapture doctrine is a very cleaver scheme of Satan to fool the masses about who he is. He has fooled most of the church leaders who mean well, but are too busy to study the Father's Word. In so doing, these same leaders are leading their flocks down a false path and both will worship anti-Christ thinking he is Jesus. That is what the Bible says will happen and that is what will happen. This is so sad because all that is needed is knowledge of what the Bible tells us will happen and acting on this knowledge. We are told in church to believe what our denomination tells us and they will get us there. We are told in school in order to be successful you must get a good education. While this is true, the education they want you to get leaves God and His kingdom out of your education. As though God was not the God of church, state, business and all aspects of life. We have some religions that take a piece of wood or metal and form a figure, cover it with gold, call it a god and worship it. There is nothing new about this. Man has done this all through history. Isn't it amazing, that people, sincere people, will worship something that has no life that was made by men? If it wasn't so sad, it would be laughable.

Most people must be indoctrinated at a very early age in order to get them to believe some of the things that are taught by religious leaders. When it comes to religion most people just accept what they are taught. They never go to the trouble to check out their teachers or what their teachers are teaching. It seems that if a person calls themselves Reverend So-N-So, most people just accept what they say as gospel truth. In the first place no one is reverend but God. It is an insult to our Father to call another man reverend, yet it is done all the time. HE and HE alone is worthy of reverence. We can respect someone but to reverence them is an abomination to God.

68. QUESTION: How can I know that I have been saved? What evidence should I look for?

ANSWER: The new life which you and every person needs begins when you accept Jesus Christ as your Saviour. When you know that He made the sacrifice of love as atonement for your sin and accept the Word of God as the rule of your life. When you notice yourself becoming one with His Word, you will also notice that you are being changed from the inside. The ways of the world, which use to be so important, are being replaced by an inner peace that you never knew. You still have problems, but you handle them differently and make more mature decisions. Your priorities are not so selfish and you know that God is in charge. What use to be so important, like being politically correct, now seems foolish, false and untrue. You find yourself with a deep desire to learn all you can about your Creator. As you learn, you are amazed at how intelligent God is and compared with man's wisdom, there is no contest. You will also find that when you think about or are asked by a friend about death you are no longer afraid. "When you come to the last hour of life and the turbulent waters splash at your feet; when the shadows of the night of death begin to gather and the sun of life is setting and the chilling damp of the grave reaches our brow and the bell of Eternity begins to toll the solemn requiem of the soul—if you have this Salvation, this life hid with God in Christ Jesus, you will be happy and safe." (author of the last quotation is unknown to this writer)

69. QUESTION: Why is Jesus not taken seriously by most of the world when He paid the ultimate price. Is it the same reason that man always has a problem with something new?

ANSWER & OPINION: Jesus is special in that He was written about long before He came to earth in the flesh. David gave the exact details of Him hanging on the cross, a thousand years before it happened. You do however bring up an interesting point, in that most all extraordinary people and their ideas were not accepted at first. Harry Atwood, in his book, "OUR REPUBLIC" addresses this topic very well. Taken from Atwood's book: "The people of all ages have quite generally failed to recognize the merit of the work of the benefactors of the race and the prophets of their time..

⊀ Bell was laughed at for discovering the telephone.

⅄   Westinghouse was humiliated for discovering the air-brake.

⅄   Columbus was persecuted for discovering a new world.

⅄   They made a wandering pilgrim of Confucius in China.

⅄   They gave Socrates the cup of hemlock for philosophy that is now taught in Universities.

⅄   They crucified Christ, who came to lead the way and set the standard of right living for all mankind.

The fact our republic has not worked perfectly is not the fault of the system but the imperfect application. It is by far the best form of government that man is capable of forming. Problems in mathematics are not always worked correctly, but it is not the fault of the digits. It is the fault of imperfect application. Words are misspelled but it is not the fault of the alphabet. That belief and worship of the one God works best in one part of the world and the worship of another god works best somewhere else is like saying the same thing about the clock, the compass, the alphabet, the Golden Rule, the ten digits number system, the standards of weights and measures or the institution of marriage. Belief in the one true God and adherence to His Word will bring blessings and prosperity in darkest Africa, densely populated China, intellectual England, communistic Russia, serious Scandinavia, impulsive Mexico or anywhere else in the world." It does not matter if the population is in the millions or limited to the hundreds, God is on His throne, His ear is not deaf and His arm in not short. When we do things His way we are blessed. When we don't we bring calamity upon ourselves."

70. QUESTION: It seems more and more that many of today's preachers are more interested in my money than about me and my family. Is it just me that feels that way?

OPINION: Unfortunately there are many who feel that way. When any preacher spends the majority of their time talking about money he is not a true man of God. You don't want to be in their shoes at judgment for the scriptures tell us that God will judge the preachers first. Let's go to **Ezekiel** and see how our Father feels about these false teachers and prophets. **Ezekiel 22:25** *"There is a conspiracy of her prophets in the midst thereof, like a roaring lion ravening the prey; they have devoured souls; they have taken the treasure and precious things; they have made her many widows in* *the midst thereof."* Don't just read over these strong words from God who is showing His emotions about false preachers. You notice they devoured souls, not bodies, not flesh. Let's read on and see God's intensity increase. *26. "Her priests have violated My law and have profaned Mine holy things; they have put no difference between the holy and profane, neither have they shewed difference between the unclean and the clean, and have hid their eyes from My Sabbaths and I am profaned among them."* In other words they are not teaching my people truth. They don't even know the difference between what is right and what is politically correct. They have turned my High Sabbath, Passover, into Easter, which is not even in My Word. They have made traditions of men their teaching rather than My Word. *27. "Her princes in the midst thereof are like wolves ravening the prey, to shed blood and to destroy souls, to get dishonest gain."* How many preachers beg for money in the name of God? Jesus told His disciples; take no begging bag with you. Many of these preachers use all kinds of gimmicks to get people to send them money. God is not happy with them and if they don't repent and change their ways, woe unto them. *28. "And her prophets have daubed them with untempered mortar, seeing vanity and divining lies unto them, saying, Thus saith the Lord GOD, when the LORD hath not spoken."* They say "I talked to God today and He told me to tell you to give me a thousand dollars." Wake up! A man of God will not do such a thing. If the man is in the will of God, he will not have to resort to trying to intimidate people to have his needs met. God blesses those who please Him. Any preacher that does these sorts of things is not a man of God. He is a phony, a deceiver, a false prophet and we know that God is not happy with him. If you read carefully you see that God is telling us that these false teachers are daubing the people with untempered mortar, false doctrine that will not sustain them when the going gets rough. They are destroying the souls of innocent people with their selfish money grubbing lies. *29. "The people of the land have used oppression and exercised robbery and have vexed the poor and needy: yea, they have oppressed the stranger wrongfully."* They have oppressed the people. They are robbing even the poor and needy. The biggest robbery that makes people poor is they are not taught the word of God. They get a verse or two a week and are never taught our Father's word, verse, chapter and book at a time. They are taught that they don't have to understand the Bible. "You just listen to me and I will get you there," they say. These guys read a passage or two and then blow hot air for almost an hour. They make us laugh and cry and get chill bumps up our spine, but they don't teach the word of God. Let me tell you that pretty story will not sustain you and you will die a slow spiritual death if you don't get help. Remember what Jesus will tell them at the end of this age. When they say, *"Lord we have cast out devils in your name and we have healed the sick in your name."* And the Bible tells us Jesus will tell them, *"You get out of My sight, I never knew you."* He is telling all those who do such things, you did not love me enough to get into My Word and learn what I wanted you to say and do. You think more of what you think and spend most of your time teaching your words, not Mine. So you get out of My sight! In the next verse we find what God is looking for in His preachers. **30.** *"And I sought for a man among them, that should make up the hedge, and stand in the gap before Me for the land, that I should not destroy it; but I found none."* God is saying I'm looking for someone to teach my people My truth so that they will not be deceived when false teaching is handed out. I'm looking for someone that loves Me and My Word and My people. A man, women or child of God that is not afraid of Satan because they know how he operates and are not fooled by his pretty lies. My true followers will not fall for this fly-a-way doctrine called the rapture. We find that God is against those who teach such things. **Ezekiel 13:20 *"Wherefore thus saith the LORD GOD; Behold, I am against your pillows, wherewith ye there hunt the souls to make them fly and I will tear them from your arms and will let the souls go, even the souls that ye hunt to make them fly."*** God is telling us there will come a time when some people, who are supposed to be church leaders, will cover His outstretched saving arms with their pillow cases of deception to hide His truth and sub-stitute their twisted truth. Revelations tells us that Satan will deceive the whole world when he returns as anti-Christ. He will tell all those misinformed, untaught people to join him, because he has come to fly them out. The only people that will not fall for his lies are those who are sealed with God's word. Those who know what "ole pretty boy" will do before he does it. Those who study the Word for themselves and don't take someone else's word for it. People who know the truth that is written in the book of instruction, the Bible. Have you read it?

Are you ready? We are led to believe that the Bible is hard to understand. Though it does take some effort, it is not difficult if you get your priorities in order and ask God to take the scales off your eyes.

71. QUESTION: I know this may not be a religious question, but it sure does affect our lives. What is your opinion of the Legal and Political Professions today? They seem to do more harm than good at times.

OPINION: Let me start off by quoting something I wrote several years ago. "There is something fundamentally wrong with a system that continues to knowingly put society in harms way in the name of justice. There is something wrong when a society is severely restricted from being able to change a system that the overwhelming majority of the people are sick and tired of. Many of the people you voted to be your representative servants have become your self-serving masters. They put up for sale critical votes to the highest bidder. They look the other way when obvious wrong is done. They wink in the name of sophistication. They laugh behind your back as their ill-gotten gains roll in. They smile sweetly and talk tough. They say all the things you want to hear. But, when push comes to shove, they bargain and compromise you and your children's future in order to go along with their so-called leaders. What is right, what is best is set aside in the name of progress and political correctness."

You can tell who a politician is by the way they vote much better than listening to what they say. National politics today at its very core is being run by socialist. They try to hide the fact that they are socialist by masquerading as liberals. The first thing socialism wants to do is remove God and guns from the people. Without guns the people can't defend themselves. Without the freedom to worship God, all progress is put on hold and a downward spiral begins. Morals decline, crime increases, homosexuality grows rampant and conditions in general grow increasingly worse. They don't want private citizens to own land and property. They want their voice to be the only voice allowed in the media. They are trying to control the economy, religion, education and the political arena by controlling the military and the media. Look at how the major media lies and slants the news toward favoring those who would best serve their socialist and Islamic causes. Most are pawns; a few know exactly what they are doing. Even they don't know who is really pulling their strings. For the most part they just think they are smarter than everyone else. Power is the only tonic that fulfills their cravings. Socialism has never worked anywhere at anytime because it is anti- God. Without the blessings of God no system will last very long. One of the very vital tests that should be applied to prospective candidates as to their fitness is whether or not they understand thoroughly what this form of government is and the stern importance of adhering strictly and literally to it in nation, state, county and city.

So the answer to your question is that politics and the legal profession in themselves are not so much the problem, but some of the politicians and lawyers who abuse the system are the real problem. There are four hidden dynasties controlled by Satan that are alive and well in the earth today. Politics is just one of them. The other three are Education, Economics and Religion. When you get to the hierarchy of any of these four, you will find corruption and abuse of power. Powerful men think they are controlling these areas, when in reality Satan is the one pulling the strings. Let not your heart be fearful, God is in control and will have the last say.

72. QUESTION: I have come to the Lord fairly late in my life. I don't believe I have time to learn enough to be of use to God. Is is possible for someone like me to make it?

ANSWER: Richard Evans said, "Don't let life or your age discourage you. Everyone who got where he is had to begin where he was." Conrad Hilton stated, "Success seems to be connected with action. Successful people keep moving, they make mistakes, but they don't quit." One step at a time, that's all you can do. But it can be more than enough. You might be intimidated by the amount of work involved, but by simply doing things, you can accomplish more than you think. Instead of thinking, I can't possible get everything done in time, just start doing what you can and see where it leads. You will also find that when you get serious about learning about God and His ways, the Holy Spirit will redeem the time and you will be able to accomplish a great deal in a short time. Remember since God led you to Him at this stage in your life, there is enough time for you to learn and accomplish what He wants from you. Charles Kettering said, "You can't have a better tomorrow if you are thinking about yesterday." Stop worrying about all the time you think you have wasted and get started. If the truth be known, God can and will use experiences from your early life to help someone else down the road. You may not have learned them in church, but Christianity is not a religion, it is a way of life. Jim Rohn said, "We must get good at one or two things: Planting in the spring or begging in the fall." And since we seem to be quoting others for this question, Confucius said: "The man who loves his job, never works a day in his life." When you realize that God shaped void that has been in your life is now being filled by God's Word, you will fall in love with the Creator of your soul and all the effort you put forth researching will seem like you are enjoying your favorite hobby. I'm not telling you, it will be a bed of roses, but your whole life will take on new meaning. Most people never give themselves a chance to fulfill their real destiny. The fact you have chosen to accept Christ is the first step, but certainly not the only step. You are on the right track, don't stop, don't quit and don't listen to anyone who tells you that you are too old. If we don't plant, we will never reap and when the people who stand before God at judgment did not take the time to partake of God's harvest by investing time, in His instruction book, they will surely be begging for mercy. You study and do and don't be found wanting. Look forward to judgment for rewards are handed to all those who please God.

73. QUESTION: What do the people who don't believe in God base their beliefs on to think that they can run the world?

OPINION: You would have to ask them that question, but to show how foolish that belief is, let's look at a few examples of their track record. If you look around the planet today, the nations that are successful are basically the Christian nations. Let's look at some of the decisions made by the so called smart folks in this nation. As they have gradually taken God out of our schools, businesses, government and even some churches we find shortsightedness, arrogance, corruption and greed. A downward spiral of the morals of our citizens who don't have a relationship with their Creator is on going. Let's look at the end result of what they thought were brilliant moves. For a country that has "IN GOD WE TRUST" printed on its money, we have slipped a long way down and removed the name of God, from just about everything else. I received this a while back and it demonstrates our U.S. Congress making decisions without prayer and instruction from God.

To The Congress and President of the United States:

1. The U.S. Postal Service was established in 1775. You have had 240 years to get it right and it is broke.
2. Social Security was established in 1935. You have had 80 years to get right and it is broke.
3. Fannie Mae was established in 1938. You have had 77 years to get it right and it is broke.
4. War on Poverty started in 1964. You have had 51 years to get right; Over one trillion of our money is confiscated each year and transferred to "the poor" and they only want more.
5. Medicare and Medicaid were established in 1965. You have had 50 years to get it right and they are broke.
6. Freddie Mac was established in 1970. You have had 45 years to get right and it is broke.
7. The Department of Energy was created in 1977 to lessen our dependence on foreign oil. It has ballooned to 16,000 employees with a budget of $24 billion a year and we import more oil than ever before. You have had 38 years to get it right and it is an abysmal failure.

   You have FAILED !!! in every "government service" you have shoved down our throats while overspending our tax dollars. And you want Americans to believe you can be trusted with a government-run health care system? I won't continue with the remainder of the email, which I have no record of who to give credit, but it clearly demonstrates how our citizens are growing increasingly uneasy about the future of this nation. When the righteous reign the people rejoice. There are not many rejoicing over the state of this nation with Godless socialist calling the shots.

74. QUESTION: What are some of the lessons in recent history that the world is ignoring that strongly indicates that we are closer to the end than many believe?

ANSWER: For this answer, allow me to quote Sebastian Vilar Rodrigez, a Spanish writer, with the following article taken from a Newspaper in Spain. "I walked down the street in Barcelona and suddenly discovered a terrible truth—Europe died in Auschwitz. We killed six million Jews and replaced them with 20 million Muslims.

In Auschwitz we burned a culture, thought, creativity, talent. We destroyed the chosen people, truly chosen, because they produced great and wonderful people who changed the world. The contribution of this people is felt in all areas of life: science, art, international trade and above all, as the conscience of the world. These are the people we burned. And under the pretense of tolerance and because we wanted to prove to ourselves that we were cured of the disease of racism, we opened out gates to 20 million Muslims, who brought us stupidity, ignorance, religious extremism and lack of tolerance, crime and poverty, due to an unwillingness to work and support their families with pride. They have blown up our trains and turned our beautiful Spanish cities into the third world, drowning in filth and crime. Shut up in the apartments they receive free from the government, they plan the murder and destitution of their naive hosts.

And thus, in our misery, we have exchanged culture for fanatical hatred, creative skill for destructive skill, intelligence for backwardness and superstition. We have exchanged the pursuit of peace of the Jews of Europe and their talent for a better future for their children, their determined clinging to life because life is holy, for those who pursue death, for people consumed by the desire for death for themselves and others, for our children and theirs. What a terrible mistake was made by a miserable Europe! A lot of Americans have become so insulated from reality that they imagine America can suffer defeat without any inconvenience to themselves. Recently, the UK debated whether to remove the Holocaust from its school curriculum because it 'offends' the Muslim population which claims it never occurred. It is not removed as yet. However, this is a frightening portent of the fear that is gripping the world and how easily each country is giving in to it. It is now more than sixty years after the Second World War in Europe ended. This post is being sent as a memorial chain, in memory of the six million Jews, twenty million Russians, ten million Christians and nineteen hundred Catholic priests who were murdered, raped, burned, starved, beaten, experimented on and humiliated. Now, more than ever, with Iran, among others, claiming the Holocaust to be 'a myth,' it is imperative to make sure the world never forgets. How many years will it be before the attack on the World Trade Center 'NEVER HAPPENED' because it offends some Muslim in the United States or Canada? If our Judeo-Christian heritage is offensive to Muslims, we sincerely invite them to pack up and move to Iran, Iraq, Syria or some other Muslim country. Albert Einstein said "The world will not be destroyed by those who do evil, but by those who watch and do nothing." I will continue this answer by quoting a retired Marine who is tired. He plays the coroner on CSI if you watch the show. He also is a Marine Vietnam War Veteran, but does not mention that he had his legs blown off in that war. This should be required reading for every man, woman and child in the United States of America.

"I'm 63 and I'm Tired" by: Robert A. Hall

I'm 63. Except for one semester in college when jobs were scarce and a six-month period when I was between jobs, but job-hunting every day, I've worked hard since I was 18. Despite some health challenges, I still put in 50-hour weeks and haven't called in sick in seven or eight years. I make a good salary, but I didn't inherit my job or my income and I worked to get where I am. Given the economy, there's no retirement in sight and I'm tired. Very tired.

- **I'm tired** of being told that I have to "spread the wealth" to people who don't have my work ethic. I'm tired of being told the government will take the money I earned, by force if necessary and give it to people too lazy to earn it.

- **I'm tired** of being told that I have to pay more taxes to "keep people in their homes." Sure, if they lost their jobs or got sick, I'm willing to help. But if they bought McMansions at three times the price of our paid-off, $250,000 condo, on one-third of my salary, then let the left-wing Congress critters who passed Fannie and Freddie and the Community Reinvestment Act that created the bubble can use their own money to help them.

- **I'm tired** of being told how bad America is by left-wing millionaires like Michael Moore, George Soros and Hollywood Entertainers who live in luxury because of the opportunities America provided to them. In thirty years, if they get their way, the United States will have:

1. the economy of Zimbabwe,
2. the freedom of the press of China,
3. the crime and violence of Mexico,
4. the tolerance for Christian people of Iran,

200

5. the freedom of speech of Venezuela.

    I'm tired of being told that Islam is a "Religion of Peace," when every day I can read stories of Muslim men killing their sisters, wives and daughters for their family "honor"; of Muslims rioting over some slight offense; of Muslims murdering Christian and Jews because they aren't 'believers'; of Muslims burning schools for girls; of Muslims stoning teenage rape victims to death for 'adultery'; of Muslims mutilating the genitals of little girls; all in the name of Allah, because the Qur'an and Sharia law tells them to.

    I'm tired of being told that "race doesn't matter" in the post-racial world of Obama, when it's all that matters in affirmation actions jobs, lower college admission and graduations standards for minorities (harming them the most), government contract set-asides, tolerance for the ghetto culture of violence and fatherless children that hurts minorities more than anyone and in the appointment of U.S. Senators from Illinois.

    I think It's very cool that we have a black president and that a black child is doing her homework at the desk where Lincoln wrote the Emancipation Proclamation. I just wish the black president was Condi Rice, or someone who believes more in freedom and the individual and less arrogantly in an all-knowing government.

    I'm tired of being told that out of "tolerance for other cultures" we must not complain when Saudi Arabia uses the money we pay for their oil to fund mosques and madras Islamic schools to preach hate in America, while no American group is allowed to fund a church, synagogue or religious school in Saudi Arabia to teach love and tolerance.

    I'm tired of being told I must lower my living standard to fight global warming, which no one is allowed to debate. My wife and I live in a two-bedroom apartment and carpool together five miles to our jobs. We also own a three-bedroom condo where our daughter and granddaughter live. Our carbon footprint is about 5% of Al Gore's and if you're greener than Gore, you are green enough.

    I'm tired of being told that drug addicts have a disease and I must help support and treat them and pay for the damage they do. Did a giant germ rush out of a dark alley, grab them and stuff white powder up their noses while they tried to fight it off? And I'm tired of harassment from "cool" people treating me like a freak when I tell them I never tried marijuana.

A **I'm tired** of being told of illegal aliens being called "undocumented workers", especially those who aren't working, but living on welfare or crime. What's next? Calling drug dealers, "Undocumented Pharmacists"? And, no, I'm not against Hispanics. Most of them are Catholic and it's been a few hundred years since Catholics wanted to kill me for my religion. I'm willing to fast track citizenship for any Hispanic who can speak English, doesn't have a criminal record and who is self-supporting without family on welfare, or who serves honorably for three years in our military. Those are the kind of citizens we need.

A **I'm tired** of the trashing of our military by latte liberals and journalists, who would never wear the uniform of the Republic themselves, or let their entitlement-handicapped kids near a recruiting station. They and their kids can sit at home, never having to make split-second decisions under life and death circumstances and bad mouth better people than themselves. Do bad things happen in war? You bet. Do our troops sometimes misbehave?" Sure. Does this compare with the atrocities that were the policy of our enemies for the last fifty years and still are? Not even close. So here's a deal for those folks. I'll let myself be subjected to all the humiliation and abuse that was heaped on terrorist at Abu Ghraib or Gitmo, while the critics of our military can be subject to captivity by the Muslims, who tortured and beheaded Daniel Pearl in Pakistan, or the Muslims who tortured and murdered Marine Lt. Col. William Higgins in Lebanon, or the Muslims who ran the blood-spattered Al Qaeda torture rooms our troops found in Iraq, or the Muslims who cut off the heads of school girls in Indonesia because the girls were Christian—then we'll compare notes. British and American soldiers are the only troops in history that civilians came to for help and handouts, instead of hiding from them in fear.

A **I'm tired** of people telling me that their party has a corner on virtue and the other party has a corner on corruption. Read the papers; bums are bipartisan. And I'm tired of people telling me we need bipartisanship. I live in Illinois, where the "Illinois Combine" of Democrats has looted the public treasury for years. Not to mention the tax cheats in Obama's cabinet.

⅄ **I'm tired** of hearing wealthy athletes, entertainers and politicians of both parties talking about "innocent" mistakes, "stupid" mistakes or "youthful" mistakes, when all of us know they think their only mistake was getting caught.

⅄ **Speaking of poor, I'm tired** of people with a sense of entitlement who have air-conditioned homes, color TVs and two cars called poor. The majority of Americans didn't have that in 1970, but we didn't know we were "poor." The poverty pimps have to keep changing the definition of poor to keep the dollars flowing.

⅄ **I'm real tired** of people, rich or poor, who don't take responsibility for their lives and actions. I'm tire of hearing them blame the government or discrimination or big-whatever for their problems. I'm tired of hearing that the Obama's are going on another vacation. This is their fortieth vacation since they moved into the White House seven years ago. Enough already!

⅄ **Yes, I'm tired,** but I'm also glad to be 63, mostly because I'm not going to have to see the world these people are making. I'm just sorry for my granddaughter.

Robert A. Hall is a Marine Vietnam Veteran who served five terms in the Massachusetts State Senate.

This writer has included the letters of frustration by Mr. Sebastian Vilar Rodrigez, of Spain and Mr. Robert A. Hall, of the United States, to illustrate the world wide concern and fear that is growing in the world today. Let not your heart be troubled, God is still in charge and the Omega point is drawing closer with each passing day. We are in the final stages of the Fig Tree Generation.

75. QUESTION: In some of your other books, you have come down strongly about saying there will be no rapture. Are there any others who also believe this to be true? The reason I am asking is that a lot of the material in most Christian Book Stores definitely teaches there will be a rapture.

ANSWER: I will take part of this answer from one of my other books, "The Fig Tree Generation," and quote myself. Some of this will repeat what has already been talked about in previous Myths and Questions, but this subject is too important to leave any stone unturned.

From **"The Fig Tree Generation"** Chapter 9 Rapture

"The rapture doctrine has become a tradition in some church families and is one of the most controversial subjects believed by many Christians to be actual fact. **This is one tradition that is not harmless.** This is one teaching if believed and followed through to the end will cause one to worship antichrist. I know that this is a very touchy subject with some of you. Rapture is your security blanket. Rapture is your escape hatch. Books endorsing the rapture doctrine make up a large percentage of sales in Christian book stores. If you firmly believe in the rapture, I still love you and want you to know that I was once in your camp. I could quote all those scriptures that certainly meant this doctrine was sound. Dave MacPherson states in his book about the rapture theory: **"The Incredible Cover-Up"** "Like the kid with the red hair, many things have a traceable origin." A Fruit tree does indeed have a root and if you want to understand the fruit, you must find and look at the root. **Romans 11:6** (ASV) says that *"if the root is holy, so are the branches."* And it follows that the fruit on such branches is also holy. Sure we're fruit inspectors. But how many of us are root inspectors?" His book is put out by Omega. Before we go any further let me state for the record what most people believe with regard to what is called "rapture."

The second coming of Christ is in two stages. First He comes for the saints and then later He comes back with the saints. The day of Christ is the first stage and the day of the Lord is the second stage. The rapture is the first stage, when Christ comes for the Church. The second stage is when He returns in judgment. There are some variations depending on who you are talking to, but this description satisfies most people.

Now let me quote from "The Incredible Cover-Up" with regard to what was taught concerning the Second Advent up until the second quarter of the nineteenth century.

1. The approaching Advent of Christ to this world will be visible, personal and glorious.

2. Believers who survive till the Advent will be transfigured and translated to meet the approaching Lord, together with the saints. Immediately following this, Antichrist and his allies will be slain.

3. No distinction was made between the Coming of our Lord, and His Appearing, Revelation and Day, because these were all held to be synonymous, or at least related, terms, signifying always the one Advent in the glory at the beginning of the Messianic Kingdom."

We have not listed all of the points that are made in his book, but feel it is important to insert two more.

4. "Whilst the Coming of Christ, is the true and proper hope of the church in every generation, it is nevertheless conditioned by the prior fulfillment of certain signs or events of the history of the Kingdom of God: the gospel has first to be preached to all nations; the Apostasy and the Man of Sin be revealed and the Great Tribulation come to pass. Then shall the Lord come.

5. Hence Christians of that generation will be exposed to the final affliction under Antichrist."

He closes this with these words.

6. "Such is a fair statement of the fundamentals of pre-millennialism as it has obtained since the close of the Apostolic Age. There have been differences of opinion on details and subsidiary points, but the main outline is as I have given it."

An early Brethren scholar, Samuel P. Tregelles stated "belief in the secret pre-trib rapture originated about the year 1832. (actually 1830) In his book "The Hope of Christ's Second Coming" written in 1864 he writes: "I am not aware that there was any definite teaching that there would be a secret rapture of the Church at a secret coming, until this was given forth as an "utterance" in Mr. Irving's Church, from what was there received as being the voice of the Spirit. It came not from Holy Scripture, but from that which falsely pretended to be the Spirit of God, while not owning the true doctrines of our Lord's incarnation in the same flesh and blood as His Brethren, but without taint of sin. After the opinion of a secret advent had been adopted, many expressions in older writers were regarded as supporting it; in which, however, the word "secret" does not mean unperceived or unknown, but simply secret in point of time. Sometimes from a hymn being altered, writers appear to set forth a secret rapture of which they had never heard or against which they have protested." The above was taken from MacPherson's book as is the following. "Until the second quarter of the nineteenth century, general agreement existed among per-millennial advocates of our Lord's Coming were:

Now listen up, pay close attention to what is said on page 240 of Alexander Reese's book "The Approaching Advent of Christ" "Only in eighteen thirty did a school arise that treats with intolerance and often with contempt, the attitude of those who had looked for Him in the manner just named. Not the slightest respect was paid to a view that had held the field for eighteen hundred years." A comment heard in a London congregation: "This rapture is a curious belief, practically unknown in earlier Church history."

John Nelson Darby was born in November eighteen hundred in London, England. He eventually led a group known as Brethren and touted the rapture doctrine after hearing the dream that Margaret Macdonald had in the year eighteen thirty. There was another man named Irving who taught this same message after hearing the dream.

The only reason for bringing any of this up is for you to see that before eighteen thirty no one ever heard of the rapture doctrine. As stated before without this evil dream, no one had come up with this idea. You see, what you believe is the result of someone hearing the dream and then coming up with the reasons why certain scriptures are supposed to mean rapture.

Let me ask you, do you believe in the rapture because you searched the scriptures and came up with this theory on your own? Be honest, you have bought into this idea based on what some man has written. Just like I did until I checked it out for myself using the manuscripts for evidence, not some demonic dream. I want you to give serious consideration to the following: Satan is a deceiver. He is a con artist. He knows he will have a short time to pull the wool over everybody's eyes when he returns. He knows if he comes back killing people and scaring people, he will deceive no one. But if he comes back looking exactly like you think Jesus should appear and doing good deeds and miracles, he will be able to continue the deception he has already started. Satan also knows that the evil dream he caused this woman in Scotland to have about not having to go through the tribulation will fool most everyone. Especially when he comes back, saying "Come get on my wagon, I've come to fly you out of here. I've come to rapture you out before the tribulation of antichrist." He will make himself seen by the people of the Islam religion as their messiah. Revelations tells us he will deceive the whole world.

He will fool most people so badly, that mother will turn against daughter; son against dad. How can this be? It is really quite simple, either the parent or the son or daughter will accept antichrist as being Christ. When "ole pretty boy" shows up, the one who believes he is the true Christ will go to this look alike Jesus and plead with him and say, "Jesus, my son is a good boy, he just doesn't believe you are Christ, would you help me convince him you are who you say you are?" And he will tell them, "My child I will be glad to help them see the light."

Convenient how this rapture doctrine appeared in the year eighteen thirty; expedient, how this would give this doctrine time to be absorbed into the Christian community and feed a thirsty multitude with a good sounding way to avoid the tribulation. An opportune way to scratch the itching ears of a people who do not check out information as long as it is given by people with the "proper credentials." After all, Satan knows most of the people who call themselves Christians are too busy to study for themselves. There is an old saying among con artist "the bigger the lie, the more they will believe it." All I am saying is, without the evil dream, there would be no rapture doctrine. Without the dream, Hal Lindsey, Tim LeHay and others would not have had the foundation to base their books on. If for no other reason the question begs to be asked, "Why was there no mention of rapture before eighteen thirty?" There was an attempt to say that Darby had mentioned it, but that was found to be false even in his lifetime.

If this is your baby; your belief, I know that what is being said is offensive to you. But, beloved I had rather offend you now and make you mad enough to get into your Father's Word and see for yourself, than see you deceived and follow Satan in ignorance. You don't have to reinvent the wheel, if nothing else, obtain a copy of MacPherson's book, "The Incredible Cover-Up" and receive the benefit of some intensive research by a researcher and journalist who did not know what he would find when he started.

OK, now I want to give you some points that are used by people who have bought into the rapture doctrine theory. When a "rapturest" reads certain scriptures, they say "see, this is another proof of the rapture." Well if you are so convinced it is true, then you shouldn't mind proving it in light of the manuscripts. We are going to look at some of the scriptures that are used to prove this theory is true. To be fair I must warn you that you will have to at least pay attention to what is written. You will have to learn to count again, at least up to seven. You will have to follow subject and object and not pull things out of the atmosphere. If you have already made up your mind; if you are so sure that you know what is going to happen that you are willing to trust your soul to a tradition that was started by a woman in Scotland in the year 1830, then that's your decision.

I'm telling you right now the rapture doctrine could never have been constructed from just reading and studying the Bible. It could only have taken root by having a picture painted in the minds of two preachers who took an evil dream by a sick lady and saw a way to short cut our Fathers' Word and appeal to lazy Bible students in the process.

Let's read the most famous rapture scripture: **I Thessalonians 4:17** *"Then we which are alive and remain, shall be caught up together with them in the clouds to meet the LORD in the air; and so shall we ever be with the LORD."* Hey, that sure sounds like rapture. Now in order to find out what is being discussed, let's back up a few verses and get the subject. What is being talked about did not inaugurate in **verse 17**. Let's begin in **Verse 13.** *"But I would not have you to be ignorant, brethren, concerning them which are asleep,* (those that are dead) *that ye sorrow not, even as others which have no hope."* The subject here is what happens when you die. I don't want you badly informed as to what happens to you when this flesh body dies. Those that don't know the Lord have no hope at this time in their life. I don't want you to be like them. **Verse 14.** *"For if we believe that Jesus died and rose again, even so them also which sleep in Jesus will God bring with Him."* The word *sleep* goes to the Strong's 2738 **taking of rest.** The subject is still death of the physical body, but since we are spirit beings this verse will make more sense if it read: **even so them also which are resting in Jesus will God bring with Him**. If we believe that Jesus died and arose again even so them which are dead in Jesus will God bring with Him when He returns. **15.** *"For this we say unto you by the word of the Lord, that we which are alive and remain unto the coming of the Lord, shall not prevent them which are asleep."* God is telling us

208

right here, when I return you which are alive and still here at My coming shall not keep those who have already gone to be with Me from coming back with Me. They are already there; we can't keep them from coming back with Him. You also notice He said *"alive and remain."* Don't read over that statement. If you are alive you will be here on earth, not floating out in space. Remember **Proverbs 10:30** *"The righteous shall never be removed."* You are going to have to decide whether you are going to believe your Father's word or believe some well dressed, smooth talking, educated in man's traditions, person that has written a best selling book. It does not matter how many books that are written telling you that Christians are going to be raptured; God's Word is always correct. The Word says in **Romans 3:3** *"For what if some did not believe? Shall their unbelief make the faith of God without effect? 4. God forbid: yea, let God be true, but every man a liar."* I plan to choose our Father's Word every time. Back to **Thessalonians 4:16.** *"For the Lord Himself shall descend from heaven with a shout, with the voice of the archangel and with the trump of God: and the dead in Christ shall rise first:"* Many of those who have died and already have their spiritual bodies will appear first with Christ at the trump of God. What trump does Christ return? Christ returns at the last trump, the seventh trump. So there is no doubt when we receive our spiritual bodies when we die, let's go to **Ecclesiastes 12:7** where it is talking about what happens at the occasion of death. *"Then shall the dust return to the earth as it was: and the spirit shall return unto God Who made it."* The Bible just told us when we die our spirit man returns to God Who made it. We are not left in that grave. The body that is in the tomb returns to dust and we no longer have any use for it. Let me say that it does not matter how the body returns to dust. Let's be sure we understand which trump is the last trump. This is overlooked by those who teach and believe that Jesus comes back at the sixth trump to fly them out of here or they believe the last trump is the sixth trump. Go to **I Corinthians 15:52**. *"In a moment, in the twinkling of an eye, at the last trump: for the trumpet shall sound and the dead shall be raised incorruptible and we shall be changed."* How many trumps are there in the book of Revelations? There are seven trumps, Christ returns at the seventh trump. Does anyone show up at the sixth trump? You bet, not only the sixth trump, but the sixth seal and sixth vial. Has your body changed at the sixth trump? No! How are you going to float off in the clouds in your physical body? Now go back to **I Thessalonians 1:17** *"Then we which are alive and remain, shall be caught up together with them in the clouds (Strong's 3507) to meet the Lord in the air: and so shall we ever be with the Lord."* The same word cloud as used here is also used in **Hebrews 12:1** *"Wherefore seeing we also are compassed about with so great a cloud (3509) of witnesses,"* Paul is using the same word (one is the plural form) to tell us about this spiritual group of people that is compassed round about us. The word *"air"* in your Strong's is number **109 "aer"** to breathe unconsciously and change. Number **138 "haireomat"** means "to prefer change." The word "changed" is also number 236 **"allasso," to make different; change.** When you tie this in with **I Corinthians 15:52** *"In a moment, in the twinkling of an eye, at the last trump: for the trumpet shall sound and the dead shall be raised incorruptible and we shall be changed;"* you can get a better understanding of what is happening. This is no per-tribulation rapture; it is at the last trump. Antichrist has already been here and you were either dead and had received your spiritual body or you lived through the sixth trump and shall receive your spiritual body at the seventh trump. Did you get the part in **I Thessalonians 15:17** *"and so shall we ever be with the Lord."* What we just learned is that at the last trump when the true Christ returns we will be changed into our spiritual bodies and we will remain in our spiritual bodies with Christ right here on earth. You are not going to float around in outer space in your flesh body. So if you buy into the idea that you get your spiritual body at the sixth trump and fly off somewhere in the air; you are making it up in your mind. You are listening to poor scholarship. The New Jerusalem is coming down. God is going to set up His Kingdom right here on earth not in the air in outer space.

Let me quote **Revelation 4:1** *"After this I looked and behold, a door was opened in heaven: and the first voice which I heard was as it were of a trumpet talking with me, which said, Come up hither and I will shew thee things which must be hereafter."* This verse is quoted as evidence of rapture??? Let's look and be sure. First the *"I"* that looked is John, it is not the church. John is told to come up to the third dimension of God's Kingdom. In **Verse 2** we find that immediately John was either in his spirit body or God opened his spiritual eyes and he was allowed to see and be in God's presence before the throne of God. In order to understand what is taking place, we have to recognize that there are times in the Bible where a flesh and blood man is allowed to enter the realm of the spirit, which is the real world. Just because someone wants this to say this is talking about the rapture does not make it fact. This is clearly identifying John only.

Let's take a moment and go to **II Kings 6:17** and see an example of a flesh and blood man being able to see into this third dimension of God's Kingdom. To set the stage we find that Elisha and his servant were surrounded by a large army. **Verse 15.** *"And when the servant of the man of God was risen early and gone forth, behold, an host compassed the city both with horses and chariots. And his servant said unto him, "Alas, my master! How shall we do?" 16. And he* (Elisha) *answered, "Fear not: for they that be with us are more than they that be with them."* His servant arose early and saw that they were completely encompassed by an army of men. The servant ran to Elisha and said, master, what shall we do? Seeing his servant's fear; verse **17.** *"And Elisha prayed and said, LORD, I pray thee, open his eyes that he may see. And the LORD opened the eyes of the young man; and he saw: and behold, the mountain was full of horses and chariots of fire round about Elisha."*

The servant was allowed to gaze into the third dimension and I'm sure he was both amazed and reassured that everything was under control. Did Elisha open the servant's eyes? No, Elisha asked God to open his servant's eyes. If Elisha asked God to open his eyes, then Elisha must have had his own eyes already open and knew that God's army was there. Now, one more example is found in **Luke 2:25-30** where we find a man whose name was Simeon, who it was revealed unto him by the Holy Spirit that he should not see death before he had seen the LORD'S Christ. **Verse 27** *"And he (*Simeon) *came by the Spirit into the temple: and when the parents brought in the Child Jesus, to do for Him after the custom of the law, 28. Then took he Him up in his arms and blessed God and said, 29. Lord, now lettest Thou Thy servant depart in peace, according to thy word: 30. For mine eyes have seen Thy salvation. 31. Which Thou hast prepared before the face of all people."* Did you notice this flesh and blood man, Simeon, *"came by the Spirit"* and then held the Child Jesus.

Now back to Revelation, John not only was able to see into this unseen world, but was taken to it. Simeon was taken by the Spirit to witness and partake in a physical event here on earth. John was taken by the Spirit into the LORD'S Day in a spiritual world. Elisha's servant remained in his physical body and was allowed to see into the spiritual world. Here we have three divergent situations where this third dimension of the spiritual world is allowed to be witnessed. When you truly understand this, many scriptures and modern events will make much more sense.

Let's read **Ezekiel 13:20** *"Wherefore thus saith the Lord GOD; Behold, I am against your pillows, wherewith ye there hunt the souls to make them fly and I will tear them from your arms and will let the souls go even the souls that ye hunt to make them fly."* Just reading this in English won't get the job done. God just told us He is against those that hunt His people to make them fly. Careful study will show this verse and preceding verses are pointing out those who cover up the real truth, some through ignorance who are sincere yet use poor scholarship and some who preach for money and promise to save those who pay.

Proverbs 10:30 *"The righteous shall never be removed: But the wicked shall not inhabit the earth."* Don't read over that! Don't try to explain it away! We were just told that the righteous shall never be raptured out of here. We were also told the wicked will be removed from the earth. This will take place at the Great White Throne Judgment.

Now let's go to **Titus 2:13** *"Looking for that blessed hope and the glorious appearing of the great God and our Savior Jesus Christ 14. Who gave Himself for us, that He might redeem us from all iniquity and purify unto Himself a peculiar people, zealous of good works."* Here we have another scripture that rapturest use and declare "See this is talking about the rapture." "Blessed hope" is used many times to represent rapture when in reality it does no such thing. If read carefully it tells us that our blessed hope is the glorious appearing of God and our Savior Jesus Christ. We should already know that happens at the seventh trump.

Let's go to **Matthew 24:36** *"But of that day and hour knoweth no man, no, not the angels of heaven, but My Father only 37. But as the days of Noe* (Noah) *were so shall also the coming of the Son of man be. 38. For as in the days that were before the flood they were* *eating and drinking, marrying and giving in marriage, until the day that Noe entered into the ark, 39. And knew not until the flood came and took them all away; so shall also the coming of the Son of man be. 40. Then shall two be in the field; the one shall be taken and the other left, 41. Two women shall be grinding at the mill; the one shall be taken and the other left."* Now all the rapture people say, "See the one taken is being raptured." That may be what they want it to say, but that is not what it says. We are told it will be as in the days of Noah. Now let me ask you, who was taken and who was left? The corrupt generation was taken away in the flood. They were removed; the earth was cleansed. Who was left? Noah, his family and two of every flesh were left. They were not taken out of the flood; they were kept in the midst of it. Did you listen? The people and animals on the ark were left. The bad guys were taken. Remember the parable of the wheat and tares. Who was taken and who was left? The tares (bad guys) were taken and the wheat (good guys) were left.

The flood that is coming is a flood of lies from Satan. Remember the flood comes out of Satan's mouth. What comes out of a mouth; words, lying words to deceive? Those that believe and follow him will be removed at the Great White Throne Judgment. There is no legitimate argument about this. It is very clear to anyone who is paying attention. Now go to **Matthew 24:13** *"But he that shall endure unto the end, the same shall be saved."* Now did it say he that is taken in the rapture shall be saved; no, *"but he that shall endure unto the end?"* Let's see when the end will be. **Verse 14:** *"And this gospel of the kingdom shall be preached in all the world for a witness unto all nations; and then shall the end come.* **Verse 15.** *When ye therefore shall see the abomination of desolation, spoken of by Daniel the prophet, stand in the holy place, (whoso readeth, let him understand:)"*

In Greek **"he," "she," "her" "him"** and **"it"** are all the same word number 846 in your Strong's Concordance. So the translator must decide which to use depending on how the word falls in the sentence. In the translation of *"standing in the holy place where it ought not"* the word *"it"* was chosen talking about the abomination of desolation. Dr. Moffatt sheds more light and now this secret that God told Daniel to keep quiet about until the end days is now unveiled to those who will receive it. Let's now read **Verse 15** with the proper translation. *"When ye therefore shall see the appalling Horror spoken of by Daniel the prophet, stand in the holy place where 'he' ought not."* So there is no doubt what is being talked about here, go to **II Thessalonians 2:4** *"Who opposeth and exalteth himself above all that is called God, or that is worshipped; so that he as God sitteth in the Temple of God, shewing himself that he is God."* Antichrist will come presenting himself as God in the Temple of God in Jerusalem. The vast majority of the world will believe he is Christ and worship him. For those of you who believe this first Jesus that comes along, you will probably be in the group that will pray for the mountains to fall on you when they realize what a fool you have been. We talked about those taken from the housetop and taken from the field. The subject of those verses and the next one is in verse **11** of **Matthew 24,** *"many false prophets shall rise, and deceive many."* So the real subject is those who are the deceived. Go to **verse 19.** *"And woe unto them that are with child and to them that give suck in those days! 20. But pray ye that your flight be not in winter, neither on the Sabbath day:"* Jesus is coming back for His bride. What will He do when He finds His bride "with child?" For she will have been deceived just like Eve and in this case is nursing along the doctrine of Satan and will be worshiping antichrist. Eve lost her virginity and became "with child" in her flesh body. Those who embrace the rapture doctrine will be "with child" in their spiritual body impregnated by that same ole serpent, but using another disguise. *"But pray ye that your flight be not in winter, neither on the Sabbath day:"* What does this mean? Don't be taken out of season. If you are taken before Christ returns, then you will have followed antichrist. You must understand all of these examples are not literal, they are symbolic. They are not of the flesh but of the spirit. Just as circumcision today is not of the flesh but of the heart and is for both man and woman.

Before we get too far from the first Gospel let's be sure everyone understands what is said in **Matthew 13** beginning with the latter part of **verse 9.** *"and ye shall be brought before rulers and kings for My sake, for a testimony against them. 10. And the gospel must first be published among all nations. 11. But when they shall lead you and deliver you up, take no thought beforehand what ye shall speak, neither do ye premeditate: but whatsoever shall be given you* *in that hour, that speak ye; for it is not ye that speak, but the Holy Spirit."* Let's put these words into understandable verbal communication. This is a message that God's elect will deliver. This message will be spoken directly to anti-Christ with world wide Network coverage. That which will be spoken through these sold out ones will come directly from the Holy Spirit of God. These rulers and kings are Antichrist and his cohorts. These events that will be broadcast around the world will be understood by everyone on the face of the earth regardless of what language they speak or where they are from. There will be enough of God's elect to give God's message enough times that everyone will see and hear and understand the message. There will be no doubt what the message is about. We live in a time when this type of worldwide coverage is already possible.

Now so we know what the Bible has to say about how long antichrist will be here; we know in **Mark 13** He tells us that He has shortened the days. So we know it will not be seven years or even three and one half years. Let's read **Revelation 9** to get a little background on what is taking place. **Verse 3.** *"And there came out of the smoke locusts upon the earth; and unto them was given power, as the scorpions of the earth have power. 4. And it was commanded them that they should not hurt the grass of the earth, neither any green thing, neither any tree; but only those men which have not the seal of God in their foreheads."* Did it say they had permission to destroy or blow up the earth? No, we were just told antichrist, his angels and his followers can't hurt the grass or the trees. They can't hurt God's people that have the truth of God in their heads. They can only hurt those people that do not have the truth of God in their awareness. In other words, like the five foolish virgins, they don't have oil in their vessels. In the next verse we find his bunch can't even kill the foolish ones. **5.** *"And to them it was given that they should not kill them, but that they should be tormented five months: and their torment was as the torment of a scorpion, when he striketh a man."* If we go to the trouble to understand the scorpion; we find it paralyzes his victim by injecting a fluid that dissolves the backbone. Taking this to the spiritual realm; have you ever been paralyzed with fear to the point you could not speak or move? Many times this is referred to as a person with no backbone. So the torment of a scorpion is symbolized to represent the type of suffering that man will experience during this time.

215

Overwhelming fear will be for those who don't have their vessels full of oil or truth. Now, so we may better understand what is being discussed here, let's read **verse 7.** *"And the shapes of the locusts were like unto horses prepared unto battle; and on their heads were as it were crowns like gold and their faces were the faces of men."* Now the mystery is solved. These are not locust or scorpions they are co-harts and followers of anti-Christ looking just like men, because they are men, but capable of supernatural acts to overwhelm those who don't know who or what they are dealing with. When you sell your soul to the devil, he may allow you short term glory or short term gain which will result in long term pain. In **verse 5** and **verse 10** we find the time has been shortened to five months. Before you open your month to argue; let's go to Genesis and get the rest of the story about Noah and the Ark. Didn't Jesus say the only sign He would give us was that it would be the same as in the days of Noah. **Genesis 7:23** *"And Noah only remained alive and they that were with him in the ark. 24. And the waters prevailed upon the earth an hundred and fifty days."* How long is an hundred and fifty days? I believe that figures out to be five months. How long will antichrist lies deceive the people? One hundred and fifty days or five months is the time given in your Bible. From the first book to the last book of the Bible the plan of God is consistent. God's Word is beautiful when the pieces come together as He intended.

I will now touch on another piece of the puzzle that I could have done a chapter on. Many people are telling us that the Temple must be rebuilt in Jerusalem before Jesus can return. I am convinced the Temple for the end time, referred to in the Bible is not a brick and stone physical building, but rather a Temple of lively stones fitly framed together. Remember **1 Corinthians 15:52** tells us at the last trump, the seventh trump, we shall receive our spiritual bodies. Man's gray matter is not sufficient to completely understand exactly what is meant by us having spiritual bodies. This is simply a third dimension where God's kingdom is found. A place where mankind's physical eyes cannot see, but is more real and everlasting than these flesh bodies can ever be. Let's look at a few scriptures that witness to us about this.

Matthew 26:61 *And said, "This fellow* (Jesus) *said, I am able to destroy the Temple of God and to build it in three days."* **John 2:19** *"Jesus answered and said unto them, "Destroy this Temple* *and in three days I will raise it up.* **21.** *But He spake of the Temple of His body."* **I Corinthians 3:16** *"Know ye not that ye are the Temple of God and that the Spirit of God dwelleth in you?"* **II Corinthians 6:16** *"For Ye are the Temple of the living God; as God hath said, "I will dwell in them and walk in them; and I will be their God and they shall be my people."* **Ephesians 2:20** *"And are built upon the foundation of the apostles and prophets, Jesus Christ Himself being the chief corner stone; 21 In Whom all the building fitly framed together growth unto an holy Temple In the Lord. 22. In Whom ye also are builded together for an habitation of God through the Spirit."* **Ephesians 4:16** *"From Whom the whole body fitly joined together and compacted by that which every joint supplieth, according to the effectual working in the measure of every part, maketh increase of the body unto the edifying of itself in love."* **Mark 14:58** *"We heard Him say, "I will destroy this Temple that is made with hands and within three days I will build another made without hands."* And the verse that really tells the whole story; remember John is telling us what he witnessed. **Revelation 21:22** *"And I saw no Temple therein: for the LORD God Almighty and the Lamb are the Temple of it."* Did you really comprehend that statement? *"The LORD God Almighty and the Lamb are the Temple."*

Our Father may cause the Muslim Golden Dome of The Rock to be destroyed to bring about the necessary world events to fulfill prophesy; but to do this in order to build the Temple of the end time is an error in scholarship.

We probably have spent enough time on this for you to at least get an idea that the "Rapture Theory" is no slam dunk. It was never heard of before the year 1830 and only then as the result of an evil dream by a sick lady. Even Margaret Macdonald said she thought the dream was evil. Whatever the scripture you want to quote that you are so sure it is making a legitimate case for rapture; please do yourself a favor and check it out yourself. Put it in the correct context and be sure you know the subject and object. You are an individual, your friends, family, pastor and church will not be with you when you stand before God. If you accept this rapture doctrine to be fact then you will accept the first Jesus that shows up as being Christ. The problem is he will show up at the sixth trump and is a fake. All the world will worship him except those who are well studied in our Father's word. The real Christ will not appear until the seventh trump.

Now, I want to say a word to you Pastors. This is usually what happens when a Pastor has the light of truth shined on the failure of the rapture theory and they truly understand it is a very clever ruse to deceive, not only unstudied Christians, but the entire world. When this has happened and the Pastor begins teaching this newly found truth, some of his or her church will accept it and follow the pastor. Some of his flock will alert your denominational headquarters and you will be called on the carpet. If you have a lot of seniority, you will probably be warned to cease and desist or you will be dismissed. This can be a very difficult decision, especially if you still have children at home. You will loose your salary, your retirement and benefits. It won't be easy, but if you believe **I Corinthians 10:13** and believe what you have been preaching all these years about the faithfulness of God, it will be an easy decision to follow God's truth. If you decide to stay and keep quiet about this, after seeing the truth. You will be of all men most miserable. In the long run, you will loose more than your retirement and standing with your denomination, you will loose your standing with God.

If you still want to hang on to one of Satan's biggest lies, I hope you like the ride, because you won't enjoy the destination.

76. QUESTION: Is there any mention of the people actually offering their children to be burned in sacrifice to a god?

ANSWER: Yes, several places, but we will use **Ezekiel 20:31** *"For when ye offer your gifts, when ye make your sons to pass through the fire, ye pollute yourselves with all your idols, even unto this day: and shall I be inquired of by you, O house of Israel? As I live, saith the Lord God, I will not be inquired of by you. 32. And that which cometh into your mind shall not be at all, that ye say, 'We will be as the heathen, as the families of the countries, to serve wood and stone.'* (Traditions of men) *33. "As I live, saith the Lord God, surely with a mighty hand and with a stretched out arm and with fury poured out, will I rule over you:"* The fire-god Molech was the deity of the children of Ammon and essentially identical with the Moabitish Chemosh. Fire-gods appear to have been common to all the Canaanite, Syrian and Arab tribes, who worshiped the destructive element under an outward symbol, with the most inhuman rites. The brass image of Molech was situated in many places in and around Jerusalem. His face was that of a calf and his hands stretched forth like a man to receive something. The Molech priest kindled the image with fire and then placed their babys into his hands, this sacrificing an innocent to this horrible death. (Taken from Smith's Bible Dictionary by Nelson) As terrible as this was, a form of molecism is being practiced today. In many ways it is even worse because people are being led to worship anti-Christ and be blotted in the lake of fire at the Great White Throne Judgment. This is how dangerous the "Rapture Doctrine" is.

77. QUESTION: If both the Hebrew people and the Muslim people are both descendants of Abraham, other than terrorism by the Muslim, what is the difference in these two races of people?

ANSWER: The global Islamic population is about one billion, two hundred million or twenty percent of the world's population. Islamic people have produced seven Nobel Prize winners. **Literature:** 1988 Najib Mahfooz **Peace:** 1978 Mohamed Anwar El-Sadat * 1990 Elias James Corey * 1994 Yaser Arafat * 1999 Ahmed Zewai **Economics:** Zero **Physics**: Zero **Medicine**: 1960 Peter Brian Medawar * 1998 Ferid Mourad **for a total of seven.**

The Global Jewish population is about fourteen million or about point zero two of the world's population. They have received **a total of one hundred twenty nine** Nobel Prizes: **Literature**: 1910 Paul Heyse 1927 Henri Bergson * 1958 Boris Pasternak * 1966 Shmuel Yosef Agnon 1976 Saul Bellow * 1978 Isaac Bashevis Singer * 1981 Elias Canetti Joseph Brodsky * 1991 Nadine Gordimer World **Peace**: 1911 Alfred Fried 1911 Tobias Michael Carel Asser 1968 Rene Cassin 1973 Henry Kissinger 1978 Menachem Begin 1986 Elie Wiesel 1994 Shimon Peres 1994 Yitzhak Rabin **Physics:** 1905 Adolph Von Baeyer 1906 Henri Moissan 1907 Albert Abraham Michelson 1908 Gabriel Lippmann 1910 Otto Wallach 1915 Richard Willstaetter 1918 Fritz Haber 1921 Albert Einstein 1922 Niels Bohr 1925 James Franck 1925 Gustav Hertz 1943 Gustav Stern 1943 George Charles de Hevesy 1944 Isidor Issac Rabi 1952 Felix Bloch 1954 Max Born 1958 Igor Tamm 1959 Emillo Segre 1960 Donald A. Glaser 1961 Robert Hofstadter 1961 Melvin Calvin 1962 Lev Davidovich Landau 1962 Max Ferdinand Perutz 1965 Richard Phillips Feynman 1965 Julian Schwinger 1969 Murray Gell-Mann 1971 Dennis Gabor 1972

William Howard Stein 1973 Brian David Josephson 1975 Benjamin Mottleson 1976 Burton Richter 1977 Ilya Prigogine 1978 Arno Allan Penzias 1978 Peter L kapitza 1979 Stephen Weinberg 1979 Sheldon Glashow 1979 Herbert Charles Brown 1980 Paul Berg 1980 Walter Gilbert 1981 Roald Hoffmann 1982 Aaron Klug 1985 Albert A. Hauptman 1986 Dubley R. Herschbach 1988 Robert Huber 1988 Leon Lederman 1988 Melvin Schwartz 1988 Jack Steinberger 1989 Sidney Altman 1990 Jerome Friedman 1992 Rudolph Marcus 1995 Martin Perl 2000 Alan J. Heeger **Economics:** 1970 Paul Anthony Samuelson 1971 Simon Kuznets 1972 Kenneth Joseph Arrow 1975 Leonid Kantorovich 1976 Milton Friedman 1978 Herbert A Simon 1980 Lawrence Robert Klein 1985 Franco Modigliani 1987 Robert M. Solow 1990 Merton Miller 1992 Gary Becker 1993 Robert Fogel **Medicine:** 1908 Elie Metchnikoff 1908 Paul Erlich 1914 Robert Barany 1922 Otto Meyerhof 1930 Karl Landsteiner 1931 Otto Warburg 1936 Otto Loewi 1944 Joseph Erianger 1944 Herbert Spencer Gasser 1945 Ernst Boris Chain 1946 Hermann Joseph Muller 1950 Tadeus Reichstein 1952 Selman Abraham Waksman 1953 Hans Krebs 1953 Fritz Albert Lipmann 1958 Joshua Lederberg 1959 Arthur Kornberg 1964 Konrad Bloch 1965 Francois Jacob 1965 Andre Lwoff 1967 George Wald 1968 Marshall W. Nirenberg 1969 Salvador Luria 1970 Julius Axelrod 1970 Sir Bernard Katz 1972 Gerald Maurice Edelman 1975 Howard Martin Temin 1976 Baruch S. blumberg 1977 roselyn Sussman Yalow 1978 Daniel Nathans 1980 Baruj Benacerraf 1984 Cesar Milstein 1985 Joseph L Goldstein 1985 Michael Sturat Brown 1986 Stanley Cohen & Rita Levi-Montalcini 1988 Gertrude Elion 1989 Harold Varmus 1991 Erwin Neher 1991 Bert Sakmann 1993 Richard J. Roberts 1993 Phillip Sharp 1994 Alfred Gilman 1995 Edward B. Lewis .....

Israel is not promoting brain washing children in military training camps, teaching them how to blow themselves up and cause maximum deaths of Hebrew and other non Muslims. The Hebrews don't hijack planes, kill athletes at the Olympics or blow themselves up in German restaurants. There are no Hebrews that have destroyed a church. They don't protest by killing people. They don't neuter their young girls or kill them for adultery when they have been raped. They don't traffic slaves, nor have leaders calling for Jihad and death to all the infidels. The Muslims should consider investing more in standard education and less in blaming Israel for all their problems. Muslims must ask what they do for humankind before they demand that any peoples respect them. Regardless of your feelings about the crisis between Israel and Muslims neighbors, if you believe there is more culpability on Israel's part, the following two sentences really say it all: **"If the Arabs put down their weapons today, there would be no more violence. If the Jews put down their weapons today, there would be no more Israel"** Benjamin Netanyahu. (Nobel Prize facts taken from private email)

So we have a people that make up less than one percent of the Global population producing 129 Nobel Prize winners and a nation with twenty percent of the population that have produced seven. For my part, this is a no-brain, slam dunk decision, a people that follow God are a blessed people and people that follow the devil with a name of Allah are a foolish people. Also, remember **Revelation 2:9** *"I know the blasphemy of them which say they are Jews and are not, but are the synagogue of Satan."* Not everyone that claims to be of Israel is authentic and actually works for the other side. **Jeremiah 24:2** symbolically uses two baskets of figs. One with very good figs and one with very naughty figs which could not be eaten, they were so bad. The good figs are the peoples of Israel which unknowingly inhabit the Christian nations of today. **Jeremiah 24:7** *"And I will give them an heart to know Me, that I am the LORD: and they shall be My People and I will be their God: for they shall return unto Me with their whole heart.* And regarding the bad figs, we go to *Verse* **9.** *"And I will deliver them to be removed into all the kingdoms of the earth for their hurt, to be a reproach and a proverb, a taunt and a curse, in all places whither I shall drive them."* Also, for the serious student, remember the fig tree that Jesus cursed in **Mark 11:14** because it bare no fruit. If you think that God is unfair, you need to continue to study and find that everyone gets what they deserve.

78. QUESTION: Do you consider a prayer to open a session of Congress to be a violation of Church and State?

ANSWER: This nation was founded by men of prayer. Let me share with you what Pastor Joe Wright said when he was asked to open the new session of the Kansas Senate. Everyone was expecting the usual generalities, but this is what they heard: "Heavenly father, we come before you today to ask your forgiveness and to seek you direction and guidance. We know Your Word says, *"Woe to those who call evil good,"* but that is exactly what we have done. We have lost our spiritual equilibrium and reversed our values. We have exploited the poor and called it the lottery. We have rewarded laziness and called it welfare. We have killed our unborn and called it choice. We have shot abortionists and called it justifiable. We have neglected to discipline our children and called it building self-esteem. We have abused power and called it politics. We have coveted our neighbor's possessions and called it ambition. We have polluted the air with profanity and pornography and called it freedom of expression. We have ridiculed the time-honored values of our forefathers and called it enlightenment. Search us, Oh, God and know our hearts today; cleanse us from every sin and set us free." A-men!

The response was immediate. A number of legislators walked out during the prayer in protest. Central Christian Church, Pastor Wright's church, logged more than 5,000 phone calls with only 47 responding negatively. The church is now receiving international requests for copies of this prayer from India, Africa and Korea. If you will take the time to read the Constitution, you will find the subject of your question has absolutely nothing to do with the separation of Church and State.

79. QUESTION: Is it true that the Bible talks about one of the rulers of Russia being killed, his body being burned and buried in lime?

ANSWER and OPINION: Our history books even detail this happening in 1918 when the Romanov family and last Tsar of Russia, Nicholas II and his entire family were held captive and eventually killed, burned and buried in lime by the Bolsheviks. When the four daughters, Grand Duchesses Maria, Olga, Anastasia and Tatiana were found in 1979 their DNA was linked to Prince Phillip, Duke of Edinburgh. Nicholas II was excavated in 1991 and DNA linked him to Grand Duke George Alexandrovich.(still Romanov family) This scarlet thread ties back to the tribe of Judah, the King line of Israel. We find this in **Amos 2:1** *"Thus saith the LORD; for three transgressions of Moab and for four, I will not turn away the punishment thereof; because he burned the bones of the king of Edom into lime: 2. But I will send a fire upon Moab and it shall devour the palaces of Kirioth: and Moab shall die with tumult, with shouting and* *with the sound of the trumpet:"* You notice Moab which is Russia. You notice at the sound of the trumpet God will send fire. That is the seventh trump at the battle of Hamongog and Armageddon discussed earlier in this book.

80. QUESTION: Why did God bless Abraham so much?

ANSWER: If you want to be blessed in your life, following Abraham's example is the best way I know of. Let's look at what Abraham did and how he lived his life. We find God talking and giving the reasons He blessed Abraham in **Genesis 26:5** *"Because that Abraham obeyed My voice and kept My charge, My command-ments, My statutes and My laws."* God lists five things (five is grace) that pleased Him and give Him pleasure. Now that you know, what are you going to do about it? I will make you a promise backed up by the Word of God and He cannot lie, you do these five things and your life will completely change for the better. You will be tested, but you will have peace within and a guaranteed future.

81. QUESTION: Has God ever repented for anything?

ANSWER: The answer to this question surprises most people. The Book of Exodus relates a conversation between God and Moses. God is telling Moses that He regrets He made man because of how sorry they had become. God tells Moses He is going to consume these people and start over with Moses. Moses reminds God of his prom-ises to Abraham and talks God out of destroying the people. **Exodus 32:9** *"And the LORD repented of the evil which He thought to do unto His people."* This is a great example of how much we were cre-ated with the same kind of feelings and emotions as our Creator. He is slow to anger, but He does have a boiling point.

82. QUESTION: Is there any place in the Bible that tells us it is OK to vote. I have a friend who says God does not want us to get involved in politics.

ANSWER: To my knowledge there is no place in the Bible that tells you to vote in a particular election, but the idea of voting is found in **Acts:1:26** *"And they gave forth their lots; and the lot fell on Matthias; and he was numbered with the eleven apostles."* This clearly demonstrates the disciples of Christ voted to replace Judas, who betrayed our Lord. Do you really believe that God does not want us to vote in this country? Do you realize that bad politicians get into office because good people don't vote. Don't you know that bad politicians remain in office because people only listen to what they say and don't check their record to find out what they are really about. We have a mess in Washington today because enough good people did not vote.

83. QUESTION: Why do you think Israel is so important today?

ANSWER: Mount Zion is God's favorite place in the world. Ever since King David captured the area known as Jebus at that time and renamed it Jerusalem, Israel has always been at the forefront of Bible history and prophesy. The Bible tells us to pray for the peace of Jerusalem. Since we have found that many in this nation are actually of Hebrew decent, those with eyes to see and ears to hear know that Israel is God's time table. We can gauge the pulse of the world by keeping a close eye on Israel. With all they have endured, God would have to be for this small nation for they have withstood more adversity than any other nation in the history of the world. I would like to bring in an outside opinion for the remainder of this answer. Some of his speech gives details already covered in earlier questions. Andrew Roberts, a 47 year-old British Historian who regularly appears on British television and radio, is also an award winning writer. **Here is an edited version of a speech he gave to the British Government** at the Friends of Israel Initiative in the British House of Commons on July 19. 2015. "From Morocco to Afghanistan, from the Caspian Sea to Aden, the 5.25 million square miles of territory belonging to members of the Arab League is home to over 330 million people, whereas Israel covers only 8,000 square miles, and is home to seven million citizens, one-fifth of whom are Arabs. The Jews of the Holy Land are thus surrounded by hostile states 650 times their size in territory and 60 times their population; yet their last, best hope of ending two millennia of international persecution - the State of Israel - has somehow survived. When during the Second World War, the island of Malta came through three terrible years of bombardment and destruction, it was rightly awarded the George Medal for bravery. **Today Israel should be awarded a similar decoration for defending democracy,** tolerance and Western values against a murderous onslaught that has lasted 20 times as long. Jerusalem is the site of the Temple of Solomon and Herod. The stones of a palace erected by King David himself are even now being unearthed just outside the walls of Jerusalem. Everything that makes a nation state legitimate -- blood shed, soil tilled, international agreements, argues for Israel's right to exist, yet that is still denied by the Arab League. **For many of their [Arab] governments, which are rich enough to have economically solved the Palestinian refugee problem decades ago,** it is useful to have Israel as a scapegoat to divert attention from the tyranny, failure and corruption of their own regimes. **The tragic truth is that it suits Arab states very well to have the Palestinians endure permanent refugee status;** whenever Israel puts forward workable solutions they are stymied by those whose interests put the destruction of Israel before the genuine well-being of the Palestinians. Both King Abdullah I of Jordan and Anwar Sadat of Egypt were assassinated when they attempted to come to some kind of accommodation with a country that most sane people now accept is not going away."We owe to the Jews," wrote Winston Churchill in 1920, "a system of ethics which, even if it were entirely separated from the supernatural, would be incomparably the most precious possession of mankind, worth in fact the fruits of all wisdom and learning put together."Although they make up less than half of 1% of the world's population, between 1901 and 1950 Jews won 14% of all the Nobel Prizes awarded for literature and science, and between 1951 and 2000 Jews won 32% of the Nobel Prizes for medicine, 32% for physics, 39% for economics and 29% for science. This, despite so many of their greatest intellects dying in the gas chambers. Yet we tend to treat Israel like a leper on the international scene, threatening her with academic boycotts if she builds a separation wall that has so far reduced suicide bombings by 95% over three years. Her Majesty the Queen has been on the throne for 57 years and in that time has undertaken 250 official visits to 129 countries, yet has not yet set foot in Israel. **She has visited 14 Arab countries, so it cannot have been that she wasn't in the region.** After the Holocaust, the Jewish people recognized that they must have their own state, a homeland where they could forever be safe from a repetition of such horrors. **Since then, Israel has had to fight five major wars for her existence.** Radical Islam is never going to accept the concept of an Israeli State, so the struggle is likely to continue for another 60 years, but the Jews know that that is less dangerous than entrusting their security to anyone else. I recently visited Auschwitz-Birkenau. Walking along a line of huts and the railway siding, where their forebears had been worked and starved and beaten and frozen and gassed to death, were a group of Jewish schoolchildren, one of whom was carrying over his shoulder the Israeli flag. It was a moving sight, for it was the sovereign independence represented by that flag which guarantees that the obscenity of genocide will never again befall the Jewish people. No people in history have needed the right to self-defense and legitimacy more than the Jews of Israel, and that is what we in the Friends of Israel Initiative demand here today."

84. QUESTION: Do you know of any world class scientist that called himself a Christian?

ANSWER: I will answer from a witnessed account of a Professor of philosophy class. "Let me explain the problem science has with religion." The atheist professor of philosophy pauses before his class and then asks one of his new students to stand. "You're a Christian, aren't you son?" "Yes sir," the student says. 'So you believe in God?' 'Absolutely' 'Is God good?' 'Sure! God's good.' 'Is God all-powerful? Can God do anything?' 'Yes.' 'Are you good or evil?' 'The Bible says I'm evil.' The professor grins knowingly. 'Aha! The Bible! He considers for a moment. 'Here's one for you. Let's say there's a sick person over here and you can cure him. You can do it. Would you help him? Would you try?' 'Yes sir, I would.' 'So you're good...!' 'I wouldn't say that.' 'But why not say that? You'd help a sick and maimed person if you could. Most of us would if we could. But God doesn't.' The student does not answer, so the professor continues. 'He doesn't, does he? My brother was a Christian who died of cancer, even though he prayed to Jesus to heal him. How is this Jesus good: Can you answer that one?' the professors says. He takes a sip of water from a glass on his desk to give the student time to relax. 'Let's start again, young fella. Is God good?' 'Er..yes,' the student says. 'Is Satan good?' The student doesn't hesitate on this one... 'No' 'then where does Satan come from?' The student falters. 'From God' 'That's right. God made Satan, didn't he? Tell me, son. Is there evil in this world?' Yes, sir.' 'Evil's everywhere, isn't it? And God did make everything, correct' 'Yes.' 'so who created evil?' the professor continued, 'If God created everything, then God created evil, since evil exists and according to the principle that our works define who we are, then God is evil.' Again, the student has no answer. 'Is there sickness? Immorality? Hatred? Ugliness? All these terrible things, do they exist in this world?' The student squirms on his feet. 'Yes' 'so who created them?' The student does not answer again, so the professors repeats his question. 'who created them?' There is still no answer. Suddenly the lecturer breaks away to pace in front of the classroom. The class is mesmerized. 'Tell me,' he continues onto another student. 'Do you believe in Jesus Christ, son?' The student's voice betrays him and cracks. 'Yes, professor, I do.' The old man stops pacing. 'science says you have five senses you use to identify and observe the world around you. Have you ever seen Jesus?' 'No sir. I've never seen Him.' 'Then tell us if you've ever heard your Jesus?' 'No, sir, I have not.' 'Have you ever felt your Jesus, tasted your Jesus or smelt your Jesus? Have you ever had any sensory perception of Jesus Christ, or God for that matter?' 'No, sir, I'm afraid I haven't.' 'Yet you still believe in him?' 'Yes.' 'According to the rules of empirical, testable, demonstrable protocol, science says your God doesn't exist...What do you say to that, son?' 'Nothing,' the student replies.. 'I only have my faith.' 'Yes, faith,' the professor repeats. 'and that is the problem science has with God. There is no evidence, only faith.' The student stands quietly for a moment, before asking a question of His own. 'Professor, is there such thing as heat?' 'Yes.' 'And is there such thing as cold?' 'Yes, son, there's cold too.' ''No sir, there isn't.' the professor turns to face the student, obviously interested. The room suddenly becomes very quiet. The student begins to explain. 'You can have lots of heat, even more heat, super-heat, mega-heat, unlimited heat, white heat, a little heat or no heat, but we don't have anything called cold.' we can hit down to -458 degrees. Every body or object is susceptible to study when it has or transmits energy and heat is what makes a body or matter have or transmit energy..Absolute zero (-458F) is the total absence of heat. You see, sir, cold is only a word we use to describe the absence of heat. We cannot measure cold. Heat we can measure in thermal units because heat is energy. Cold is not the opposite of heat, sir, just the absence of it.' Silence across the room. A pen drops somewhere in the classroom, sounding like a hammer. 'what about darkness, professor. Is there such a thing as darkness?' 'Yes,' the professor replies without hesitation. 'What is night if it isn't darkness?' 'You're wrong again, sir. Darkness is not something; it is the absence of something. You can have low light, normal light, bright light, flashing light, but if you have no light constantly you have nothing and it's called darkness, isn't it? That's the meaning we use to define the word. In reality, darkness isn't. If it were, you would be able to make darkness darker, wouldn't you?' The professor begins to smile at the student in front of him. This will be a good semester. 'So what point are you making, young man?' 'Yes, professor. My point is, your philosophical premise is flawed to start with and so your conclusion must also be flawed." The professor's face cannot hide his surprise this time. 'flawed? Can you explain how?' 'You are working on the premise of duality,' the student explains...'You argue that there is life and then there's death; a good God and a bad God. You are viewing the concept of God as something finite, something we can measure. Sir, science can't even explain a thought. It uses electricity and magnetism, but has never seen, much less fully understood either one. To view death as the opposite of life is to be ignorant of the fact that death cannot exist as a substantive thing. Death is not the opposite of life, just the absence of it. Now tell me, professor. Do you teach your students that they evolved from a monkey?' If you are referring to the natural evolutionary process, young man, yes, of course I do.' 'Have you ever observed evolution with your own eyes, sir?' The professors begins to shake his head, still smiling, as he realizes where the argument is going. A very good semester, indeed. 'Since no one has ever observed the process of evolution at work and cannot even prove that this process is an ongoing endeavor, are you not teaching your opinion, sir? Are you now not a scientist, but a preacher?' The class is in uproar. The student remains silent until the commotion has subsided. 'To continue the point you were making earlier to the other student, let me give you an example of what I mean.' The student looks around the room. 'Is there anyone in the class who has ever seen the professor's brain?' The class breaks out into laughter. 'Is there anyone here who has ever heard the professor's brain, felt the professor's brain, touched or smelt the professor's brain? No one appears to have done so.. So, according to the established rules of empirical, stable, demonstrable protocol, science says that you have no brain, with all due respect, sir. So if science says you have no brain, how can we trust your lectures, sir? Now the room is silent. The professor just stares at the student, his face unreadable. Finally, after what seems an eternity, the old man answers. 'I guess you'll have to take them on faith.' 'Now, you accept that there is faith and in fact, faith exists with life,' the student continues. 'Now, sir, is there such a thing as evil?' 'Now uncertain, the professor responds, 'Of course, there is. We see it Everyday. It is in the daily example of man's inhumanity to man. It is in the multitude of crime and violence everywhere in the world.. These manifestations are nothing else but evil.' To this the student replied, 'Evil does not exist sir, or at least it does not exist unto itself. Evil is simply the absence of God.. It is just like darkness and cold, a word that man has created to describe the absence of God. God did not create evil. Evil is the result of what happens when man does not have God's love present in his heart. It's like the cold that comes when there is no heat or the darkness that comes when there is no light. **The professor sat down.** The student was **Albert Einstein.** He wrote a book titled '**God vs. Science'** in 1921. There are still a few highly educated men and women in the world that believe in God and are about their Father's business.

There are hundreds of additional questions that we could address, but you have enough information in key areas that if acted upon will be a good foundation for you to begin or continue your own research. I want to end this **Question and Answer Section** with a question for you.

FINAL QUESTION: How many Christians do you know that are fluent in **ancient** Hebrew, Chaldee, Aramaic and Greek? I'm talking about Pastors, Evangelists, Sunday School Teachers, College Professors and all those who produce the quarterlies, lesson plans and study guides for the hierarchy of your church. A follow up question would be: Do you know for sure that the people preparing all of your "Christian" literature and information are Christians?

ANSWER: Everyone that I have asked the first question, over the last forty years while counseling, shook their head and replied, "I don't know any." The answer to the follow up question, sad to say, many or not Christians. The point is, the only sure way of finding what the original scriptures were talking about is to go as close as possible to the original language in which they were written. To do less is to deceive yourself out of God's plans for your life. We are made up of spirit, soul and body. God intended for us to be balanced in all three areas of our life. Most people spend the majority of their time on the body and mind, leaving their spiritual being to a third party. That would be OK, if the third party, is a true Bible scholar and servant of God. Since you and you alone will be the only one standing before your Creator at judgment and only you will give an account of your life; you need to study to show yourself approved before God; rightly dividing the Word of God and putting on the whole armor of God. Make up your mind not to be like one of the five foolish virgins. Get yourself a good study Bible that you can make notes in. I recommend The Companion Bible with ISBN Numbers: 0-8254-2240-x or 0-8254-2237-x or0-8254-2178-0 or 0-8254-2177-2 or 0-8254-2179-9 or 0-8254-2288-4 or 0-8254-2180-2 or 0-8254-2203-5 or 0-8254-2099-7. Find an original Strong's Exhaustive Concordance of the Bible with ISBN Number 0-917006-01-01 or ISBN 978-1-4185-4169-9. Get a Smith's Bible Dictionary ISBN 08407-5542-2 or 0-8407-3085-3. Having the correct ISBN number is important because many of these works have been tampered with and are now called the "New and Improved Addition" or words to that effect. These changes are just further attempts of Satan to cover his tracks and continue to fool the majority of Christians.

"My People are destroyed
for lack of knowledge."

Hosea 4:6

SECTION III

WERE THE FOOD LAWS GIVEN BY GOD IN THE OLD TESTAMENT DONE AWAY WITH IN THE NEW TESTAMENT?

WHAT THE BIBLE HAS TO SAY
ABOUT WHAT WE EAT

We have seen in Sections I and II that the spiritual well being as being taught by most today, leaves much to be desired. Sincere, well meaning people are still getting it wrong and are relying on the traditions of men and the greed based major food industries sophisticated advertizing and marketing techniques to tell them what to eat. For profits' sake, the FDA has allowed many unhealthy things to be taken from and added to our food. There are many good things about the FDA and the original intent for the most part was positive. While the secular official's policies are sometimes very harmful to the health of our citizens, the religious community does as much or more harm by poor scholarship in God's Word and relying on church traditions. The end result is confusion and "umpteen" different government regulations on the one hand and most of the ecclesiastical hierarchy giving their blessing to disregarding the food laws in the "OLD TESTAMENT." The common thread that runs through most denominations is the teaching that Jesus did away with the "Food Laws" and all of them claiming they have the truth. Yet their truths are as different as daylight and dark and most don't have a clue what the manuscripts say. There is only one God and He gives the best advise. When we learn to do it His way, we are healthy, wealthy and wise. He blesses us as only He can; we know who He is, we know who we are and why we are here.

As we look at the state of health in our nation today, we have to conclude that something is wrong with the way we eat. As I grow older it becomes more apparent that we have depended on man to tell us how to be healthy. One survey concluded that the average age for a medical doctor to die in this country is 58 years old. God gave us 120 years and many are not making it half way. We have a proliferation of disease every year. There is no doubt in the last few years there is an effort to educate us how to eat for better health. While many of these are an improvement, even some of these are flawed when we align them with the food laws in the Bible. We are what we eat spiritually and this is especially true of our physical health as well. The difference is we can look in the mirror and see the results much easier for our physical body. If a person is unhealthy, overweight, or out of shape, they are responsible. We are not talking about handicap or disabled people. If you smoke, don't complain when your health fails. If you develop disease as a result of eating the wrong foods, don't be surprised. Willing ignorance is no longer an excuse. Even our own laws state the ignorance of the law is no excuse. The average person spends more time getting their Christmas card list together than they do studying to learn how to eat, for spirit or body.

Common sense tells us we would not use the vacuum cleaner to clean the house and then take the dirty bag and use it to brew a cup of tea. We wouldn't take the filter from our air conditioning unit and use the collection of dust and hair to cook with. Yet most people have no problem eating animals that are scavengers that are just as unclean as the dirty filters. As wonderful as the body is, with all of it's filters, cleaning systems and back up systems, it can function at a high level only so long if it is abused over and over again without rest and the time to cleanse itself. This can only be done with the proper fuel for the body. God's instructions make common sense. Science and observation tells us there are plants that clean our air and water. There are certain animals, fish and birds that were created to clean the earth and sea. Man has made many things to clean and purify the environment. These creatures scavenge the earth of all the dirty, rotten, polluted material that was not intended to be eaten by man. There is nothing really complicated about it. The problem is most people don't think about it and just go along with the seductive advertizing presented to appeal to our senses and emotions. You see, we are not taught this in school; even medical school spends little, if any time teaching on what is healthy to eat. Med students are taught how to medicate symptoms. The majority of which are caused by people not eating good, clean healthy food. We are programmed to eat what taste good, not what is good for us. We have filters in our bodies like the kidneys, liver, lungs, white blood cells, the hairs in our nose and ears, sweat glands, lymph nodes etc. They only work well when we give the body proper nutrition. Stop and think about this; **there is no money in healthy people** and the food, drug and advertizing industries are only interested in profits. As a result, many people live in poor health and/ or die before their time. Many people are born, live and die and never realize their health could have been so much better if they had done their homework or money was not the leading contributor in what we are taught as the best way to go.

NO, THE FOOD LAWS GIVEN BY GOD WERE NOT DONE AWAY WITH! YES, THEY ARE STILL IN EFFECT!

God did not say don't eat certain foods to prove that we are obedient to Him. He did tell us which animals were created to clean the waste of the earth and that they are not healthy to eat. He wanted His children to be healthy and feel good. If we adhere to His standards, we don't have to buy pills to make us feel better. We don't have to go see the doctor nearly as often. Of course this would really mess up the insurance, legal and medical professions, so I guess we better not do that. It's probably better if we don't think for ourselves and have all that money left over at the end of the month. **Following the food laws in the Bible, if done by the majority, would radically change the medical, legal, pharmaceutical and insurance business around the world.** When God told us not to touch certain animals, He was just letting us know about harmful germs. When the Bible was written, man was not aware of germs. It is interesting to see what goes on under a microscope and it is also great to know that if we follow God's rules we can live healthy lives even if we don't know all the details. If you want to know about a product, you go to the person who designed the product. You go to the manufacturer who made the product. Only they have the correct guidelines to make the product function to the best that it is capable. Only they know how to keep it in perfect working order. If you want the best service you don't take your Ford to the Honda Dealer. Only Ford has the blueprint and molds for the proper parts for the Ford. Only they know how everything is supposed to work. It works the same way with our physical bodies and it only makes sense to consult the Creator of our bodies. I have a John Deer Tractor and purchased a Technical Manual and a Service Manual, that cost an extra $150 each, so I could take care of the Tractor myself. In most households, you will find your owners manual, written by God, on the coffee table or in a bookcase. Even if you take it to church every week, the section that deals with your health is seldom referred to. You see this Manufacturer thinks so much of His creation, He left precise instructions on the care and maintenance that works best when followed to the letter. Doesn't it make sense to at least make an attempt to find out what the Creator of the universe and your body says about how to take care of them both.

God is always fair, you get serious with Him and He will always take you seriously. You see, unlike the care and maintenance on my tractor, which I could let someone else do, this maintenance is best done by the individuals themselves. You are the only one who actually puts food in your mouth. The gas attendant can put gas in your car, or at least they use to, but the waitress at the restaurant does not tell you what to eat or hand feed you. You and I need to go to the owner's manual ourselves and research and find out what it says. Sometimes this requires going to the original languages to check it out and be sure that what we have been told is really true. I can tell you this, if you make an in-depth study, your world, including your health, will start making a lot more sense. In this fast paced world it does not seem to be profitable to man to follow these instructions. So the only time we hear about things in the Bible is when a preacher reads one or two verses on Sunday morning. Another problem, after reading "my text for today" the preacher teaches traditions of men the remainder of the time. Sad to say, most religious leaders have not learned how to understand the Bible. Anyone can read it, very few read with understanding. I know this may sound shocking or even radical, but it doesn't take much in depth study of the manuscripts to learn how true this is.

If we were to get one of the top advertising agencies to promote the Word of God, it wouldn't take long for most people to be familiar with it. You know, the same people that make all those foods and products seem like you just can't live without them. Why in no time, you would know what foods are not good for you and all the reasons why. They would have thirty second TV Spots with all the best colors and lighting letting you know exactly what was good for you and do it in such a way that you would believe it. It is amazing how we are led around by the nose and not question what we are told. The advertisers are so good at what they do, they can make you want something even if you know you don't. They can create a need that was not there and then convince you where to go and who to see to fix the thing that was not broke.

The love of money is still the root of all evil. Many people will do anything for money, even if they know it is not right or proper or true, as long as there is profit in it, they do it. We all praise the medical profession and hold it in high esteem; yet the modern day medical world is based more on profit than keeping people well. As we stated before, there is just not enough money in "well folks." Well people don't need pills and operations. Most doctors, if they are honest, will tell you a high percentage of sick people are in ill-health because of their diet. One doctor told me, **"most people don't die naturally, they kill themselves with their teeth."** Some studies place illness as high as 80% on improper diet. To be sure you don't misunderstand, there is a place for a dedicated doctor. There are times when they can save your life. Unfortunately in today's world, their real purpose has become to medicate symptoms. The pharmaceutical industries are controlling the medical profession and in this writers opinion, the tail is wagging the dog. Their purpose is to get you out of misery, not to inform you how to be healthy. As long as you are feeling good and looking great, you don't need their services. They can't make any money from you. As stated earlier, the death for a medical doctor is way too young on average in this country. The thing that is wrong with this picture is we need to look to more than the medical community to find how to live healthy.

Several years ago, Dr. John Barnet, spoke to our Rotary Club. At he time he was overseeing the building of a new cancer center in Cleburne, Texas. The first thing Dr. Barnet said, when he took the podium, was: **"The food laws in the book of Leviticus make the best diet."** He then said, **"if you follow these food laws, you will never need my services."** He did state, that "the American Medical Association gets a little closer to this kind of diet every year." It seems the medical profession is getting around to a healthier diet through trial and error over many years. It is also clear to anyone with an open mind that the Bible has had the information all the time.

Many people ask, "why should I read some dusty old book to find out how to live today? That book can't possible have more useable knowledge than we have today." The politicians would have us to believe that people are better off today than ever before. They tell us they have eliminated famine, poverty, sickness, wars and corruption. We don't have any disease that is a threat to society today. That is what the political leaders would like for you to believe. The fact is we have a paradox in the land; on the one hand, we have more education and prosperity than ever before. While on the other hand we still have poverty, sickness, disease, famine and tension throughout the world. The pollution of water, land, air and space is an on going problem.

Most people are programmed, through highly motivated intelligent people, to believe what they are told. That what they say is the only way to live. The truth is, if you buy what they continue to sell, you won't live healthy fulfilled lives. Instead you will unknowingly mistreat your body and health to the point you will have to use their products and services in a much greater degree that is necessary. Food plays a chief part in health and sickness. It is in your best interest to obey God's instructions now and for all of your life. All the food laws in the Bible are based on the preservation and health of the human race. Some are for sanitary reasons, some are for peculiarities of climate and some to separate a people. When you follow God's laws about what to eat and not eat, you will automatically separate yourself from most other people by being healthier. You will not have to use the medical or pharmaceutical professions nearly as much. You won't need expensive patented pills or potions for the rest of you life and you will sleep better and live longer. Dramatic results are seen when middle-age people start eating properly. Just imagine what would happen if your parents had started you out right and taught you how to eat when you were a youngster. You would really be different from most. You would look and act much younger than your age group. If you think this is impossible to do, many of us already do this for our pets and livestock. We wouldn't dare feed our cattle, horses and dogs anything but the proper diet for them. Because most animal life span is much shorter than ours, we can see the effects of improper diet much quicker in them. Most people don't pay much attention to the importance of diet on their health until they get older. Much of the damage has been done before they begin making changes in the way they live and eat. Eating healthy along with proper exercise will change your life for the better.

One of the most eaten scavengers today is the hog. Bacon, ham and ribs can be prepared to taste so good. What can possibly be wrong with pork? Most people eat pork all their lives. I grew up on a farm in east Texas and usually had pork everyday. After all, didn't Christ say it was now OK? Actually, He did not say that at all. He did say, He did not come to change one jot or tittle of the law. The vision that Peter had about unclean foods was used as an illustration of what happened to a people. God was showing Peter what is available to the Hebrew people is also available to the Gentiles. It really had nothing to do with food. Most people don't realize that except for a few in its nose, the swine has no sweat glands. Many of the wastes and poisons in our bodies are gotten rid of through our sweat glands. The Hog stores many poisons in the fat. There is a residual effect over many years of eating pork, including the poisons in the meat, that manifest themselves in our failing health. This effects people in different ways, but happens sooner or later and effects everyone. Most of us who have been around awhile realize that what we eat is directly related to the state of our health and if you have not discovered this yet, you will.

Let's face it, most Christians spend the majority of their Bible reading time in the New Testament. Most believe that Jesus did away with the Old Testament laws, especially the food laws and it is quite alright to eat most anything as long as they bless it first. Most don't realize there is a difference between statutes, ordinances and laws. Jesus said in **Matthew 5:17** *"Think not that I am come to destroy the law or the prophets: I am not come to destroy, but to fulfill. 18. For verily I say unto you, Till heaven and earth pass, one jot or one tittle shall in no wise pass from the law, till all be fulfilled."* Jesus did do away with the blood ordinance by shedding His blood once and for all. God gave us the laws in the Old Testament and much of the New Testament is taken up with quoting the Old. Let me ask you, does God change: The Bible says He changes not in **Malachi 3:6** *"For I am the LORD, I change not;"* Do the people living today have a different body than when God gave us the proper foods to eat? No, we are pretty much the same today as then. So there is no reason to assume that eating scavengers and improper food today would not do harm to our bodies and health as then. The obvious reason we know that eating improper food causes our health to decline is just a matter of looking around at the state this nation's health. Let's find a scripture to see how important it is to God what we eat. **Isaiah 65:3** *"A people that provoketh Me to anger continually to My face; that sacrificeth in gardens and burneth incense upon altars of brick. 4. Which remain among the graves and lodge in the monuments, which eat swine's flesh and broth of abominable things is in their vessels; 5. Which say, 'Stand by thyself, come not near to me; for I am holier than thou. 'These are a smoke in My nose, a fire that burneth all the day."* WOW, did you understand that? God is not happy with us when we eat things that are unhealthy. People that call themselves Christian eat unhealthy food that makes them sick. Then they ask everyone to pray for God to heal them. Is it any wonder these prayers go unanswered? In spite of this, there are times when God will heal us anyway. Then, because of poor scholarship, people go right back to the same unhealthy diet and get sick again and say: "I lost my healing." We find in **I Corinthians 6:19** *" What? Know ye not that your body in the Temple of The Holy Spirit, which is in you, which ye have of God and ye are not your own."* Do you defile your temple by disobeying God's common sense eating rules? We find in **Leviticus 3:16** *"all the fat is the LORD's. 17. It shall be perpetual statute for your generations throughout all your dwellings, that ye eat neither fat nor blood."*

From a health perspective let's think of the Bible words "Clean" and "Unclean" as "healthy" and "unhealthy." Regarding the food laws, every time the word clean is used we will substitute the word healthy and doing the same with the word unclean, we will use unhealthy. This should make it more user-friendly, yet still very correct, in today's world.

NOTE: If you wish to skip the detailed description of the

clean and unclean, take a detour here and pick it back up two pages down. See "Detour Resumed"

In this first reference we find God is telling Moses and Aaron to tell the people what animals are healthy to eat and the ones that are unhealthy. Remember, The Lord is speaking directly, this is not something Moses or Aaron came up with on their own. **Leviticus 11:3** *"Whatsoever parteth the hoof and is cloven footed and cheweth the cud, among the beasts, that shall ye eat." 4. Never the less these shall ye not eat of them that chew the cud, or of them that divide the hoof: as the camel, because he cheweth the cud, but divideth not the hoof; he is unclean (unhealthy) unto you. 5. And the coney,* (the old English name for rabbit) *because he cheweth the cud but divideth not the hoof; he is unclean* (unhealthy) *unto you. 6. And the hare* (not yet identified) *because he cheweth the cud, but divideth not the hoof; he is unclean unto you." 7. And the swine, though he divide the hoof and be cloven footed, yet he cheweth not the cud; he is unclean to you. 8. Of these flesh shall ye not eat and their carcase shall ye not touch: these are unclean to you. 9. These shall ye eat of all that are in the waters: whatsoever hath fins and scales in the waters, in the seas and in the rivers, them shall ye eat.* (they are healthy) *10. And all that have not fins and scales in the seas and in the rivers, of all that move in waters and of any living thing which is in the waters, they shall be abomination unto you"* (they are unhealthy for you to eat) Now don't get mad at the messenger, we are just quoting the Bible. What was just quoted means any scavenger; shrimp, lobster, crab, catfish, shark etc. God did not say it is OK if you can prepare these to taste good? Also, keep in mind disobeying these food laws is a sin against your body, it will not send you to hell.

If you go against God's rules and break them it will cost you sooner or later in failing health. Beginning in **Verse 13,** God deals with the fowls of the air. Some are familiar to us and some or not. Some have been identified in modern terms, others are still in doubt. We will attempt to clarify where possible based on the findings of Dr. E.W. Bullinger. **Leviticus 11:13** *"And these are they which ye shall have in abomination among the fowls; they shall not be eaten, they are an abomination;* (unhealthy) *the eagle (or vulture) and the ossifrage"* (bone-breaker, from taking their prey up in the air and dropping it on a rock to break it) *14. "And the vulture* (kite) *and the kite* (falcon) *after his kind. 15. Every raven after his kind;* (black birds of all kinds) *16. And the owl and the night hawk and the cuckoo* (probably sea-gull) *and the hawk after his kind. 17. And the little owl and the cormorant,* (darter) *and the great owl* (night bird) *18. And the swan,* (not our swan, it is rendered ibis, bat, heron) *and the pelican and the gier eagle,* (little vulture) *19. And the stork, the heron after her kind and the lapwing* (better the hoope, a dirty bird) *and Bat."* (Verse 20 is a little confusing in English until we look up the root word "oof" in Hebrew which is to cover with wings, to fly) This will explain the four legs. **Verse 20.** *"All fowls that creep, going upon all four, shall be an abomination unto you. 21. Yet these may ye eat of every flying creeping thing that goeth upon all four, which have legs above their feet to leap withal upon the earth; 22. Even of these of them ye may eat; the locust* (swarming locust) *after his kind and the bald locust (devouring locust) after his kind and the beetle* (chargol or wingless locust) *after his kind and the grasshopper after his kind. 23. But all other flying creeping things, which have four feet, shall be an abomination unto you."*

"Detour Resumed"

To sum up the detour portion:

⌅ Don't eat scavengers – fish, fowl or animal
⌅ Don't eat fat or blood

Leviticus 3:16 *"All the fat is the LORD'S 17. It shall be a perpetual statute for your generations throughout all your dwellings, that ye eat neither fat nor blood."*

Now let's go to the New Testament and look at some scriptures that many people quote to justify eating things that were not approved. **I Timothy 4:1** *"Now the Spirit speaketh expressly, that in the latter times some shall depart from the faith, giving heed to seducing spirits and doctrines of devils; 2. Speaking lies in hypocrisy; having their conscience seared with a hot iron. 3. Forbidding to marry and commanding to abstain from meats, which God hath created to be received with thanksgiving of them which believe and know the truth."* Do you understand what was just said? Have you been seduced into believing that God changed His health laws. Think about who the devil used to seduce you. We were just told that there are some people who will tell you it is OK to do things that the Word says not to. The key phrase is in verse 3. *"meats, which God hath created to be received" with thanksgiving of them which believe and know the truth."* Have you been taught the truth? Do you know that God created some animals, birds and fish that are good and healthy for you to eat in moderation? God did not create all animals, birds and fish to be eaten by man. That was not and is not their purpose. Using common sense we can eliminate some things. The thought of eating a buzzard is enough to make you sick. This scavenger is too filthy to consider. God said, He made some animals, fish and birds to keep the earth clean. We find this in all of His nature. From the dung beetle, to the catfish, to the vulture, all nature was intended to be kept clean and pure. Our bodies are wonderful creations, intended to function at a high level for over a hundred years. Just as we see the pollution in our air, water and land when people do not take care of it. We find our health threatened by improper diet, mold, fungus, parasites and pollution of all types. Is it any wonder modern man is dying long before his or her time? With medical doctors dying at middle age, we should look to more than the medical community for our daily health. Please take note: Emergency health care in this country is second to none and can save your life when there is no time to do it any other way. This work is not an attempt to disparage the doctors, it is a plea for them to look to more than the pharmaceutical companies to keep us in good health.

Medical school teaches how to medicate symptoms. "When in doubt, cut it out" is the thinking too much of the time. A doctor has to be smart to get through medical school. The problem is they have bought into the idea that medical school has all the answers. This is simply not true. Many people and cultures have had people through the ages that have lived long healthy lives with out the help of modern medicine. When we understand the power and control over the Doctors by the pharmaceutical companies, we begin to understand how the system has gotten out of control. It is mostly about money. You see they can't make big money on natural foods and herbs because they haven't figured out a way to patent them without a public uprising. If they are unable to patent them, **and they are trying to do this,** they can't charge high prices. Let's look at a few examples of how science and the medical profession is sometimes wrong and is slow to admit it. In the sixteenth century when Galileo invented the telescope and stated the truth of the Copernican theory (planets revolving around the sun) he was condemned for heresy by the so-called scientific community of that day. When Dr. W.T. Blunt told his fellow doctors that they needed sterilize their instruments and the operating room before each operation, he was laughed at and ridiculed. Dr. Blunt was the State of Texas Health Officer in the late 1800's. He was the son of Dr. Fred P. Blunt who was the first Surgeon General of the United States, appointed by Andrew Jackson, seventh President. Dr. W.T. Blunt based his findings on France's Dr. Louis Pasteur discovery of bacteria found using a microscope. Until this finding, it was a badge of honor for a doctor to have as much blood on his white coat as possible. The more blood on the coat, floor and operating area the busier and more successful the doctor appeared. Even with this information it took until the early part of the 20th century for change to take place. England's Dr. Joseph Lister, during the early nineteen hundreds, introduced the first Antiseptic surgery.

What are we saying? It took many years for the medical profession to change their ways after the first knowledge of a better way to do surgery was known. Dr. Pasteur found the world of Bacteria. Dr. blunt said, "we need to clean up our act." Dr. Lister said, "Now that you have found the bacteria, I will show you how to kill it." Fifty years ago the majority of doctors smoked cigarettes. Not too many years ago the dental community said it was not necessary to use tooth paste, but said to rinse your mouth out with warm water. They changed this a short time later. The point is, they are not always on the cutting edge. This is further clouded by the tremendous wealth that can be accumulated by using artificial things and ways for which they can charge a huge price. Let's face it, there is not much incentive to look for inexpensive ways and products to keep us healthy. There is tremendous incentive to make and push drugs and products that can be patented and marketed for huge profits. The fact that these drugs and products are not always the most healthy choice doesn't seem to matter as long as there is big money to be made. Man will look the other way as long as it is not "his ox" that is getting gored. I don't claim to be a doctor or nutrition expert, but I do read and observe what goes on and it doesn't take a rocket scientist to figure out that there are alternative ways and things people can do to help themselves. At this point in time, most anyone who educates themselves, will be better informed about nutrition and alternative healing methods than the average doctor. There are a few doctors and food experts that are telling the truth and showing there is a better, less expensive, life enriching and life extending way to get the job done.

Man putting profit ahead of health is not what God had in mind for you. There are many reasons given as to why modern man has to alter, change and modify the foods and medicine we use today, but right now we are not talking about the masses. We are talking about you, your life and your health. God tells us in the great Book of Revelation that He created all things for His pleasure. This includes you and me. If we give Him pleasure, He is honor bound to bless us. You can believe in Jesus to save you, but if you disobey God's health laws, you will not live as well or as long as you could by being a "doer" as well as a "hearer" of the Word. With computers, we say "garbage in, Garbage out." It works the same way with our bodies. Healthy food, life-style, exercise "in," good health and length of life "out." Unhealthy food, sedentary life-style "in," and poor health and shortened life "out."

If we continue to do things the way we have always done them, we will continue to get the same results. If we eat bread made from moldy grains and drink milk from cows that are drugged that produce milk that is drugged and heated to 160 degrees, we will not enjoy good health. Nothing wrong and everything right about eating good healthy food, not only in Bible times, but as it was done in this country not too many years ago. The body was created to handle a certain amount of pollution, but when it is overwhelmed it can't keep up, especially as we get older. In the book of Genesis after Adam was removed from the Garden of Eden, he was informed that he would earn his bread by the sweat of his brow. While most people don't actually plant and harvest their own food today, we still have to put forth more than a little effort in order to find proper nutrition today. Many people will argue that the government and food companies have allowed preservatives and anti-biotic in our food and drink in order to make it last longer and to be sure to kill all the bad bacteria. While it is true they do this, it is also being proven unhealthy on a daily basis. One example of a healthy food is raw honey. This is honey that has not been heated to 160 degrees which kills most of the beneficial, health giving properties. Did you know that no bacteria can live in the presence of raw honey. Did you know that a single bee produces about a tablespoon of honey in it's short lifetime. Did you know the average bee hive produces about five pounds of honey a year: God in His wisdom made the bee to produce the honey and in the process cross pollinate the flowers that produce the fruits, vegetables, grains and flowers for us to enjoy. Greedy man comes along and says, "I know how to improve on this so I can make more money. I will heat it and mix additives and even feed the bees sugar so they will produce more. What does it hurt if it is not pure the way God intended. Who will ever know?" This is just one example, but the formula is repeated over and over with similar results. **Isaiah 29:15** *"Woe unto them that seek deep to hide their counsel from the LORD and their works are in the dark and they say, 'who seeth us?' And who knoweth us? 16. Surely your turning of things upside down shall be esteemed as the potter's clay: for shall the work say of him that made it, "He made me not?" or shall the thing framed say of him that framed it, "He hath no understanding."*

Did you know that more than a few of our early rural relatives were raised with the knowledge that a few drops of mother's breast milk would clear up eye problems in their children. In most cases the eyes cleared up by the next morning. They also could place a couple of drops of their milk in the nose when the child was congested and reported the problem had gone in a short time. I have a friend that would put fresh cows milk in calves eyes with pink eye and the problem was solved without using expensive drugs. Eating the comb of honey from your area has helped many people, especially children, two years old and above with breathing problems. It requires effort to find fresh grains and fruits that are not polluted with pesticides. It takes effort to filter your water so you don't drink chlorine or breath chlorine gas as you take a shower. All of these measures cost very little or nothing. No one made an unreasonable profit and the participants enjoy better health. Also, these simple solutions don't cause other problems. The side effects of many prescribed medicines cause even more problems. There are times when these modern drugs can save your life, but many times they are given too often.

With the explosion of information available today, no one should sit around and wish they felt better. There are answers out there and you are not the only one with your problem. There has been someone that has been there and done that. Sometimes you have to go beneath the surface to find the real answer, just as you have to go to the original languages to find what the Bible really says. If you have not gotten relief from your health problem, then change what you have been doing. This does not work in every case, but try going back in your own mind and find when and where the problem started. Something happened that started the problem. Just because it did not show up right away does not mean that it didn't begin earlier in your life. Could be the air you breathed was polluted which started bacteria growing in your body and you just did not think about connecting the incident.

I have been around horses many years and sometimes I think a Vet has to be smarter, in some ways, than a human doctor. The Vet's patients can't tell him where it hurts and the problem is not always obvious. The Vet has to look for the real problem. He or she will check the horse's waist and check the hay or grain for mold or parasites. The Vet has to read the body language of the animal. They check mucus membranes, gut sounds, temperature, how the horse is holding its head, the position of the ears etc. Another thing about Vets, they know if they don't get results quickly they will be replaced. I know some people go to the same doctor year after year, faithfully filling those prescriptions and never seem to feel any better. If you have a good doctor, stick with him or her. If you are running to the doctor every time you turn around, there is room for improvement. Hopefully, we will see a time when medical schools will teach nutrition with much more emphasis on how to keep a person well instead of just how to medicate symptoms and get a person out of trouble. A Doctor friend of mine was at the ranch a few years ago and I asked him, "How much nutrition did you get in medical school?" He held up his thumb and forefinger forming a circle. He got nada, none. There are exceptions, but I would venture to say the majority of doctors in this country don't know much about nutrition unless they have taken it upon themselves to learn on their own. Most of us realize the health care in this country has evolved, both good and bad. There is increasingly more health information available to us and yet we still find the best information about what we should eat is in the Bible. This short food and health portion of the book was added because of all the misuse and abuse and poor teaching about what the Bible says to eat. There are many more scriptures that relate to food and I hope you will get into the Word and find them for yourself. If you don't understand what the Bible is saying, look until you find a Biblical Herbalist and/or Biblical Nutritionist to help you with a good healthy eating regimen. Find a good health food store that stays on the cutting edge of nutrition. Start an exercise program that fits your age and requirements. We all are made up of Spirit, Soul and Body and we must be balanced in all three areas of our lives if we are to live happy, healthy lives and reach our full potential.

Bibliography

The Companion Bible: a King James Version of the Bible and was used for this book. The scriptures, some of the side notes and the Appendixes from this Bible were used. The Companion Bible © Copyright 1999: by E.W. Bullinger, Published by Kregel Publications, Grand Rapids, MI.

Strong's Exhaustive Concordance of the Bible: by James Strong. Published by Hendrickson, Peabody, Massachusetts. Used to reference Hebrew and Greek words from the English.

Smith's Bible Dictionary: by William Smith Last © Copyright 1999. Published by Nelson -Nashville * Atlanta * London * Vancouver

Dr. Arnold Murray: Senior Pastor of Shepherd's Chapel Church Opened doors about: Three World Ages, What happened in the Garden of Eden and who the Kenites are. This book would probably not be without his influence.

Moffett Bible: Acknowledgment given when used.

"Our Republic" by Harry Atwood Acknowledgment given when quoted.

Greens Interlinear Hebrew-English Old Testament Jay P. Green Sr., General Editor and Translator Sovereign Grace Publishers, Lafayette, IN 47903

The Apocrypha: by Edgar J. Goodspeed, Published by Vintage

One Man's Destiny: by C.R. Dickey, Published by Destiny Acknowledgment given when quoted.

Webster's New World Dictionary: Second College Edition Published by Prentice Hall Press

"The Law and the Constitution": Speech by Howard B. Rand Acknowledgment given when quoted.

Number of Bible Books Quoted from: Old Testament 34 New Testament 24 Total 58

Number of Bible Verses Quoted or Referred to: Old Testament 541 New Testament 586 Total 1127

Note: With all the information available today, it is difficult and sometimes seemingly impossible to find the originator of an email or social media information. This writer has attempted to give credit for any and all information contained in this book and does apologize if there has been any oversight.

About the Author

David Murdoch has read and studied the Bible most of his life. He was the pastor of a small church in Baytown, Texas in the early seventies where he began counseling people with all manner of problems. Thus began the journey of deeper study to find what the Bible had to say about all of life's situations. David was a student of the David Ebaugh Bible School and considers David Ebaugh as one of his mentors. His other mentor is Dr. Arnold Murray of Shepherd's Chapel, which is the largest TV ministry in the world, broadcasting from a small church in Gravette, Arkansas. David considers Shepherd's Chapel to be the spirit of Elijah ministry of the end times. Neither of these men begged for money, in fact they hardly ever mentioned it. They both taught from the manuscripts. Mr. Murdoch is mostly self-taught as far as Biblical research is concerned. David has found that others can open a door for you, but you still have to study and allow a truth to become reality to you. David is proof positive that most anyone can learn from the manuscripts without knowing the ancient languages.

In the 1980's he and his wife, Martha, raised Egyptian Arabian Horses. The importance of keeping the pedigrees accurate by his wife, led David to better understand the importance of paying close attention to all details, including names and families in the Bible. This of course led to an even closer study of the manuscripts, which broadened his understanding of what the Bible really says.

David can be found at the ranch much of the time where they still raise Cross-Bred Angus cattle.

Books by David Murdoch

GOD'S Eternal Purpose Published by MEI 2003 (Out of Print)

Understanding GOD'S Overall Plan Published by GOM Press 2004

The Fig Tree Generation Published by WingSpan Press 2007

The Bible Was Not Written in English Published by WingSpan Press 2015

Available on line from: Amazon, Barnes & Noble, most e-book readers and the Author

Send Comments to: P.O. Box 771, Cleburne, Texas 76033

A complimentary copy of this book given to anyone requesting financial assistance.

www.probingthebible.com

www.ingramcontent.com/pod-product-compliance
Lightning Source LLC
Chambersburg PA
CBHW031244090426

42742CB00007B/311